WE ARE THE MARKET

The Commercial City Center as the Final Commonplace

ALL ON OFFER

PRIVATE

a stop-motion of added relics

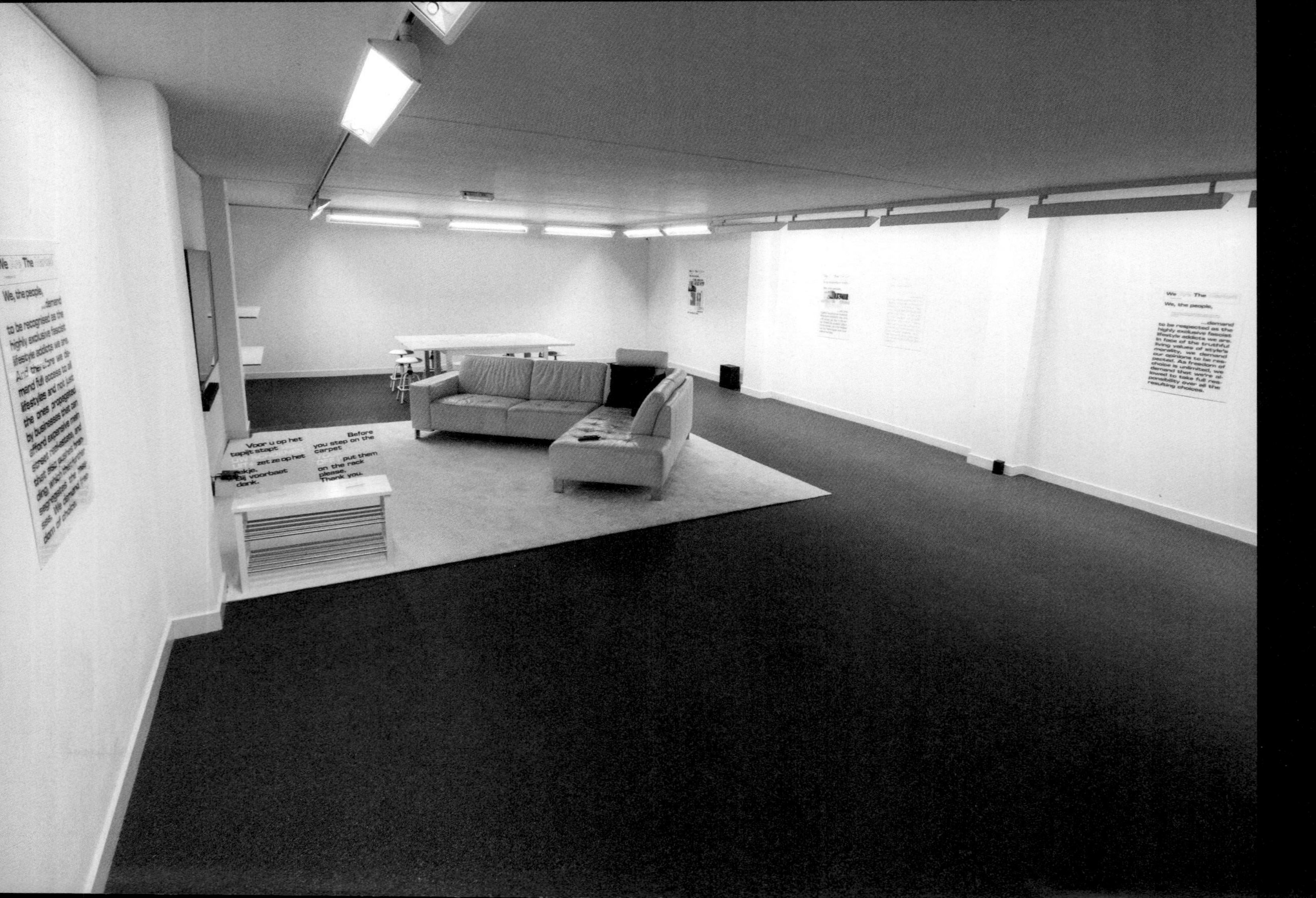
We, the people,
...demand
to be recognised as the
highly exclusive fascist
Voor u op het
tapijt stapt
zet ze op het
rekje.
Bij voorbaat
dank.
Before
you step on the
carpet
put them
on the rack
please.
Thank you.
We The
We, the people,
...demand
to be respected as the
highly exclusive fascist
lifestyle addicts we are.
In face of the truthful
living values of style's
morality, we demand
our opinions to be res-
pected. As freedom of
choice is unlimited, we
demand that we're al-
lowed to take full res-
ponsibility over all the
resulting choices.

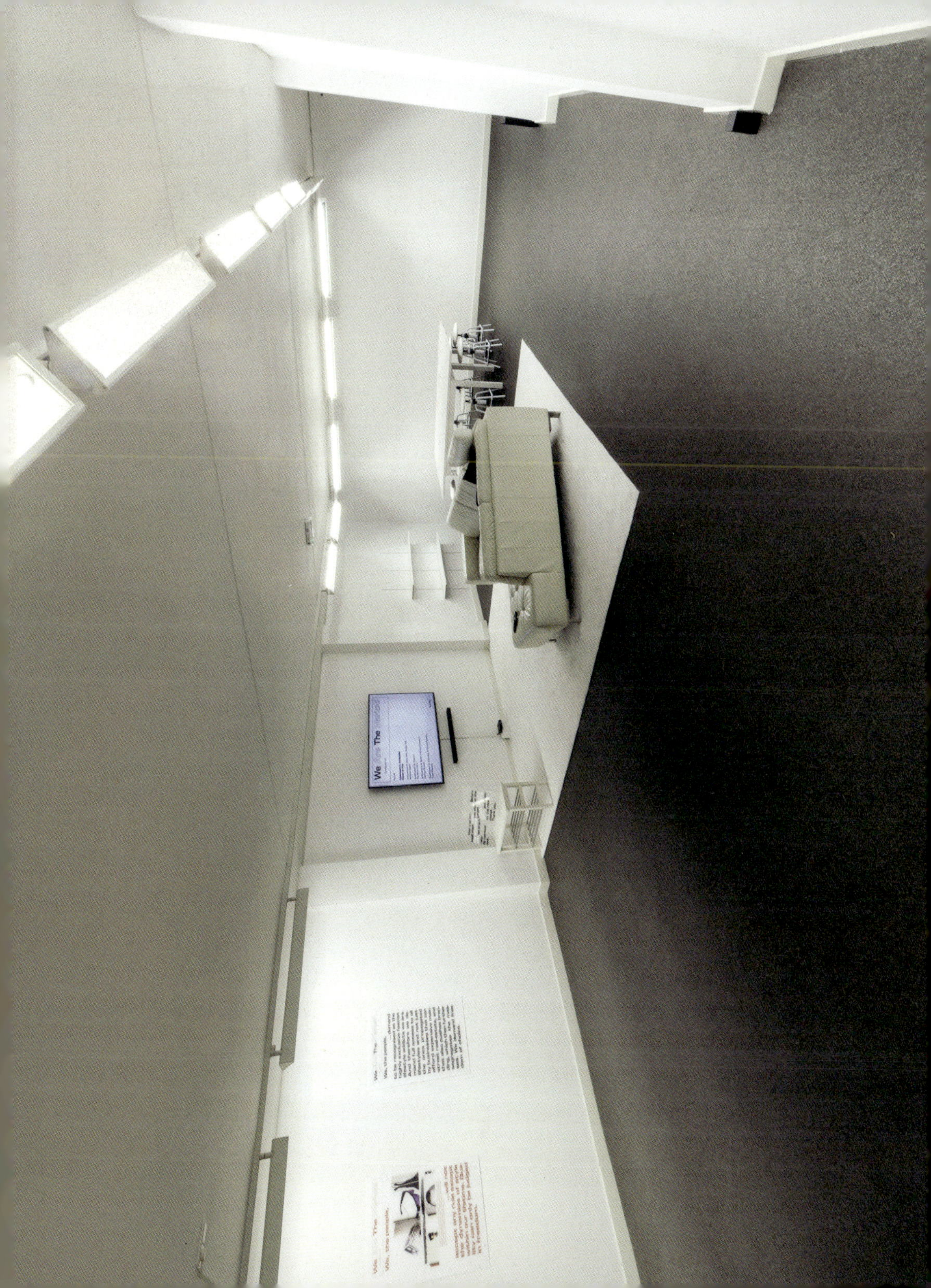

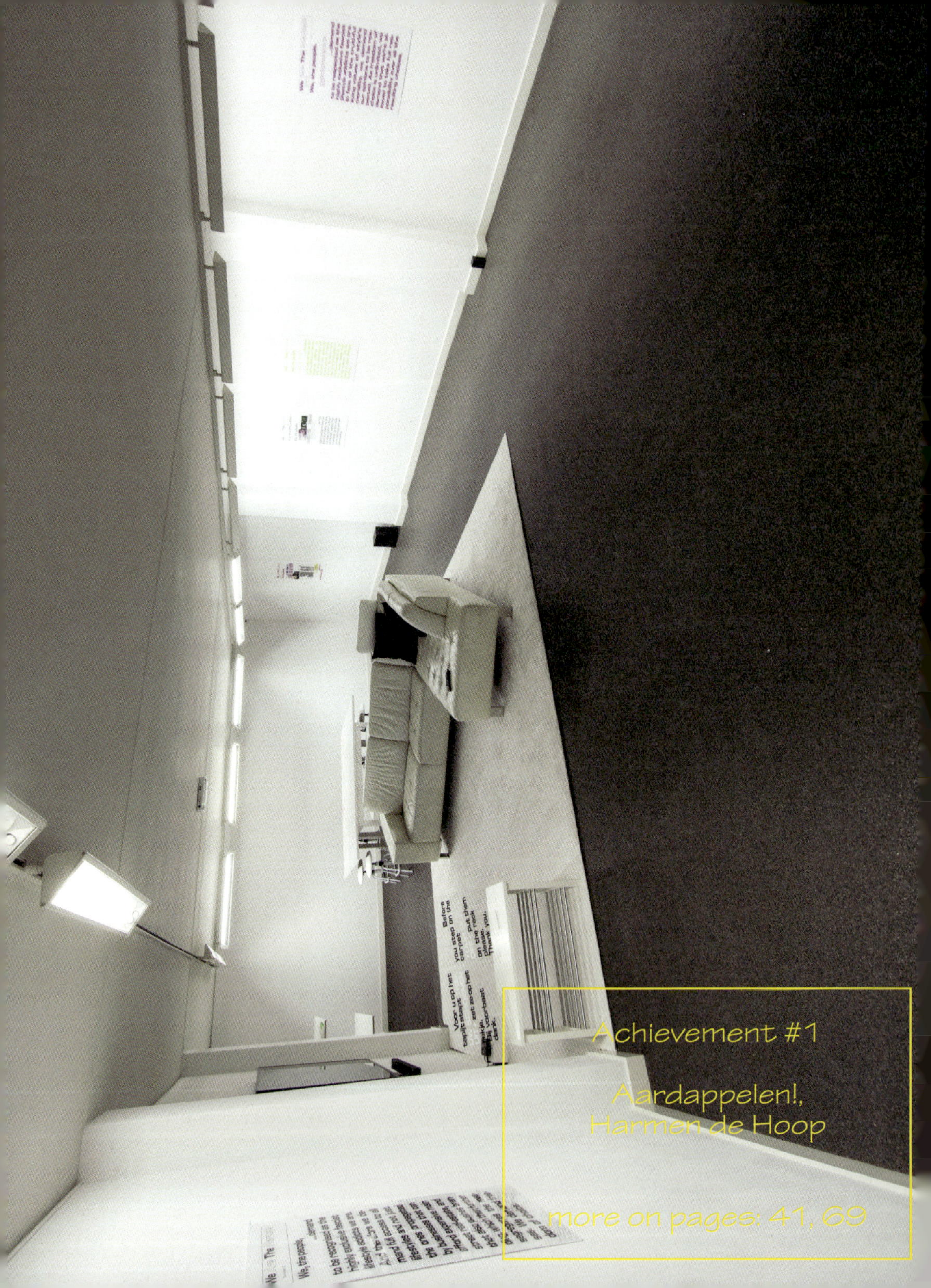

Achievement #1

Aardappelen!,
Harmen de Hoop

more on pages: 41, 69

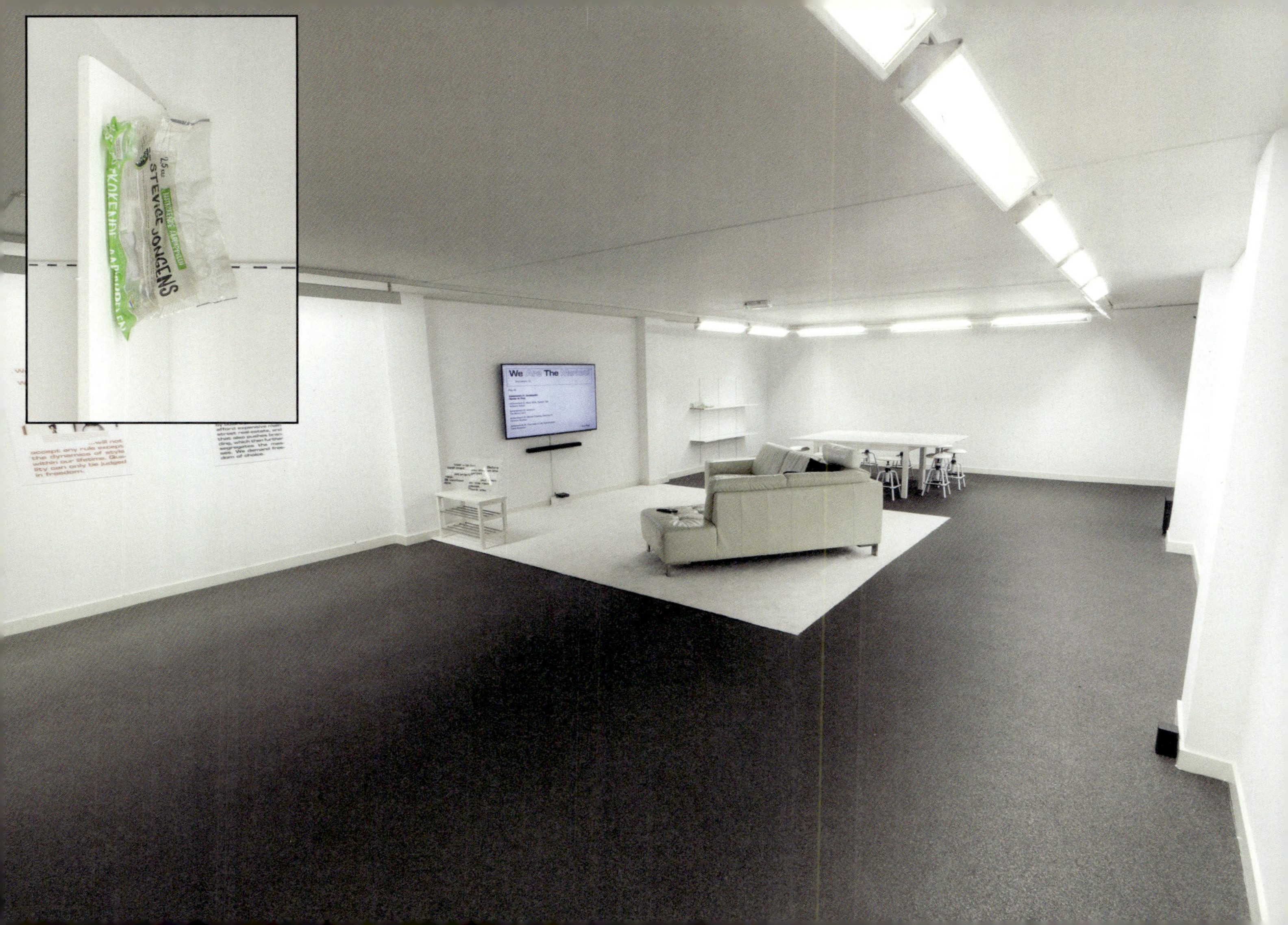
STEVIGE JONGENS
We Are The Market
...will not
accept any rule except
the dynamics of style
within our lifetime. Qua-
lity can only be judged
in freedom.
afford expensive main
street real-estate, and
that also pushes bran-
ding, which then further
segregates the mas-
ses. We demand free-
dom of choice.

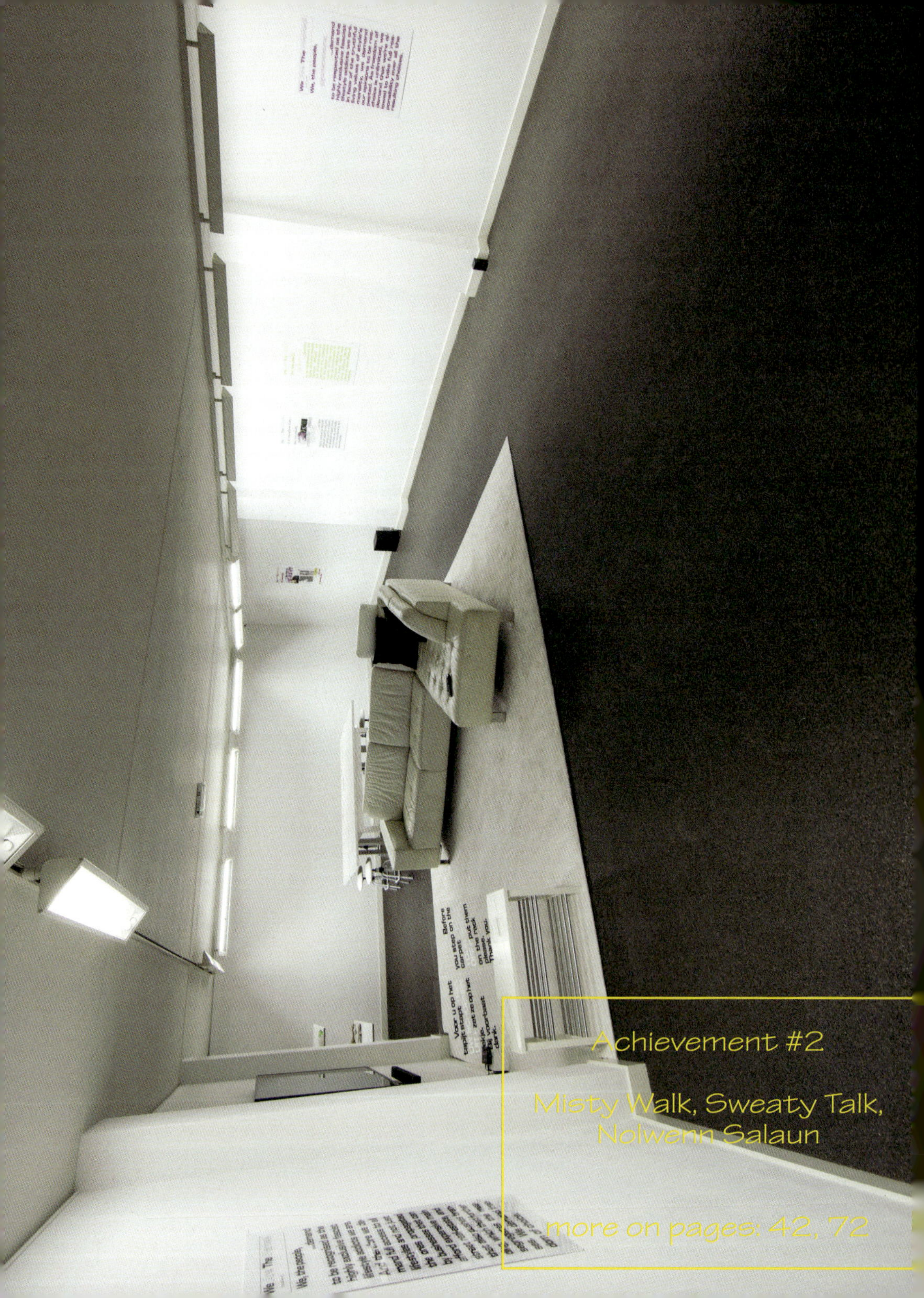

Achievement #2

Misty Walk, Sweaty Talk,
Nolwenn Salaun

more on pages: 42, 72

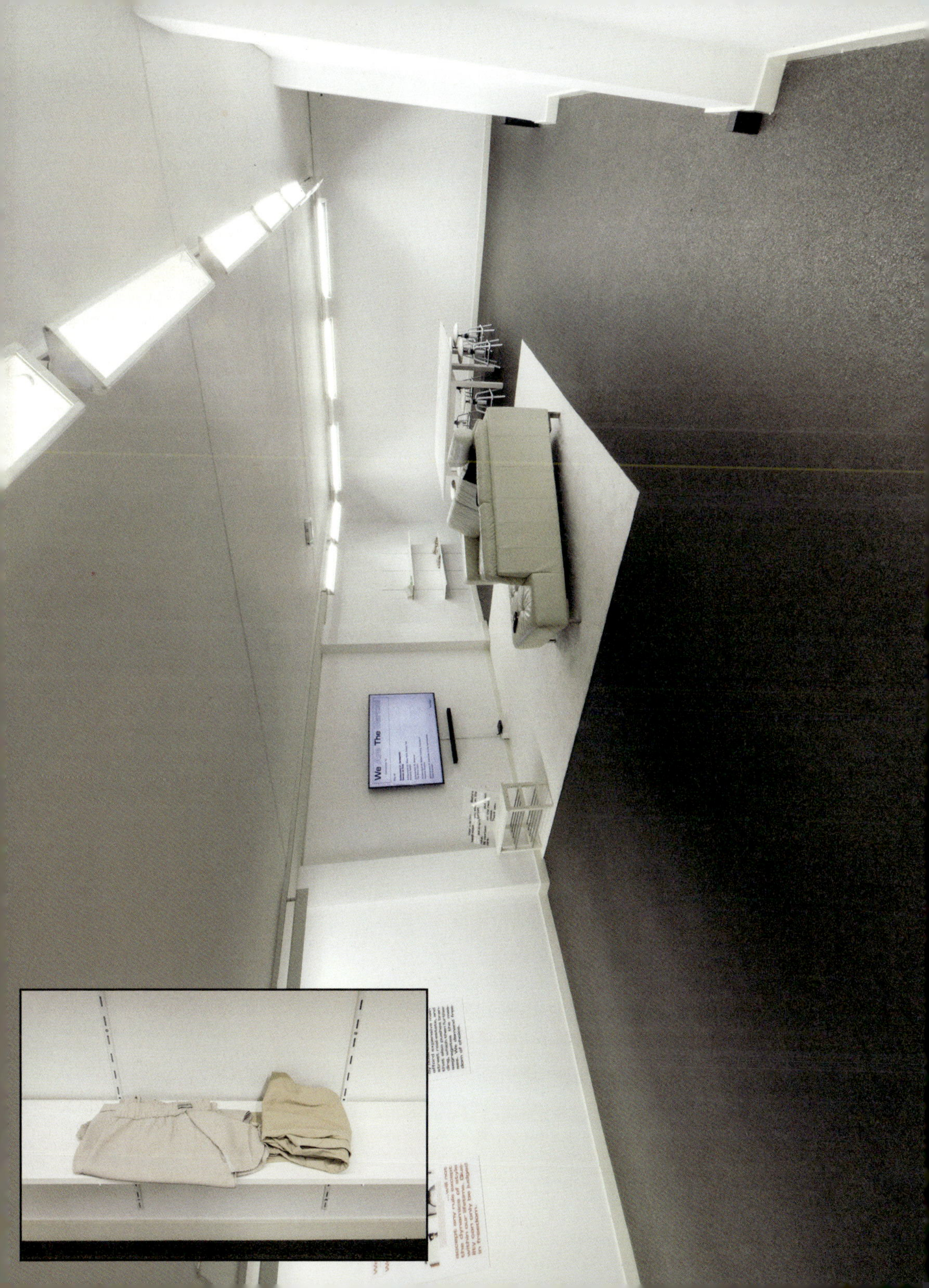

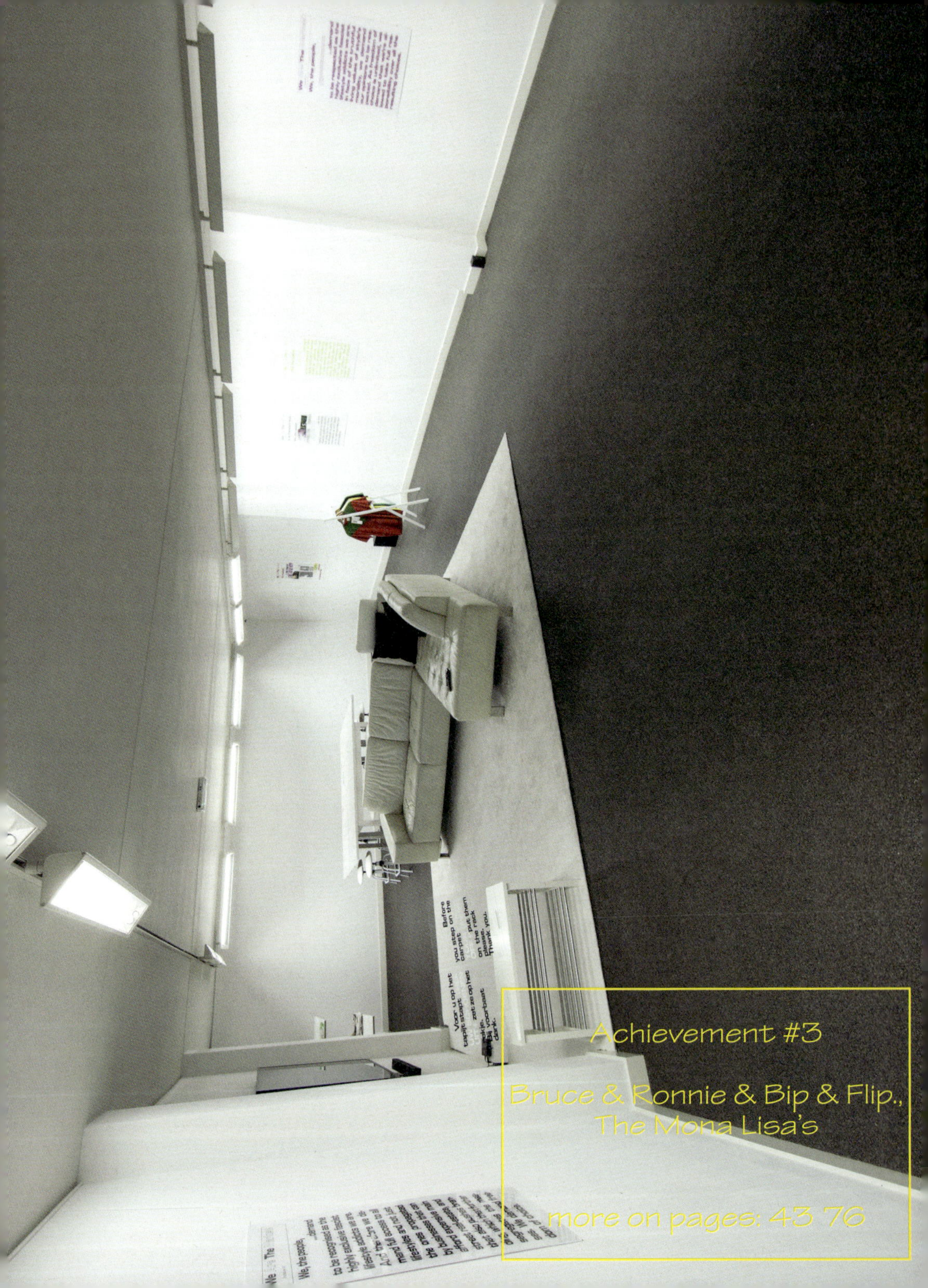

Achievement #3

Bruce & Ronnie & Bip & Flip., The Mona Lisa's

more on pages: 43 76

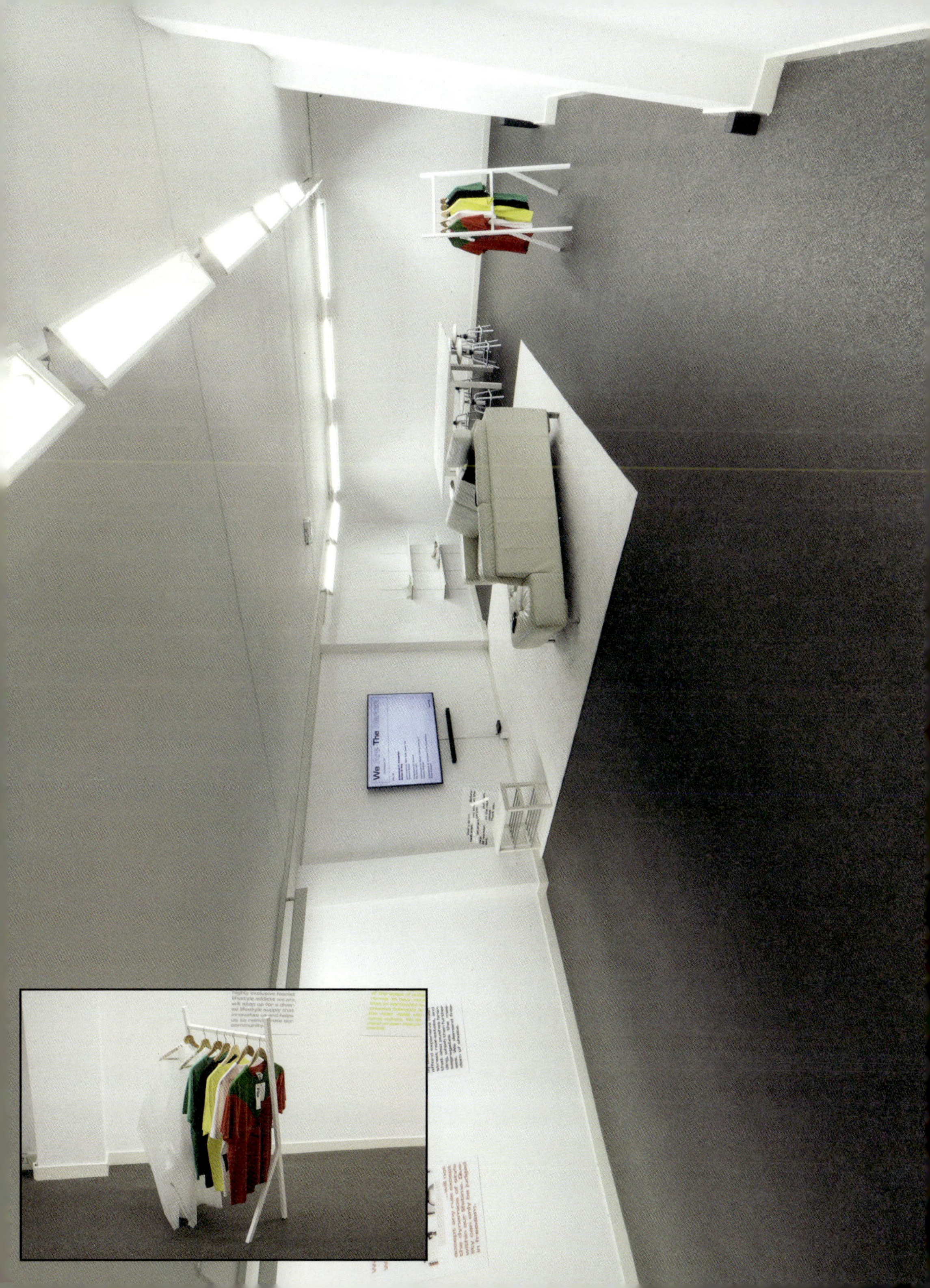

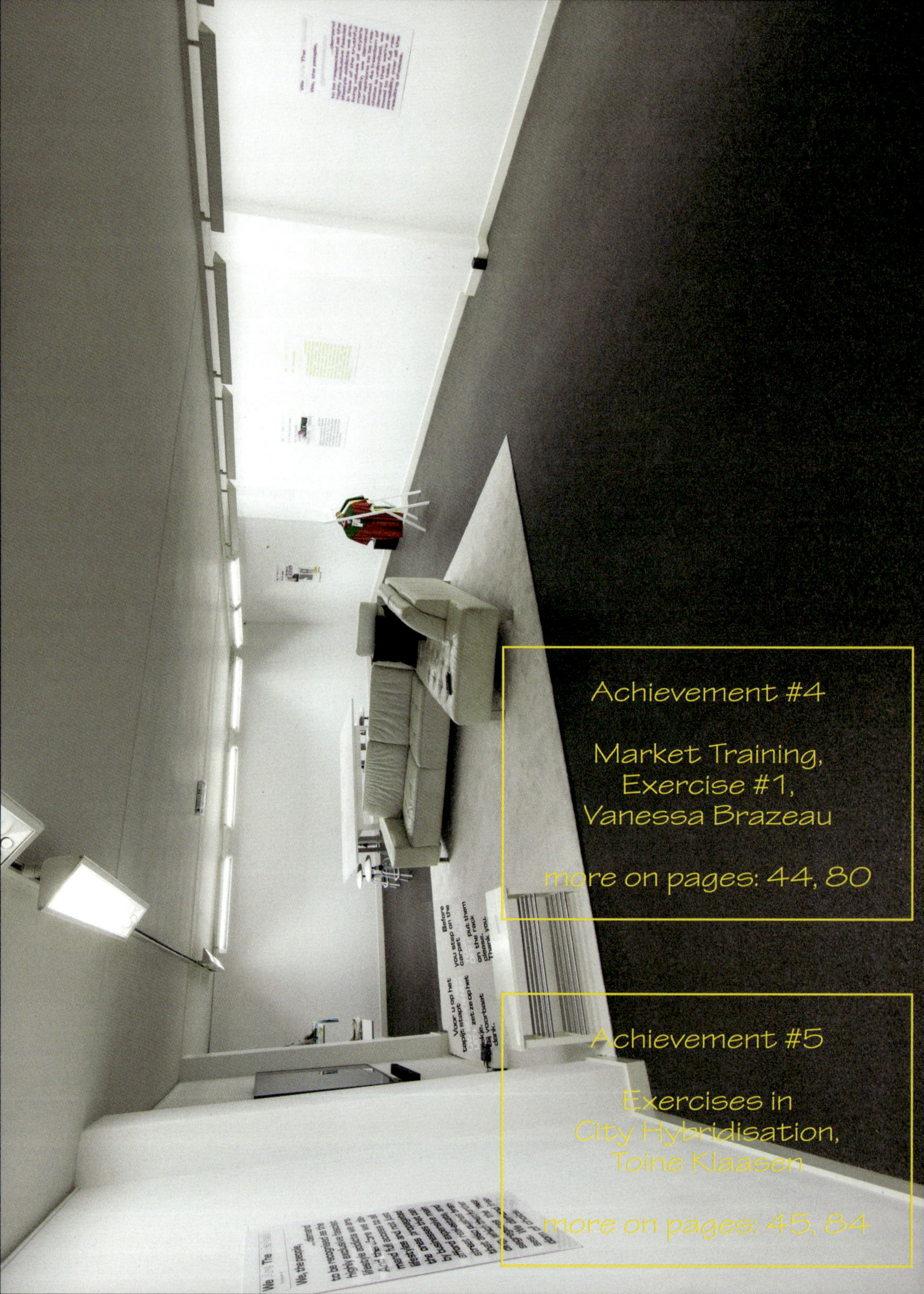

Achievement #4

Market Training,
Exercise #1,
Vanessa Brazeau

more on pages: 44, 80

Achievement #5

Exercises in
City Hybridisation,
Toine Klaasen

more on pages: 45, 84

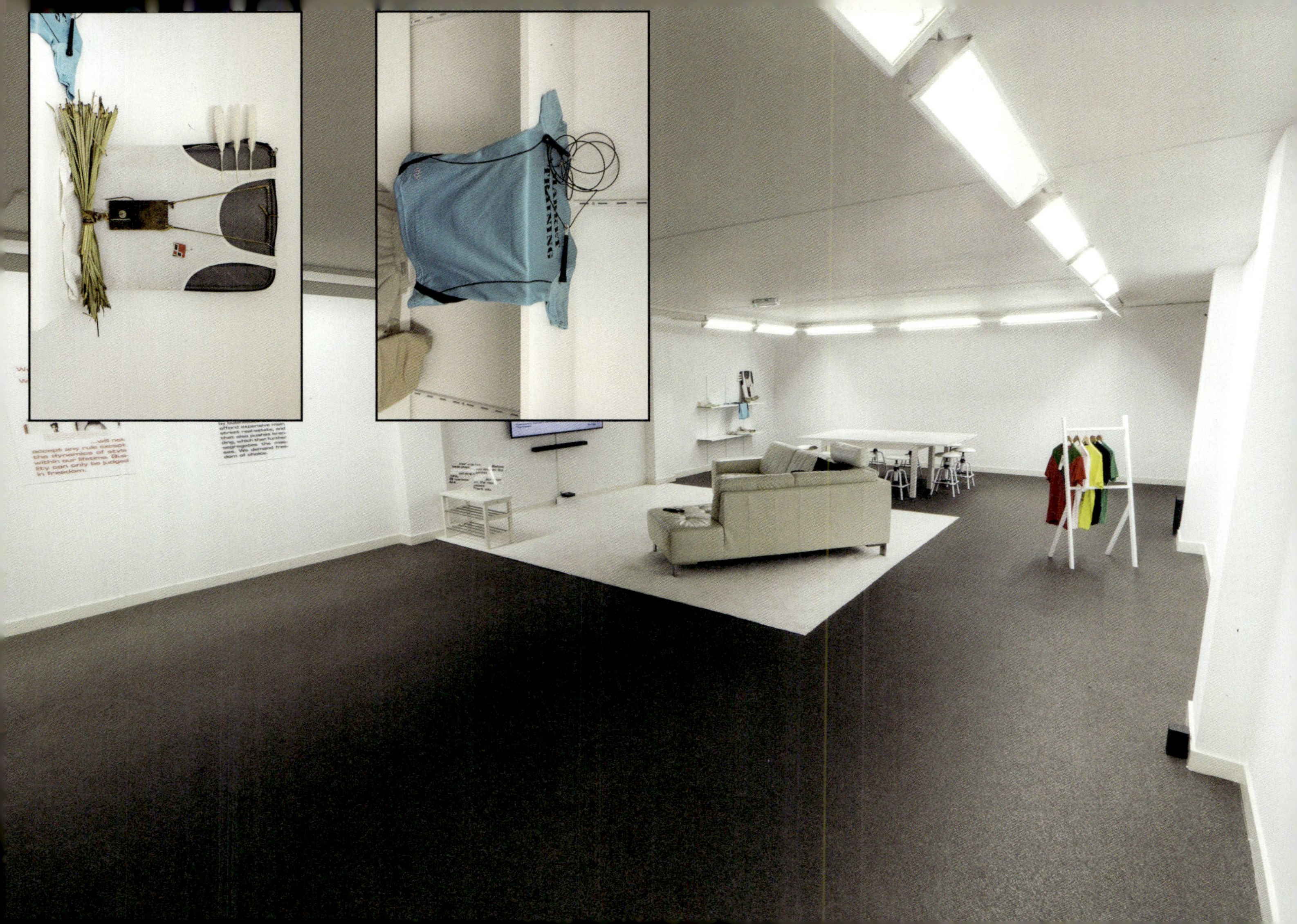
will not
accept any rule except
the dynamics of style
in freedom.
afford expensive main
street real-estate, and
that also pushes bran-
ding, which then further
segregates the mas-
ses. We demand free-
dom of choice.

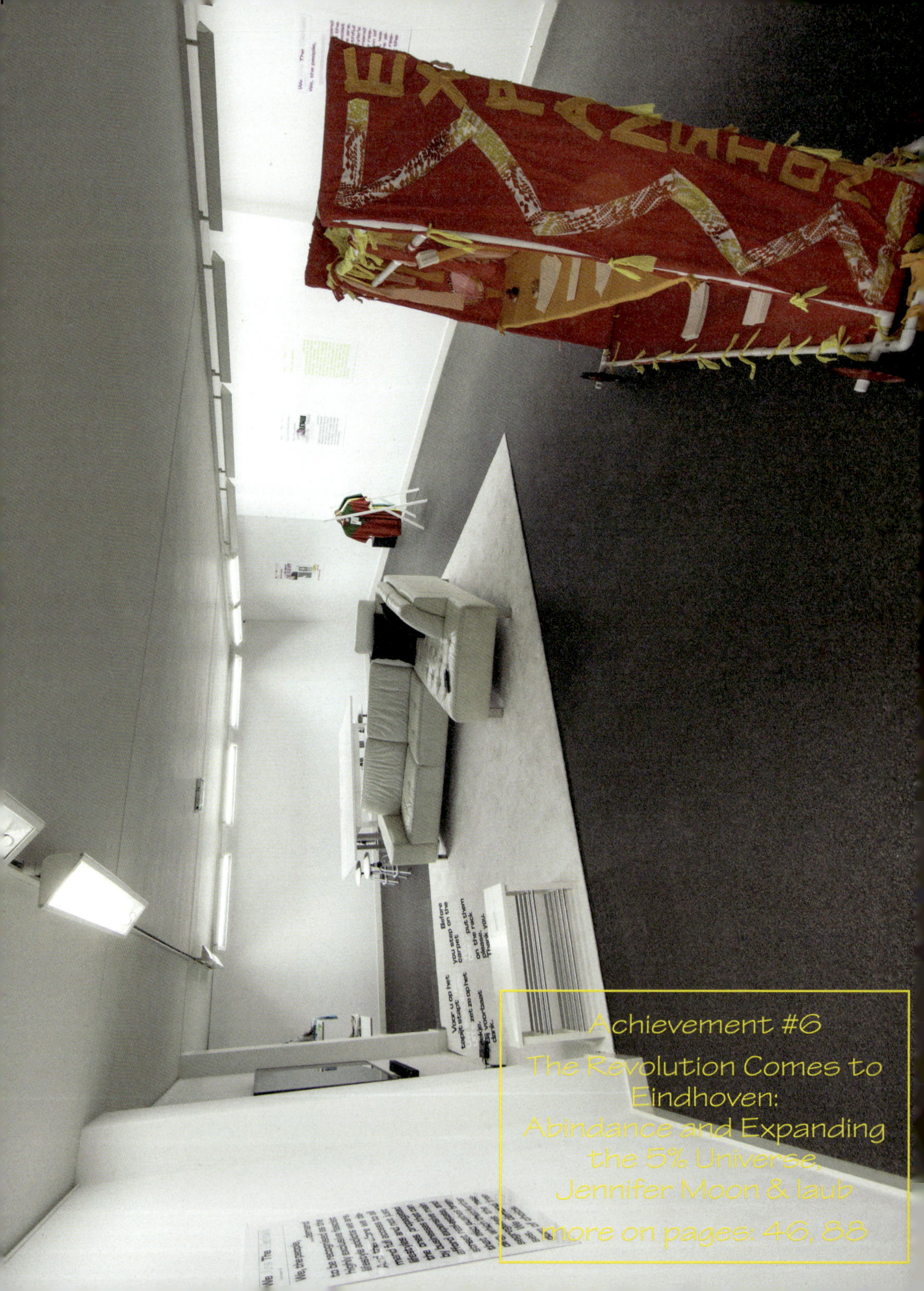

Achievement #6
The Revolution Comes to Eindhoven: Abindance and Expanding the 5% Universe, Jennifer Moon & laub

more on pages: 46, 88

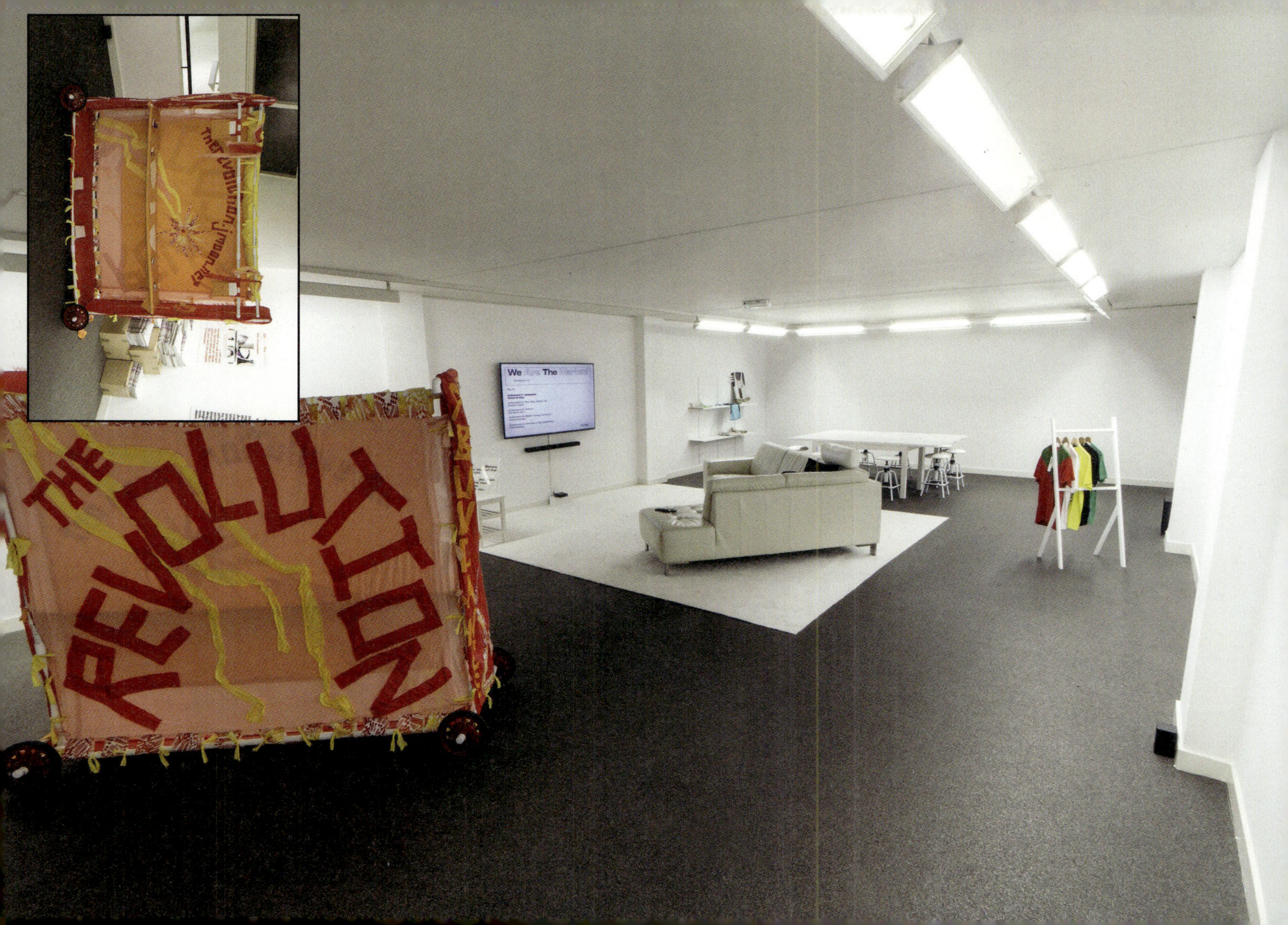
THE REVOLUTION
We Are The

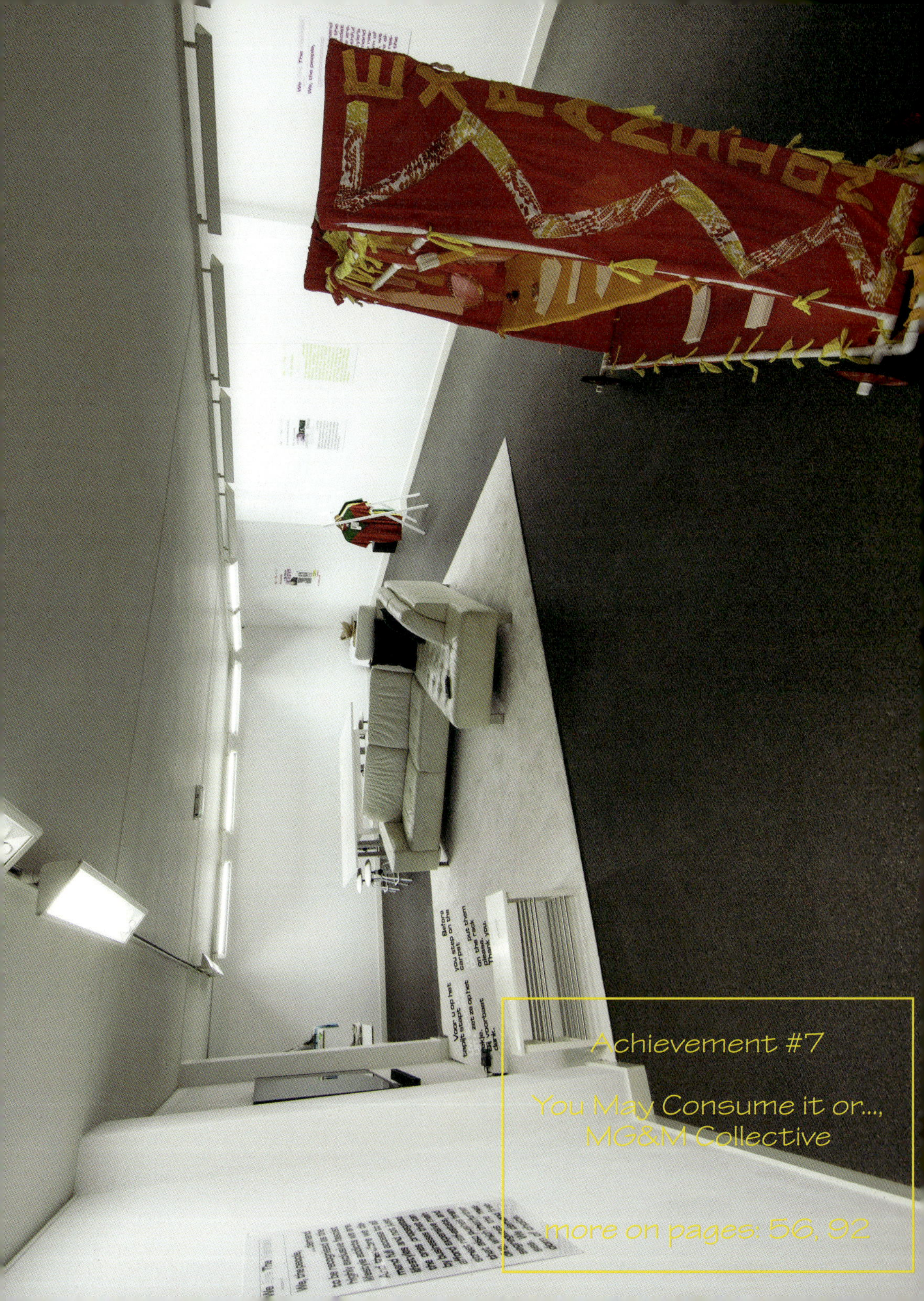

Achievement #7

You May Consume it or...,
MG&M Collective

more on pages: 56, 92

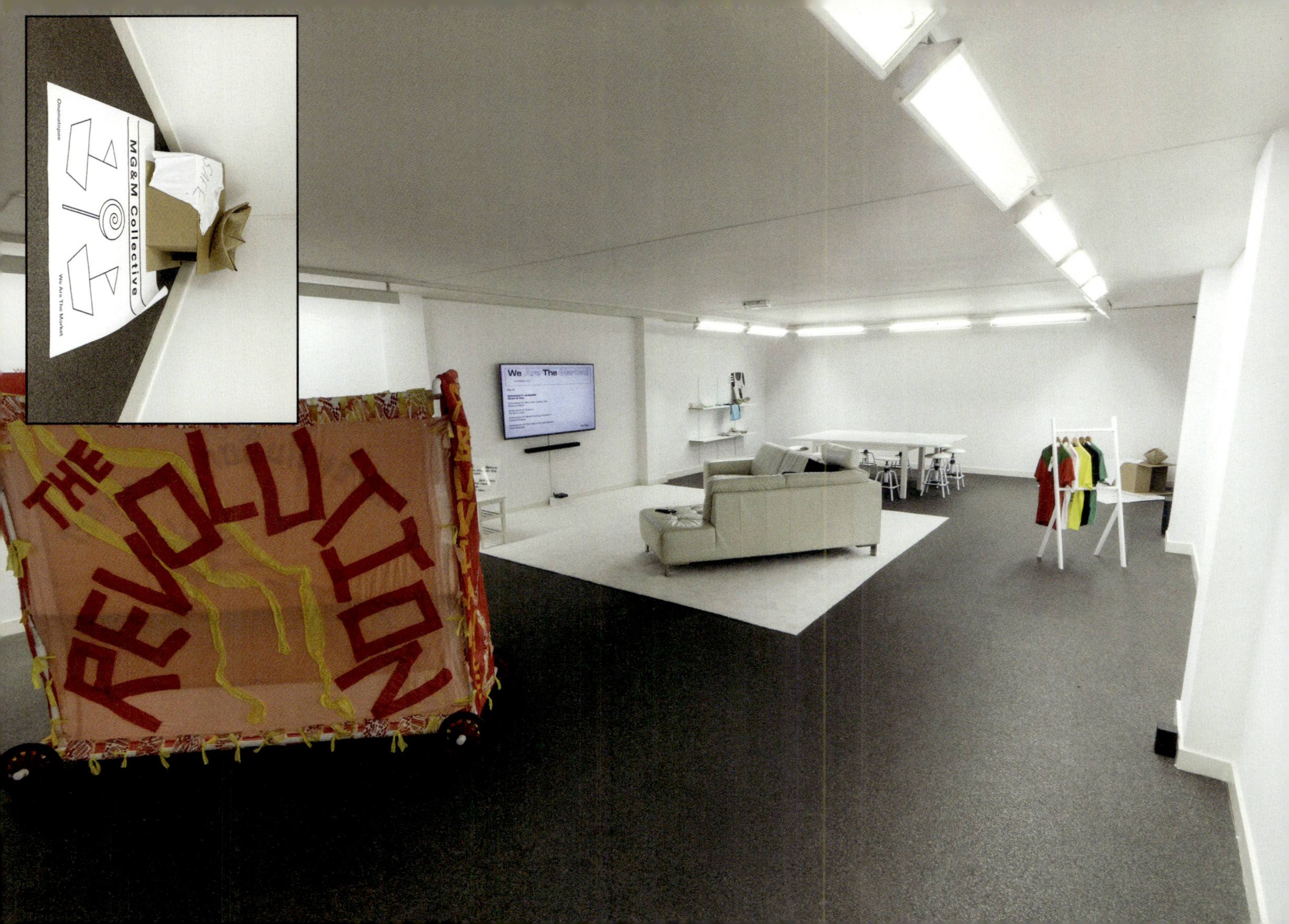
THE REVOLUTION
SAFE
MG&M Collective
Onomatopee
We Are The Market

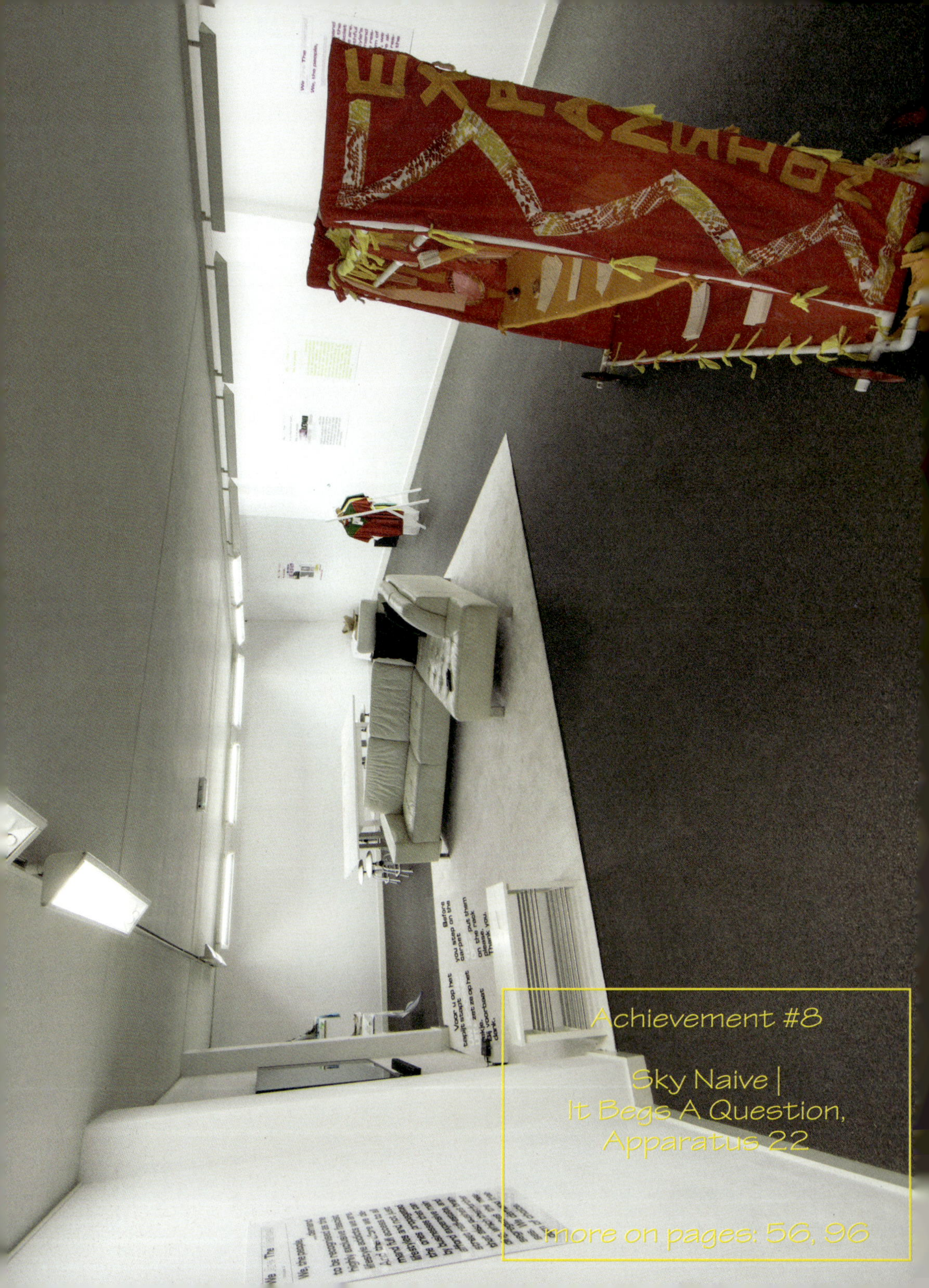

Achievement #8

Sky Naive |
It Begs A Question,
Apparatus 22

more on pages: 56, 96

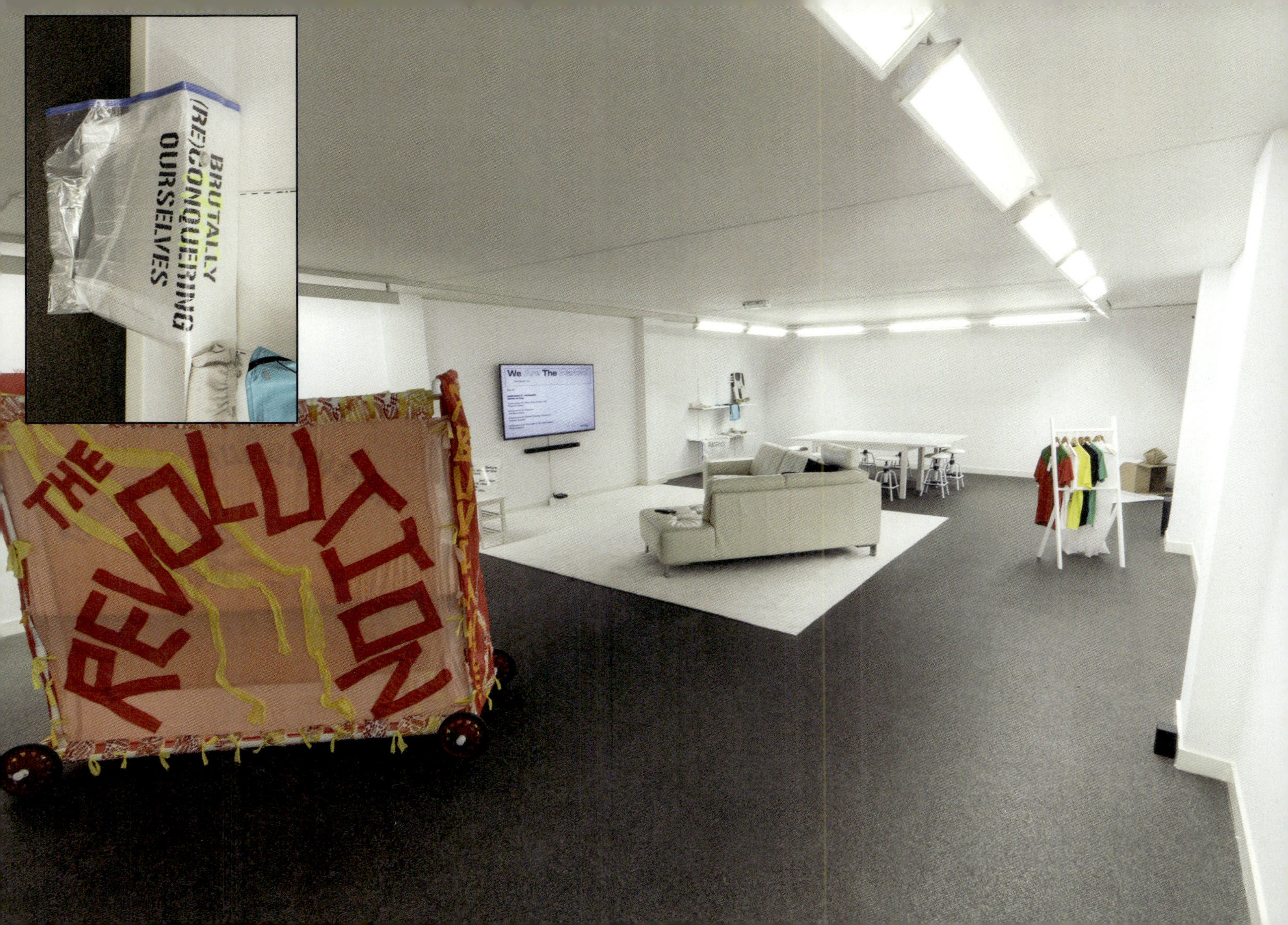
BRUTALLY
(RE)CONQUERING
OURSELVES
THE
REVOLUTION

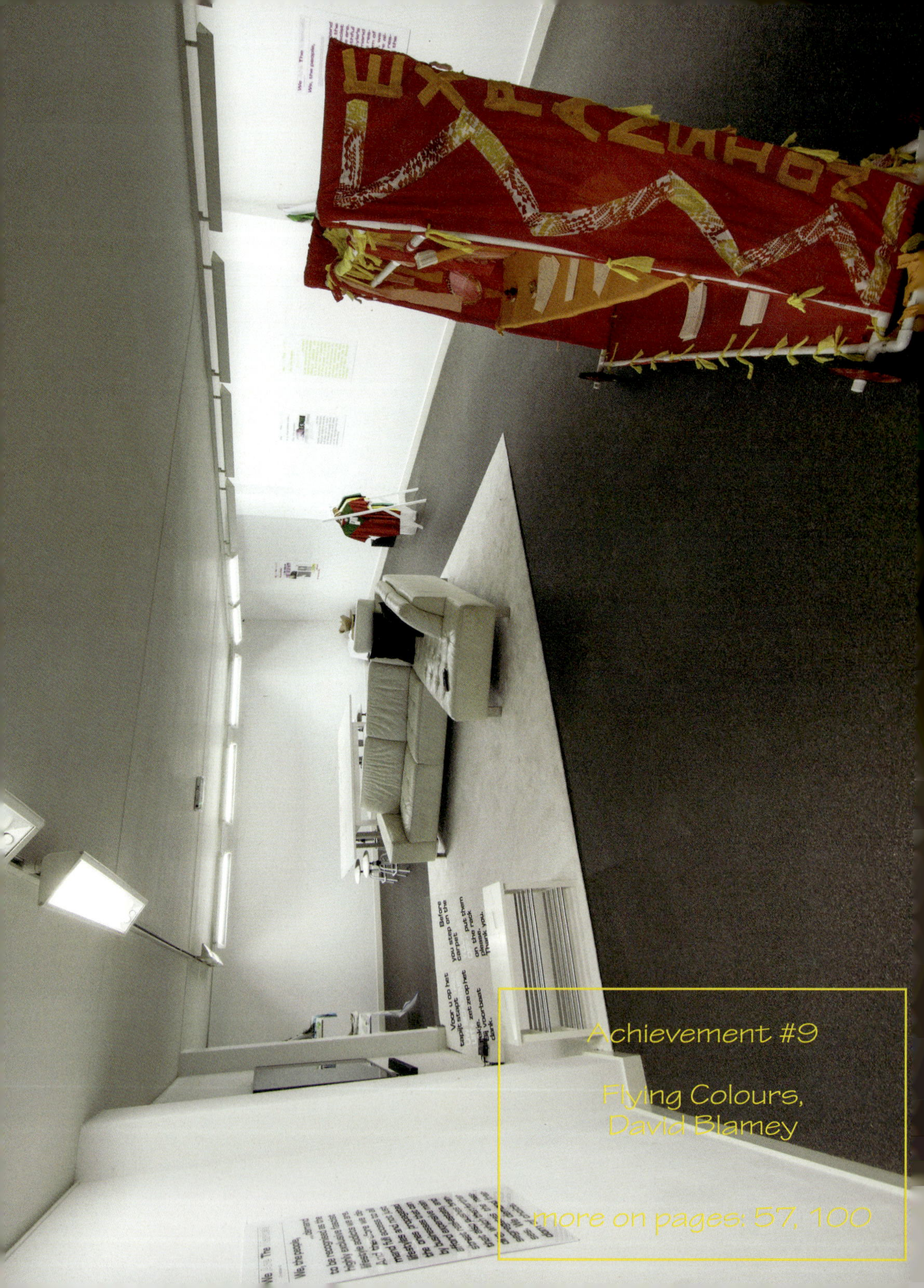

Achievement #9

Flying Colours,
David Blamey

more on pages: 57, 100

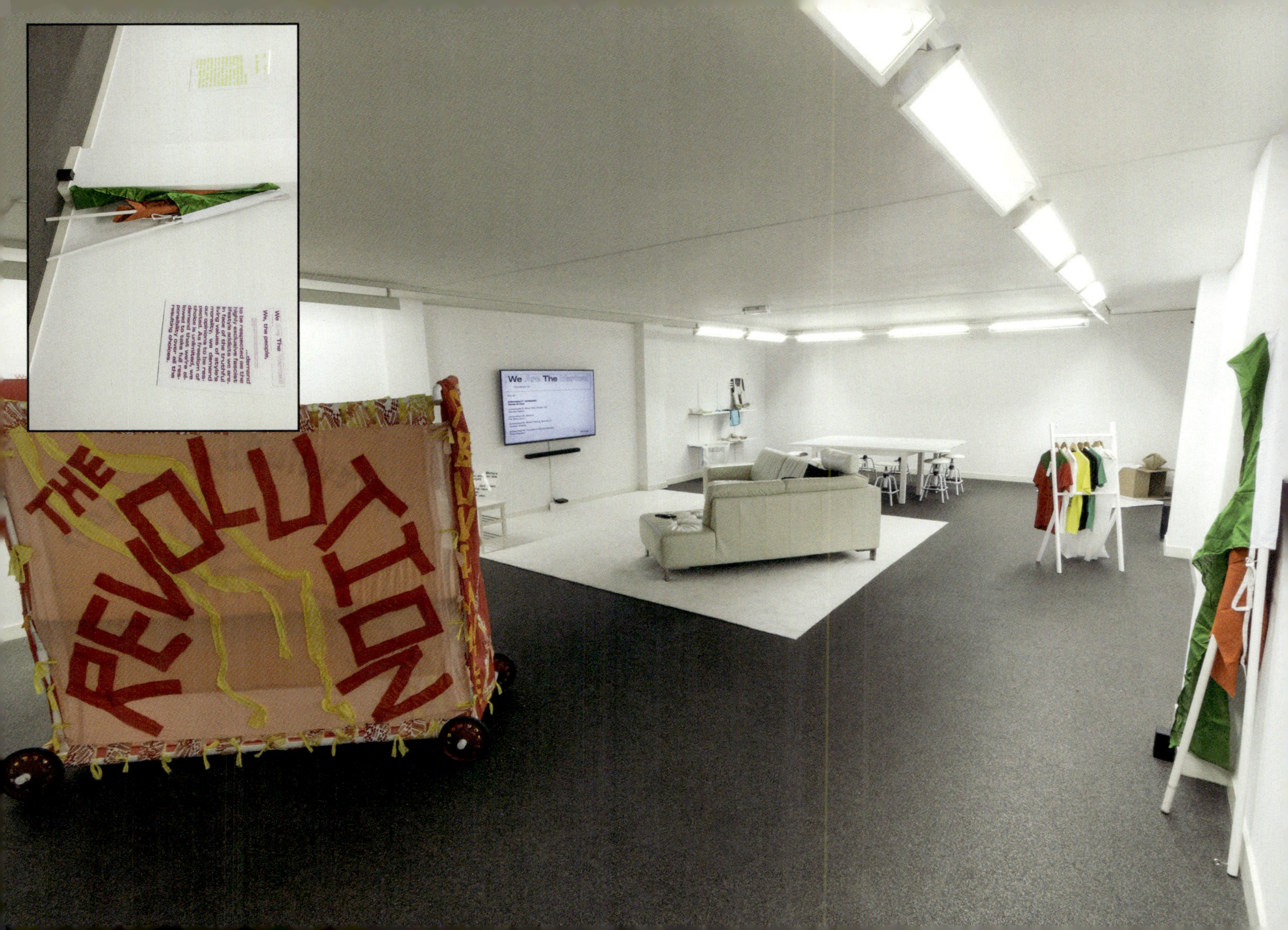
THE REVOLUTION
We, the people,
...demand to be respected as the highly exclusive fascist lifestyle addicts we are. In face of the truthful living values of style's morality, we demand our opinions to be respected. As freedom of choice is unlimited, we demand that we're allowed to take full responsibility over all the resulting choices.

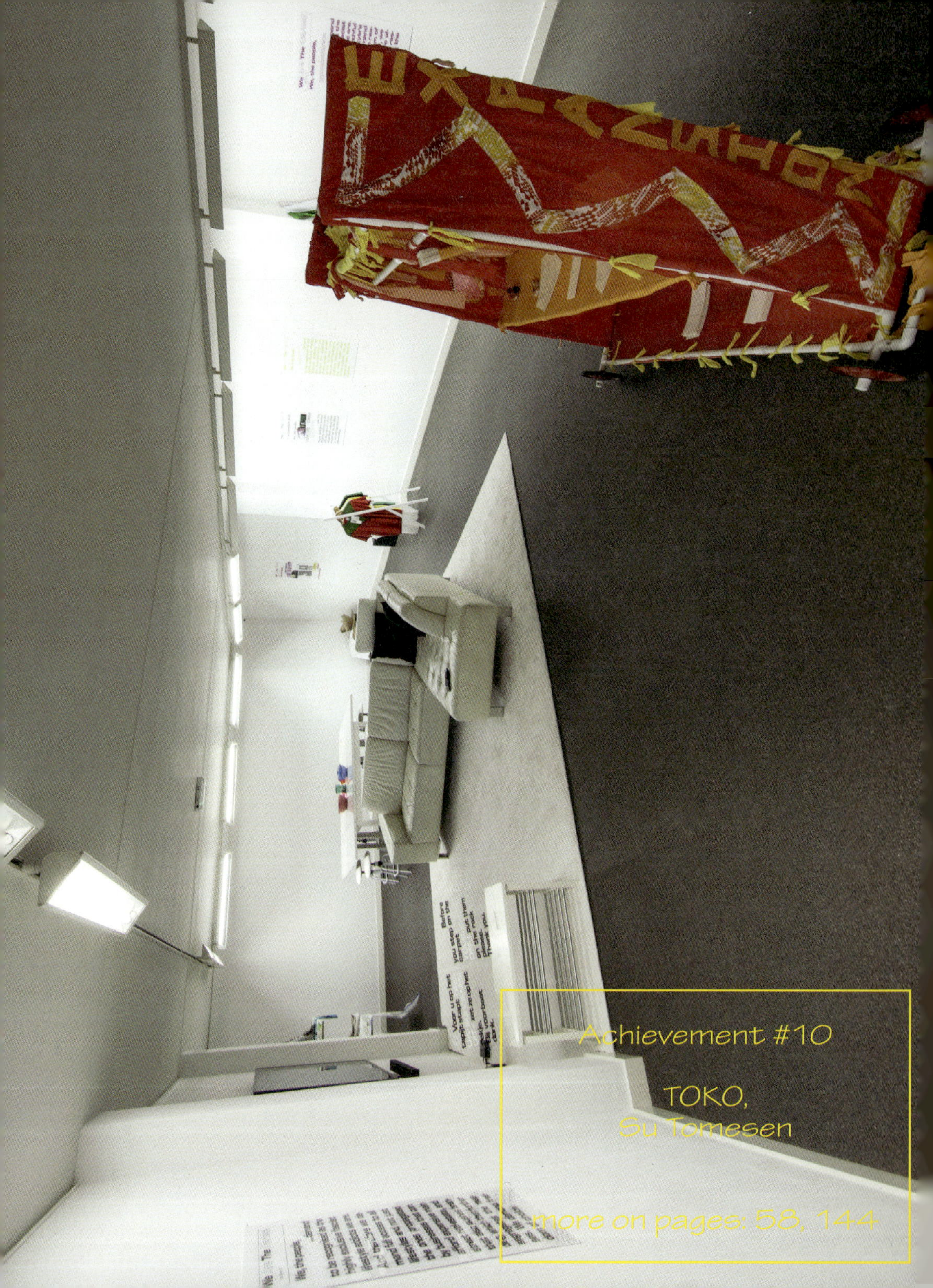

Achievement #10

TOKO,
Su Tomesen

more on pages: 58, 144

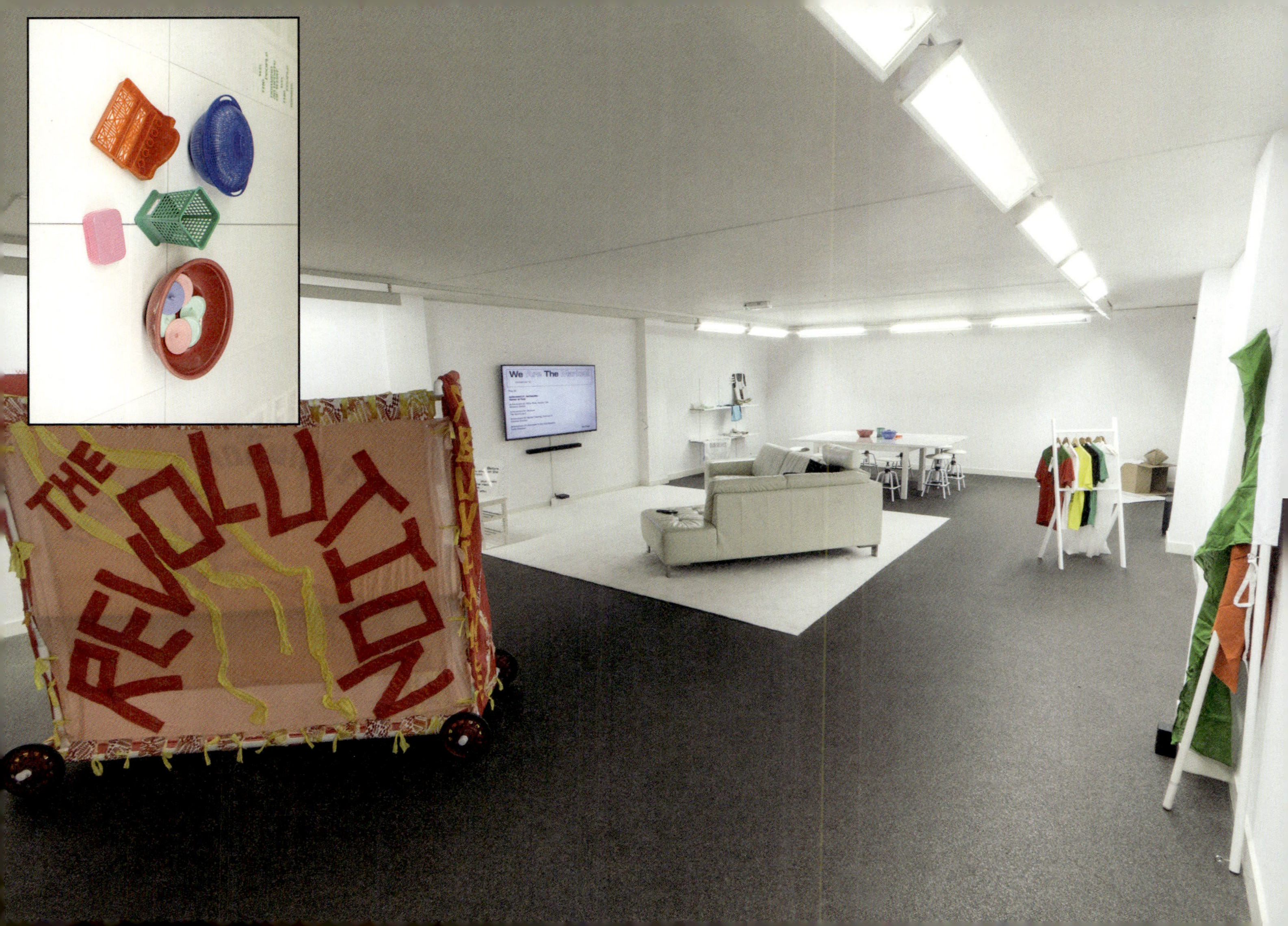
THE REVOLUTION

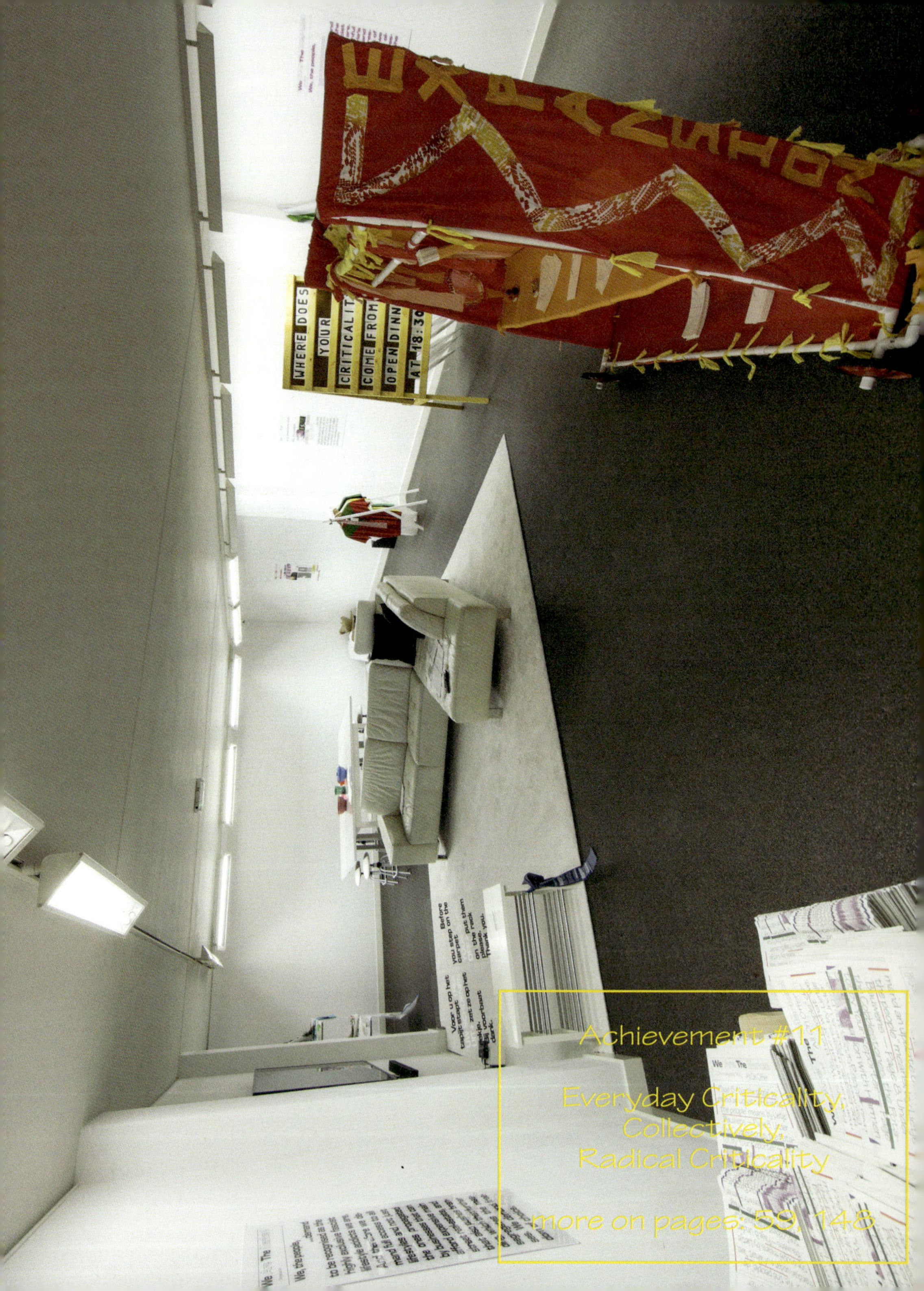

Achievement #11

Everyday Criticality,
Collectively,
Radical Criticality

more on pages: 59, 148

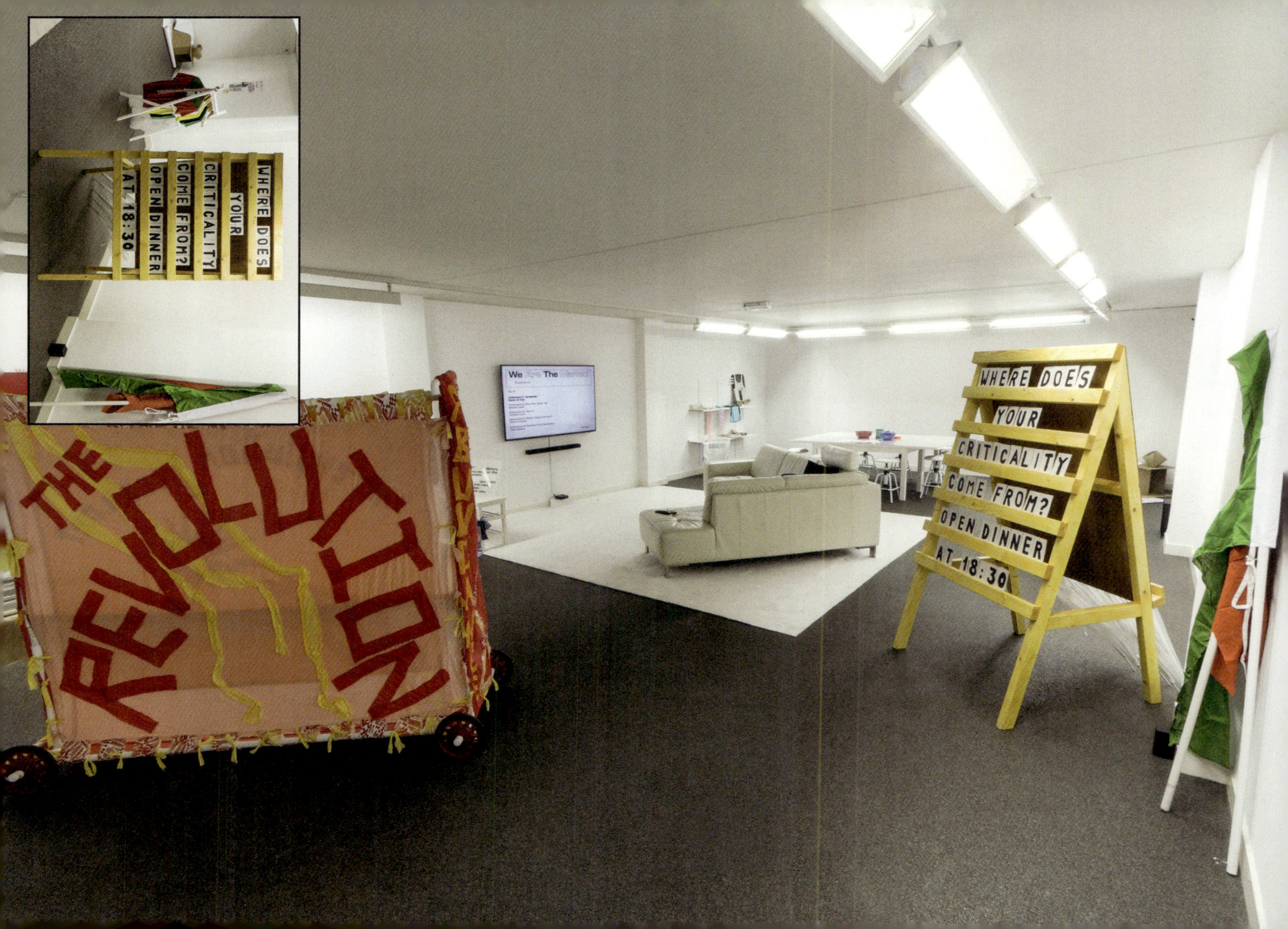
THE REVOLUTION
WHERE DOES
YOUR
CRITICALITY
COME FROM?
OPEN DINNER
AT 18:30

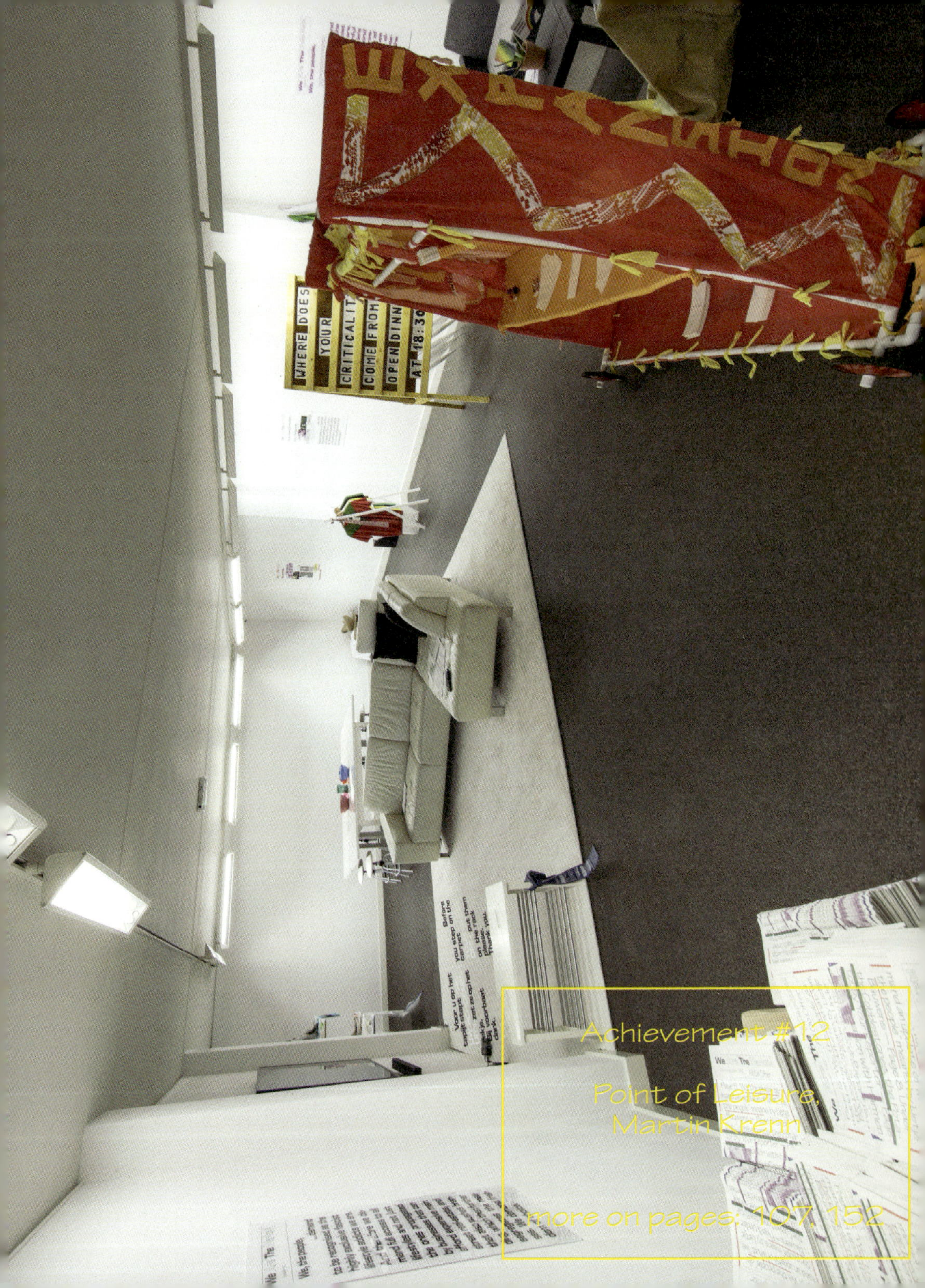

Achievement #12

Point of Leisure,
Martin Krenn

more on pages: 107, 152

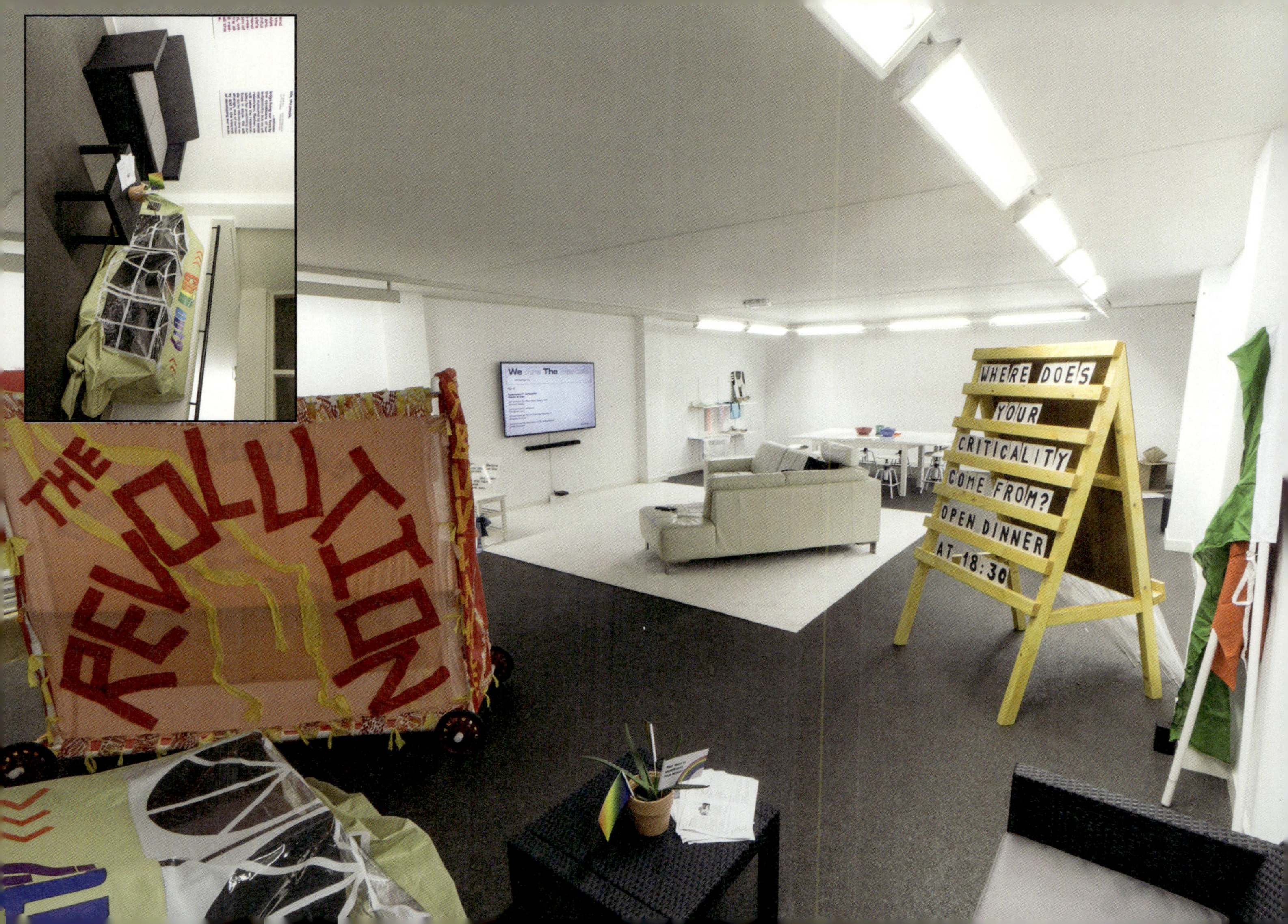

THE REVOLUTION
WHERE DOES
YOUR
CRITICALITY
COME FROM?
OPEN DINNER
AT 18:30

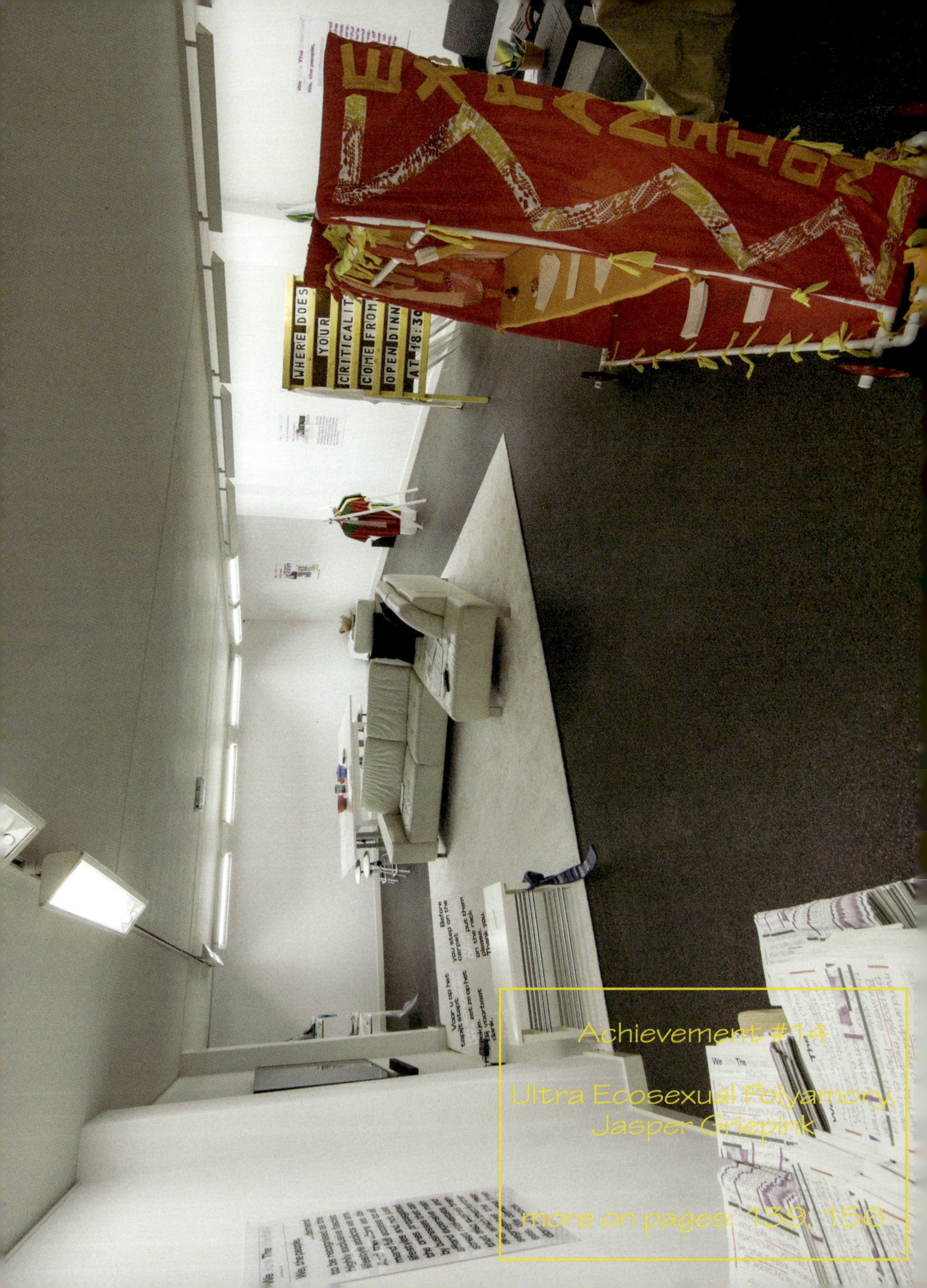

Achievement #14

Ultra Ecosexual Polyamory,
Jasper Griepink

more on pages: 139, 156

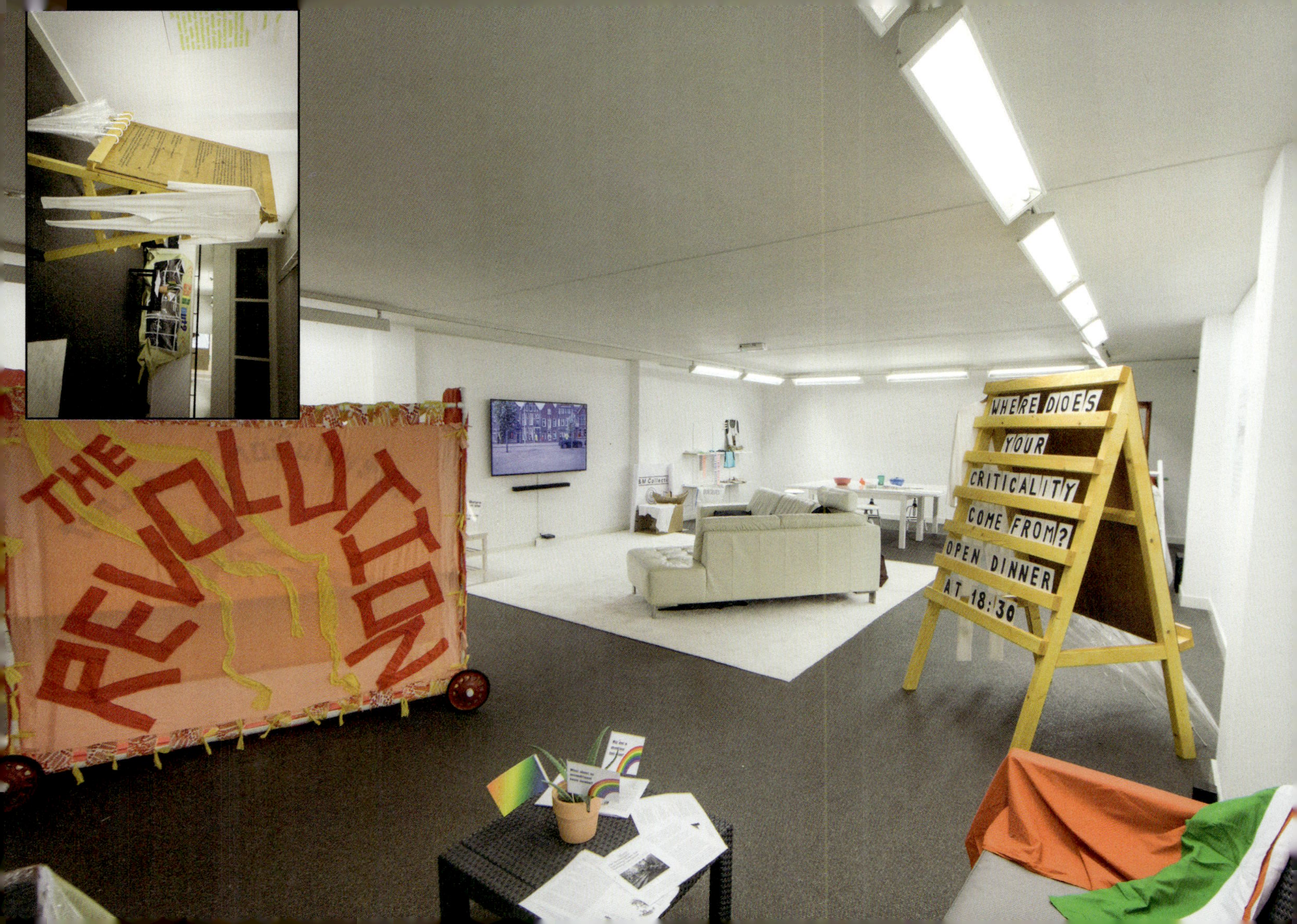
THE
REVOLUTION
WHERE DOES
YOUR
CRITICALITY
COME FROM?
OPEN DINNER
AT 18:30

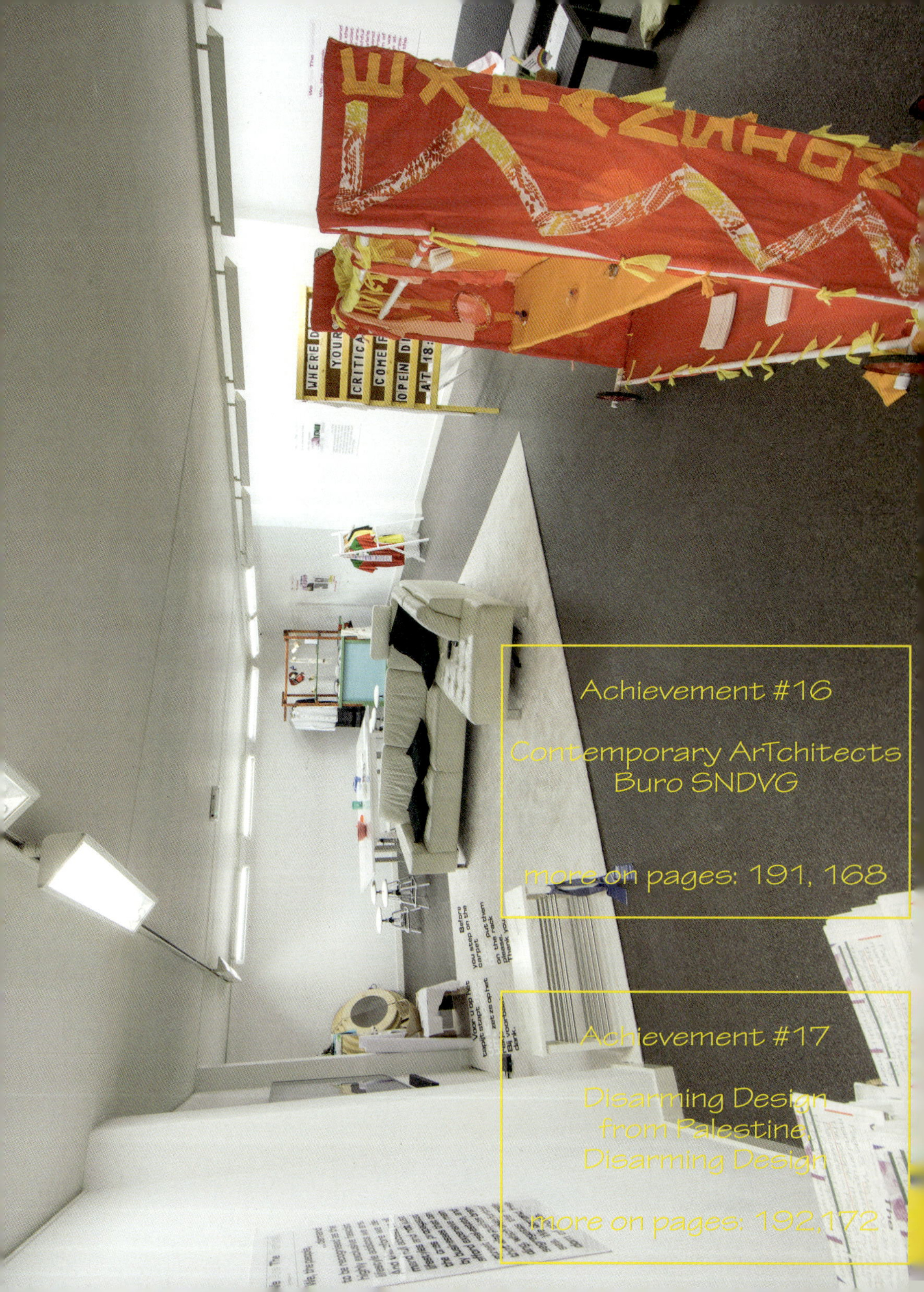

Achievement #16

Contemporary ArTchitects
Buro SNDVG

more on pages: 191, 168

Achievement #17

Disarming Design
from Palestine,
Disarming Design

more on pages: 192,172

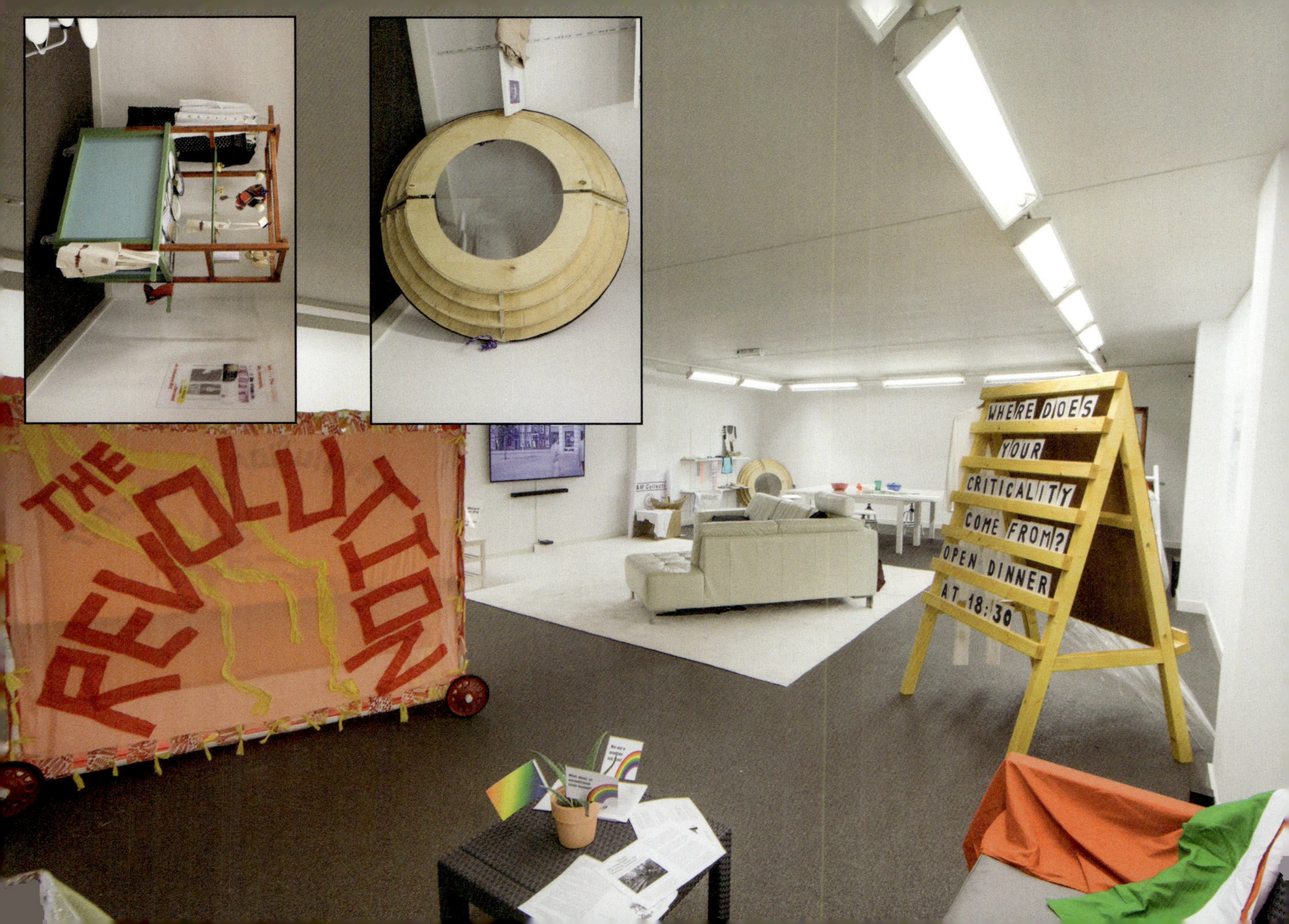
THE REVOLUTION
WHERE DOES
YOUR
CRITICALITY
COME FROM?
OPEN DINNER
AT 18:30

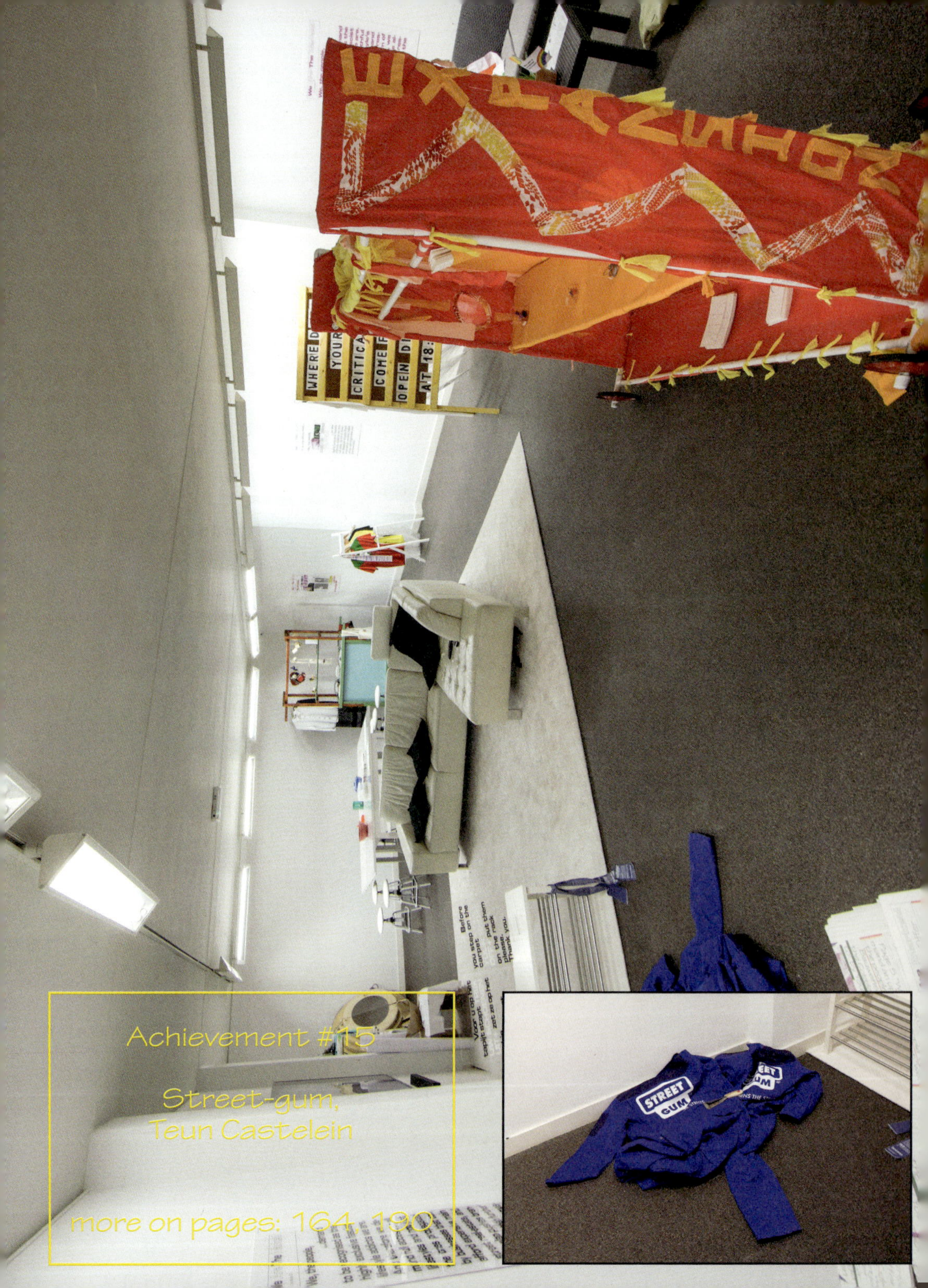

Achievement #15

Street-gum,
Teun Castelein

more on pages: 164, 190

IN THE BEGINNING...

IN THE BEGINNING...
by Freek Lomme

Pushing the stretch of our cultural offer We Are The Market! claims a liberal ALL-INCLUSIVITY. It does so right in the eye of the final commonplace: the capitalist commons of the high street.

As the relatively unmarked solidarity of "the masses"—both online and offline—are segregating as "publics" and whilst they are increasingly exposed as targeted; the high street and the city centre emerge as the "neo-traditional" hotspot of cultural production. These might be the last places to give way to a truly public scene, that is, a place built on the foundation of collective premises whereupon diversity is lived. But also here, or even more so here, the invisible hand of capitalism pushes its influences as cultural producer to its "diverse audiences". As we live the "capitalist commons", are we the last ones to wonder where the disinterested sphere of public engagement lies? Are we the last of our kind to experience a life without economic interests tagging our cultural life?

We Are The Market! wonders what the public role of cultural production could be beyond the likes of them, be it through art, design, philosophy, poetry or whatever—and what challenges the institutional frame of a not-for-profit that serves a public mission beyond the one the government sets for itself... Since capitalism already stole guerrilla marketing and public practice, engaged live art may soon be an equally obsolete cultural strategy in promoting an offering beyond our presumed and conditioned likes. Revolt—a rather inelegant and often not particularly eloquent form of engagement—might soon be the only alternative for civil and grassroots engagements.

Indeed, the disinterested sphere of art is under siege. A general interest that could collectively produce quality seems remote. As public space is nevertheless open for all to wonder in the heart of the city with a unique offer, Onomatopee Projects has to step up by any means available and show that it is not just another shop but rather a different incarnation of public space with free services. We Are The Market! did so by promoting and commissioning the production of an alternative offer on the streets of Eindhoven.

We Are The Market! might just be the final convulsion of a dying organisation unable to uphold its public engagement while enduring a decadent and arrogant provincialism that does not put faith into people's capacity to cope with diversity. This is even more painful as we were only able to deliver this project as a publicly funded organisation. We are extremely grateful for this and are presumably more aware than others may be because of it. People should be aware of the unique qualities the public sector (still) exercises when moderating the cultural bandwidth on our behalf. All people engaged with public service should promote this very capacity, it should inspire public pride and dignity over and again as these involved logics—as was expressed by the many true, receptive and critical exchanges we had with so many people on the streets—offer so much of the true backbone of our dignity.

The progressive cultural producers—artists, designers, writers, makers and others invited—contributed by concentration, specific means and abilities, sourced by their all too often precarious engagement fuelled practices. This publication does not showcase the evident and globally established art-world entrepreneur incorporated into the clientelism of the scene, but the relatively unknown engaged practitioner out there pushing for a difference through alternative postures. I hope you judge what people here achieved yourself and consider their ease of access. Something that is helped along with some introductions and articles written fora newspaper we previously published in an edition of 10.000—all distributed for free on the streets of Eindhoven.

As we reached the end of the project by finishing the last pieces of public engagement, we can also look back upon the result of the mission and ask, to what extent did the developed content serve the goal? Intended to step up for an alternative offer, we can now say the offer was not that prominent in establishing a collective awareness in the people. Rather it sharpened the individual's tolerance and awareness when engaging with the achievements and conversations. When looking back through all the content it is unquestionable that we connected with so many people, either through direct contact or as a bystander. We built relations with neighbouring shops and others living and working nearby and made people curious for what Onomatopee Projects is all about. Furthermore the involved cultural producers mingled in and around the white cube, both amongst themselves and with other people working on projects; either risographing or simply hanging out at Onomatopee. In that sense, the objective to promote Onomatopee as a public space that's able to be used by all became more apparent.

Despite this, we can never compete with the garish and ever more forceful nudging of the invisible and culturally economic hands of whatever franchises surround us. It feels like whatever we do it well never be enough unless we first lose everything and so have all the time in the world to become a precarious mass of souls, lost on the streets. This scenario would make us the losers of globalisation, not the cosmopolite producers with a local anchoring we are supposed to be. It is also for that reason that Onomatopee is situated in Eindhoven, being the most economically flourishing region in The Netherlands; which is one of the most economically flourishing countries in Western Europe; which is one of the economically best equipped areas in the world.... At the same time it is a city where the history mainly consists of the 100-year old rise of Philips industrial manufacturing: something that is now vanishing to give way to the knowledge based economy. This change brings in new inhabitants in want of a higher level of cultural offer—a cosmopolite that is less focused on local pride. This balancing between localism and cosmopolitanism is the challenge of a globalising world and a challenge for a city in transit. Sharpening awareness supports the building of social cohesion during changing times. We Are the Market, We Are The People.

1.

UNDER THE COBBLESTONES, THE POTATO

Your reporter >> p. 69

The Dutch, if they weren't made of flesh and bones, would I'm sure be made of potatoes. This earth dwelling piece of (often) golden matter was once described by Friedrich Engels as being the equal of iron in its 'historically revolutionary role'. This subversive tuber has once again been caught up in a political act that obscures its humble origins.

One of the most exciting aspects of humanity is our ability to give real agency to inanimate things. Just through the act of picking up a potato and not eating it, we imbue it with an almost extra terrestrial purpose. To defenestrate a potato is akin to humans walking on the moon, while one obviously requires more money, they are both in fact examples of humankind's capability for imagination. Both those actions represent our ability to think abstract thoughts and reach for tools to solve problems.

This act of reaching for tools is exactly what the Rotterdam based artist Harmen de Hoop did when creating his achievement Aardappelen. On a disingenuously sunny day in May the artist arrived in the southern Dutch city with a trowel in his hand and an empty rucksack on his back. With these basic gadgets he walked into the supermarket to purchase a bag of Dutch potatoes. This was a blatant disruption of the equilibrium. For a farmer had to plant these vegetables, let them grow, package them, transport them, and finally sell them; only for them to then be picked up by an artist and placed back into the ground. But this is what happened, and Eindhoven will be a greener place for it. This is because Aardappelen is a project that challenges the idea of public space: de Hoop finds a piece of public land, which very often turns out to be private, and grows vegetables and wheat on it for the people of the city, as he explains:

'The whole concept of public space hardly exists anymore, and certainly not the romantic idea that there is a town square where you can meet people. Usually that is totally commercial, privatised or not, but certainly commercial. But there are left over spaces that you can change the function of, like here there's this very small piece of soil used for plants, and I as an individual can decide that I want to use it for a different function.'

What could be interpreted as a very banal act, is actually quite a deviant one. It harnesses an archetype, the trusted symbol that we usually pay no attention to, and uses it as a conduit. It channels debate from the dirt into the public realm. Watching de Hoop dig the holes and plant the potatoes may well be one of the most insightful aspects to this project. We're so often told how little attention people pay to their environments, but it's so evident when watching his achievement at Onomatopee. Individuals glued to screens wander pass, groups carry on talking to each other, and cyclists take no notice — all the while a man in a red shirt pushes spuds into the ground. It highlights an indifference to these spaces, as long as people can walk through they don't seem to care about the invisible forces that are at play.

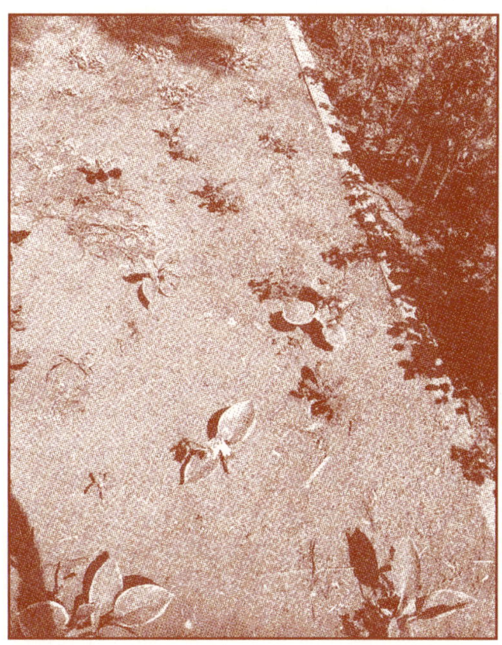

But this is where we need to stop and look, just like the masses didn't. Why does it matter that we as a whole don't care about the erosion of public space, and more increasingly soil? As long as we're "free" to walk through and to buy what we want, why do we need to comprehend these things? Well, de Hoop can enlighten:

'For me it's about perception and making the passer-by think for just a second about elements of public space, of their life, of the city, just thinking about it. So just twenty seconds of philosophy without any change, and without changing their lives or getting other people to do something.'

But what is this twenty seconds worth? As it's already been mentioned, they are just potatoes and it is just time. How can an act like that be effective in the wider city? How will it change the public's behaviour? The answer is that it probably won't, not this single act anyway. Yet what Onomatopee has done is document the whole process while also evaluating and critiquing it. For the most part this is what has the potential to change the people's minds, and to force them into asking questions they wouldn't usually.

So why are there potatoes planted on Willemstraat? Go and find out for yourself

2.

MISTY WALK, SWEATY TALK

Anon >> p. 72

Dear Sir,

First of all, I'm worried.

What's makes someone write to a newspaper to complain, argue or to just vent? I'll tell you and your readers.

Art.

The Dutch masters would be turning in their graves. I don't know what passes for art these days but what I saw in Eindhoven's city centre made me feel nothing. I want a visceral reaction from my art, I want to get lost in a beautifully composed reverie. What took place on Rechtestraat in July was no more art, than if I were to walk around the town centre covered in sweat having just come back from a run.

Next, when I shop it is my time to relax, to just enjoy myself, to take my family out and spoil them. Eindhoven has a great selection of public sculpture, but I can encounter it on my own terms. Why then must these 'artists' insist on encroaching on my space? If I'm to believe that this is what passes for art these days, then we dear editor, are in worse cultural shape than I thought. There was an absence in this 'performance', it alienated me and my family; it was not inclusive at all. That's not even mentioning the fact that it was filmed, isn't there a law against that anyway? Filming in a public space, shouldn't I have to give my consent first, and what about filming my children?

Finally, I would like to make it clear that I fundamentally disagree with the fact that this was publicly funded. The money should be put to better use. Simply, it's ridiculous.

Yours faithfully,

Anon

3.

BRUCE&
RONNIE&
BIP&
FLIP.

Your reporter >> p. 76

Absence—to many is a loss or a void, a feeling of something missing or of something that's never been grasped. We, the body, can be absent while also being present, it's our minds that are elsewhere. This absence of mind, then leads to questions of self; and it's within this division between the mind and the body that the internet can linger. An online culture has developed that is stretching what it means to be absent, our plastic lives and experiences are being simultaneously die-cast yet pulled apart. As soon as what resembles a life is visible and starts to emerge from the liquid crystal, it's immediately warped. Our physical existence becomes a kind of Pygmalion glitch: the online avatars that we sculpt gain an agency in reality, and what used to be virtual becomes actuality. Could these newly sentient parts of ourselves fully materialise and confront the original?

The Mona Lisa's, a Rotterdam based art collective, are the people who could potentially start to answers questions like these. Dealing with internet memes and folklore, as well as pagan rituals and anonymous expressions of cyber subcultures.

What was recited in Eindhoven was a paean to the commercial gods. Who according to The Mona Lisa's, help form our collective memories and therefore our identities under consumer capitalism. Our thoughts are no longer held by the fear of what lurks in the woods, but by what we consume, or more accurately what we don't consume. Our insecurities about identity are laid bare as the communities that helped define us are replaced by transient systems of people. It's no surprise then that as the self is eroding, people are seeking out online groups to belong to; thus helping to (re)define themselves in the process.

The collective's contribution to the ongoing exhibition of We Are The Market was to hang up second hand t- shirts with fake logos on them in the local square. The reason for this was that their research revealed people dressing up as these "gods"; there were Ronald McDonalds and Incredible Hulks, aplenty. This prompted the question what becomes of the self when you put these costumes on? The Mona Lisa's wanted to challenge our idea of identity under globalisation by hijacking the utilitarian nature of the t-shirt and creating the most minimal of costume changes. It was while these t-shirts hung in the empty square that the absence between selves was most noticeable. Each one was strung out on a line, as if waiting for an individual to pass by the nonexistent market and take it home. They hung forlornly in the square reminding the would be consumers of the dream that they could become someone else. While this was a very physical critique of the self, it can still highlight the debate about how we act online.

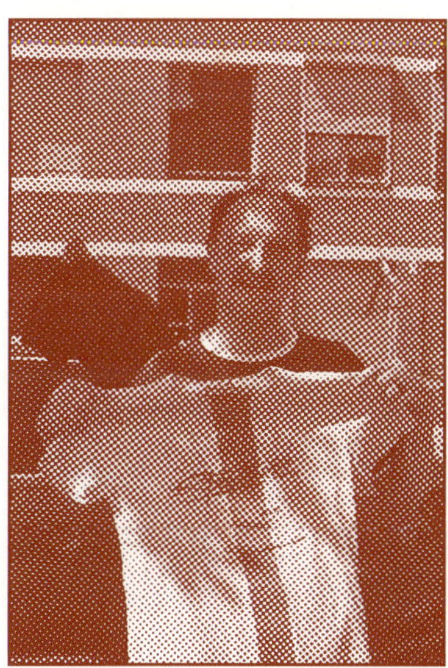

This also ties in with another fascination of the group's, LARPING, or Live Action Role Playing. This activity takes people out of the chat room and transports them back into this world; while still being in full fantasy mode. The individual becomes part of something bigger, an offline network which trades in fictions of self.

What The Mona Lisa's did was challenge the construction of the individual set by the invisible yet tangible powers of the economic market. They force us to remember and chant Barbara Kruger's slogan: 'I Shop Therefore I Am, I Shop Therefore I Am'. If we challenge these ideas offline first, then hopefully we will have some answers to help us when we're on the other side; because it seems more and more likely that we'll be chanting 'I Click Therefore I am'. However we haven't quite stood face to face with these online avatars yet despite them getting closer and closer. All you have to do is search for the online rhetoric and behaviour of the alt-right, and then switch on a television to see that the two worlds are starting to blend. Yet, what still remains is the intangibility of the self, whether defined by the systems that we live under or through the decisions we make online—It feels that it's as elusive as ever.

4.

MARKET TRAINING, EXERCISE #1

Your reporter >> p. 80

When listening to what happened on Willemstraat one Saturday lunchtime the public would be forgiven for thinking there was an impromptu street festival going on, or more in the spirit of the 21st century; an outdoor fitness bootcamp, complete with a lycra clad Gunnery Sergeant Hartman. Except the disembodied voice that forced its way across the square was that of the Canadian born, Berlin based artist Vanessa Brazeau, not a fictitious character from the film Full Metal Jacket.

It was a performance commissioned by the public gallery Onomatopee, where a long and cyclical list of shoe brands were yelled through a PA system as unassuming members of the public were asked to jump rope. The individuals fit enough to take part had to skip until they stumbled, fell, or simply couldn't go on any longer; all all the while a benevolent North American voice chanted:

Saucony, Adidas, Nike, New Balance!
Saucony, Adidas, Nike, New Balance!
Saucony, Adidas, Nike, New Balance!

Brazeau's voice lent a certain authority to the piece, it was reminiscent of the infomercials and shopping channels that can be found in the labyrinth of satellite TV; that liminal space constantly selling us something twenty four hours a day. If consumer capitalism had a voice, it would be North American. Situated outside of the sports shop Runners World, Brazeau blended into the performance with a uniform of brightly coloured lycra. A uniform, that in this instance commanded power and allowed the wearer to take certain liberties, like asking people to start sweating in the name of art.

Sixteen people took part in this absurdist spectacle, some laughing and falling at the first hurdle, some taking it very seriously and actually buying the make and model of shoe that they quite literally landed on. It was an exercise that forced the consumer to make choices about the shoes they would buy based on their corporeal success or failure. The choices were almost a blur, highlighting what we all already have a sneaking suspicion about, that it doesn't really matter which one we land on anyway. The shoes are most likely to be made in the same kind of factory, out of the same kind of material, under the same kind of working conditions. All that's different is the logo.

Yet a round of applause is heard after each jump rope intervention, continuously adding to the carnivalesque atmosphere. The louder and more frenzied the rhythm, the bigger the crowd that was drawn in. What happened on Willemstraat not only engaged the public, but yanked them out of their object inspired reverie. Being stopped in the street usually comes with the stock phase of 'spare change?', or 'excuse me do you know the way to..?' But here people were made to take part in an almost regressive exercise act, the jump rope. It's this surrender and relapse through a perceivably childish act that lulls us, and them in to an almost infantile state of mind. It surrenders us to chance, to serendipity.

This act satirises the current industry direction of product customisation. Many

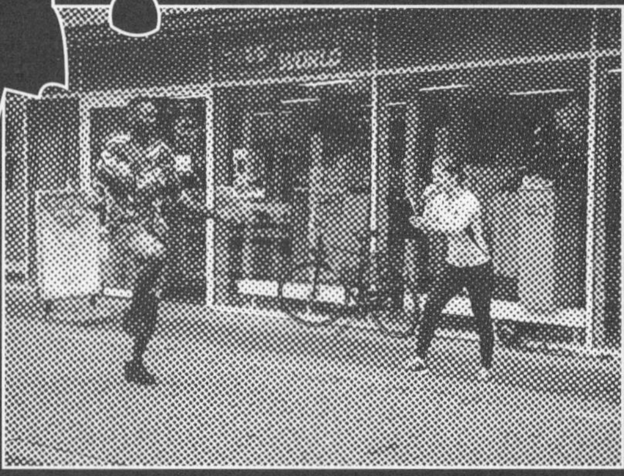

trend forecasters have written extensively on how brands can attract more consumers by apparently giving them more power over their choices. Except this choice isn't an individual choice, because you've already decided to buy their products. They've hooked you with the sales pitch 'You're free to choose', while in fact you actually lost that freedom as soon as wandered into their (web)shop seeking the exact thing you are now devoid of. Reducing these choices to chance, lays bare the blatant apathy the system has for us so long as we keep buying their stuff.

Vanessa Brazeau's performance was a surreptitious one, one that snuck in a critique of neoliberal ideology and consumer capitalism under the guise of one of the most democratising acts: sport. Using this medium as a way of starting a debate is nothing new for her as the majority of her work uses this same technique. While people could say that doing so is discriminatory against the less abled, it would detract from what Brazeau is doing. This is mainly because her work and techniques are incredibly personal to her own experiences, and they represent her own struggle with fitness and body image; because of this the project develops yet another layer of humanity. A generosity that is in sharp contrast to what is an incredibly impersonal experience—shopping.

5.

EXERCISES IN THE CITY HYBRIDISATION

Your reporter >> p. 84

There is another city, sat right on top of Eindhoven. It's the exact same size, has exactly the same buildings, and has precisely the same amount of people living in it, except there is something not quite right with this one. It doesn't quite fit the narrative we're sold about modernity and what a future gazing smart city should be like. This 'Eindhoven' is where the City Buffalo Hunters reside, a tribe so far consisting of two members. But it is also a place where the city hybrids dwell, and the only way to experience this world is though the mushrooms.

If this all sounds bizarre and fantastical, then it means that you've entered the world of the performance artist Toine Klaassen. Inside his head, according to the artist, is somewhere you do not want to go. Yet his performance in Eindhoven this August allowed a glimpse into the the earthy spirt of the city, one that exists simultaneously with our own concrete one. Creating a visual story, Klaassen exposes us to the 'mycelium' layer that is ever present in our lives. It stretches under our feet and erupts in fungal infections that can puncture our everyday lives: only if we want them to though. They stop us in our tracks like a fly agaric on the forest floor, and tease us in with the invite of mystery. But it is here that we must leave Toine Klaassen as an entity, as he no longer exists, and introduce the character Loves Stones, an urban hunter-gatherer, born of Eindhoven, who seeks out the carcasses of old leather sofas that have been left to graze the neglected back streets of the city. Loves Stones is a personality who on first impressions could seem a little contrived. But when you take time to understand where he has come from and what his journey has been; you'll realise he could be no one else, wear nothing else, and move in no other way. But his existence is no act of cultural appropriation, and no other civilisations have had their histories ransacked of ancestral knowledge. Loves Stones is Dutch, through and through. It was a photo of the artist's father in his garden that prompted the birth of the Dutch Bushman, the overarching paternal force that nurtures individual incarnations of characters like Loves Stones. The artist uses only what's at hand or abandoned materials that have been neglected, and explains that if you can find it your backyard, you don't have to go off on long plane journeys or ayahuasca trips. All you need to do is practice with your imagination: it's all about staying at home.

Using this kind of imagination means that we are all city hybrids whether we want to acknowledge it or not. Through globalisation, different cultures have crossed, mingled and settled within one another. As Klaassen explains 'the Chinese are building Catholic churches and we, the Dutch, are doing this Zen Buddhist bullshit... over the past 300 years all the Christians are living in China and all the Taoists are moving to Brabant'. The alter ego that is Loves Stones exposes us to this mycelium layer that we're all plugged into but don't realise, it is our universal bond to the rocks and dirt that binds us together, not a Transatlantic Trade and Investment Partnership. He gives us a glimpse of an absurdist reality, one in which the illusion of consumer capitalism is snagged on a branch and through these tears, Bushmen appear. These characters make fun of our wasteful habits by hunting leather sofas and making clothing from them, and they ridicule our single mindedness and notions of property in the city by creating habitable oases next to streams and railway tracks, alike.

It is this transformative ability of the artist that is key, Klaassen describes himself as a farmer, ploughing the city and sowing seeds in the furrows he creates. He literally remodels the urban landscape with his idolatrous acts: worshipping anything other than the commercial gods is often denounced as heresy. But if his work makes us reflect, how then does it make him feel? Loves Stones is a buffer, a shield as he describes it, for him to get closer to us. But he is not the only alter ego the artist has, so many are there that he asks 'Who the fuck is Toine Klaassen, anyway'? and admits that there is sometimes a sense of fear when he performs as he doesn't know how the public will react to his often invasive acts.

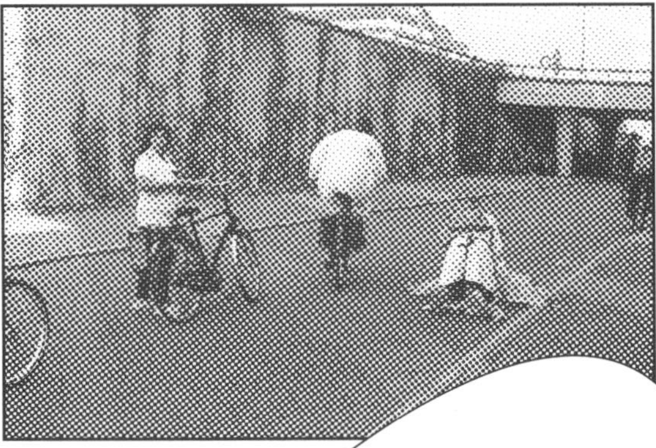

It is through the layers he applies and the objects he uses that a kind of scaffolding is put up around him, creating a chance for Toine Klaassen, or Loves Stones, to twist the normal behaviour of people.

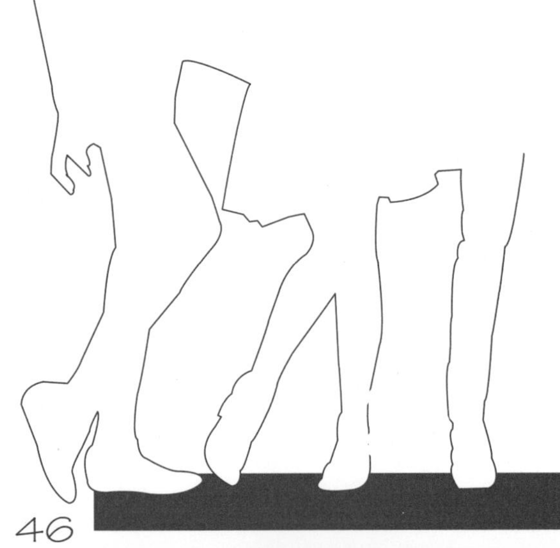

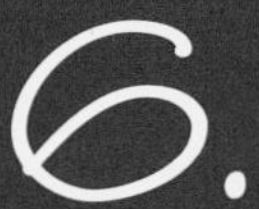

6.

THE REVOLUTION COMES TO EINDHOVEN: ABUNDANCE AND EXPANDING BEYOND THE 5% UNIVERSE

Notification of public space nuisance and violation

>> p. 88

We were dining at the 1910 restaurant on Willenstraat on Saturday August 25th when we were interrupted by two Americans screaming through a microphone. There was a blatant exorcism of emotions being carried on that square, something that we found very troubling. People were not engaging with them at all and they were just a nuisance. This performance cemented everything that I had already assumed about people from the US—they're loud, garish and earnest in their search for self.

Can you specify this subject?*

- ○ Trailers or caravans
- ● Noise disturbance
- ○ Dog disorder
- ○ Illegal commissioned city councel
- ○ Juvenile discomfort
- ○ Enviromental crime
- ○ Charge room rental
- ○ Parking overload
- ○ Stench discomfort
- ○ Permits
- ○ Other

Fields with a * are required.

THE XENO-EPISTEME AND POST-OTHERNESS

By Berit Fischer

"Decolonial thinking strives to delink itself from the imposed dichotomies articulated in the West, namely the knower and the known, the subject and the object, theory and praxis. [...] It exists in the borderland/on the borderlines of the principles of Western epistemology; of knowing and knowledge-making. The inside (Western epistemology) fears losing its status of rational mastery by promoting the importance of emotion over reason. [...] Well, that is what disobedient conservatism means: to disobey 'scientific' classifications of human beings and to conserve the fundamental role of sensing (aesthesis) and emotioning in our everyday life, as well as in the high decisions by the actors leading states, corporations and banks and the production of knowledge".

Walter D. Mignolo[1]

In the quest for musing on what post-Otherness might be, let's begin with the question of what or who is the "Other"? The Oxford English Dictionary defines it as: "to refer to a person or thing that is different or distinct from one already mentioned or known about" or "that which is distinct from, different from, or opposite to something or oneself". Talking about the social Other, thus implies a person that is different from one already mentioned or known about; in this context I'd like to concentrate on the notion of the Other as "different from the already known".

Who defines who and what is known or not known? Who sets the parameters for familiarity, "the already known about" and the registers that define it? Obviously it's a matter of perspective. Am I not the Other if I shift myself beyond the border of what is defined as the assumed "known", but that counts as allegedly unfamiliar and not

1 Mignolo, Walter D., Coloniality Is Far from Over, and So Must Be Decoloniality, Afterall Issue 43, Central Saint Martins University of the Arts London, 2017, P.42

known on the other side? Questions like "What is that Other from the other side of the imaginary borderline? Is it frightening, scary, threatening? Or maybe the Other might even be desirable, intriguing, sexy and appealing? Mysterious, challenging, enriching, enlarging?" are not productive in this exploration and just reconfirm the binary thinking structure, engrained in the lens of discrimination and which fosters social distinctions. Otherness is "a quality or fact of being different" as the English dictionary reveals. Is Otherness enrichment, a chance, and an opportunity to widen one's set apparatus of knowledge?

Is the Other only defined within the dichotomy between biotic and abiotic? Political theorist Jane Bennett reflects beyond this dualism and ponders upon: "We are, rather, an array of bodies, many different kinds of them in a nested set of microbiomes. If more people marked this fact more of the time, if we were more attentive to the indispensable foreignness that we are, would we continue to produce and consume in the same violently reckless ways?"[2] With Bennett— and as a biological fact— humans are constituted by microbiomes, the Other; the human self is then made up of things, of Others that are different from ourselves.

Overcoming binary biological definitions of the Other can be one approach for thinking about post-Otherness; so can contemplating the construction of emotion (it's dualistic assumption of being interior and exterior) be productive in the exploration of the subject.

Scholar and theorist Sara Ahmed gives a complex account of the thought on emotion in her book The Cultural Politics of Emotion. In our Western cultural history, emotions have been devalued, denoted as soft and reduced as blurring one's capacity for judgement, turning one's actions into reactionary and dependent and hence as inferior to rational, logical and therefore autonomous thought and action. Instead Ahmed offers an analysis "of affective economies, where feelings do not reside in subjects or objects, but are produced as effects of circulation [...]." [3]

2 Bennett, Jane, Vibrant Matter, A Political Ecology of Things, Duke University Press Durham and London, 2010, P. 112

3 See: Ahmed, Sara, The Cultural Politics of Emotion, 2004, 2014, 2nd edition, Edinburgh University Press, 2014, P. 8

Thinking about the construction of "Othering" in regards to her approach on the relationality and sociality of emotion is rather essential. She argues that emotion is not solely taking place in the interior, but also is expressed and shared (e.g. via laughter, crying etc.) and equally affected by exterior triggers that are "im-pressed" upon us (which can also be non-material, like memories, objects etc.). In this intra- or interstitial space between the subject and object in which an impression and affect is happening, judgement and evaluations are taking place that lead to an emotion.

Crucial in this consideration is therefore the understanding that emotions are relational, and circular in affect (a feeling that is ex-pressed outwards, "im-pressed" upon another surface of a body, to then re-affect); she calls this concept the "inside-out model". The "outside-in model" is the reverse approach, that emotions are not created by the individual but by the external, the social and the conditioning that comes with it. Ahmed considers both models as problematic as they reiterate the dualistic notion of "me" versus "we". With this theory she is joining sociological and anthropological approaches that emotions should not be considered psychological states, but rather as "social and cultural practices."[4]

She argues: "In other words, emotions are not 'in' either the individual or the social, but produce the very surfaces and boundaries that allow the individual and the social to be delineated as if they are objects. [...] [E]motions create the very surfaces and boundaries that allow all kinds of objects to be delineated. The objects of emotion take shape as effects of circulation. [...] [E]motions create the very effect of the surfaces and boundaries that allow us to distinguish an inside and an outside in the first place. So emotions are not simply something 'I' or 'we' have. Rather, it is through emotions, or how we respond to objects and others, that surfaces or boundaries are made: the 'I' and the 'we' are shaped by, and even take the shape of, contact with others."[5]

4 Ibid P.9
5 Ibid P.10

Her analysis of emotion as sociality and as performativity helps us to create a criticality on "how we become invested in social norms [... and] how emotions can attach us to the very conditions of our subordination"[6] and hence to "Othering" or thinking about post-Otherness.

Ahmed argues that norms surface as the surface of bodies; "norms are a matter of impressions, of how bodies are 'impressed upon' by the world, as a world made up of others. In other words, such impressions are effects of labour; how bodies work and are worked upon shapes the surfaces of bodies." [7]

In setting norms and normative standards, emotions become a working surface for manipulation by hegemonic (e.g. nationalistic or capitalist) structures of alignment (e.g. history, race, gender etc.), and for setting the criteria for "being part of/belonging to " or "not belonging to" (e.g. nationalistic, racial, gendered etc. self-identification). It allows for setting parameters for the demarcation of "the Other" which is "not us" and which can e.g. be utilized to be read as a danger to "what is ours".

Emotions work on this interstitial plane, of shaping the surface of the individual and collective bodies. They involve the subject, but are not reducible to it, they are relational to the object and then form the subject by the very contact it has had with objects or Others. Ahmed states "feelings do not belong or even originate with an "I", and only then move toward others."[8]

This momentary in-between space of "im-pression" on the surface of the individual or collective body, this moment of creating evaluation and emotion, is the space that hegemonic structures —like e.g. cognitive capitalism— dock on to, manipulating, stimulating and using it as a rhetorical instrument.

Just think about the highly complex algorithms that detect our behaviours and emotions in our digital patterns of movement; design and marketing formats that affect and lure us into further consumerism; general media and news coverage; and of course politics that can transform

6 Ibid P.12
7 Ibid, P.154
8 Ibid, P.208

emotions by projections and by defining normative practices as the parameters for belonging and not belonging and for inclusion and exclusion. "Political discourse is powerful as it can turn intangible feelings into tangible things that you can do things with."[9]

Modernist, nationalist, capitalist and hegemonic power structures in general create categorisation, binary thinking, dualisms and hence Othering to secure their self-interest. By taking the position or at least an approximation of consideration of the position of the "opposed" Other, an empathic change of perspective can become a form of resistance towards the established dichotomies.

Walter D. Mignolo reminds us that the engrained epistemological classification, the dichotomy and demarcation among human beings goes back in history to the time of formation of the nation state; back to the Age of Enlightenment when reason and logic started ruling our cultural history, and the states became secular and were no longer ruled by monarchs or the church, and when the "Rights of Man and of Citizen" became established along with it. The categorisation between "believers" (Christians) and "unbelievers" was replaced by the classification of "national" and "non-national" and thereby by "Othering"; an evaluation of higher and lesser human being was established. Mignolo states that this epistemological classification, the national, heteronormative regime of Othering, is the root to deeply engrained racism still today.[10]

"Othering" implies creating dualistic categories and structures of demarcation, mostly employed for hegemonic, normative and homogenising power constructions, for example regarding the migratory phenomena and politics (like recent European developments in the refugee crisis which is moreover a crisis of borders), but also in micropolitical everyday life dynamics and mechanisms; power structures in families, schools, or regarding gender, identity, religion etc.

The notion of binary epistemological classification can equally be expanded beyond nationalities and geopolitical borders (beyond racial and ethnic constructs of the

9 Ibid, P.227

10 See: Mignolo, Walter D., Coloniality Is Far from Over, and So Must Be Decoloniality, Afterall Issue 43, Central Saint Martins University of the Arts London, 2017, Pp. 39 - 45.

Other) to the geopolitics and the colonisation of the (social and individual) body by neoliberal and immaterial cognitive capitalist politics.

Following the logic of "us" and "Other" in regards to consumerism, there is a dichotomy between for example the "successful and rich" (the one fulfilling the normative guidelines which one is made to believe to be desirable and worthy of imitation) and the "unsuccessful and poor" who remains outside the complex system of capitalist requirements that define what "success" means and what that desirable is, and is to be worked towards.

It is particularly neoliberalist capitalism that sets the bars high for the marketable product(ion) of the self, the making of the self a successful and saleable product. In this binary system characterised by neoliberal standards of achievement, you become the Other if you don't comply.

Analogously it's the market and capitalist requirements that decide who is "in", who is "out" and who is the Other, the marginalised and inferior to the capitalist ladder of success, the one that per dictionary definition is "distinct from, different from, or opposite to something or oneself". It is a colonisation of the mental and physical body of the subject and society.

Mignolo calls for Civil and epistemic Disobedience and to delink from the Colonial Matrix Power; to delink "from foreign powers' control over lives goes hand in hand with rebuilding and re-existing under new conditions and modes of existence that are your own."[11]

Thinking with Mignolo one can start on the micropolitical level to delink from the foreign powers' control over one's live via creating critical consciousness, beginning to re-exist and to create new conditions and modes of existence that are our own. Self-empowerment. "This means to figure out how to live their/our own lives instead of giving our time and bodies to corporations, our attention and intelligence to the unbearable mainstream media and our energy to the banks [...]".[12]

11 Mignolo, Walter D., Coloniality Is Far from Over, and So Must Be Decoloniality, Afterall Issue 43, Central Saint Martins University of the Arts London, 2017, P. 44

12 Ibid, P.40

Furthermore, Mignolo pleads for Decolonial disobedient conservatism which "is the energy that engenders dignified anger and decolonial healing, and its main goals are to delink in order to re-exists, which implies relinking with the legacies one wants to preserve in order to engage in modes of existence with which one wants to engage."[13]

Inspired by Sarat Maharaj, independent curator Bonaventure Soh Bejeng Ndikung and cultural anthropologist Regina Römhild propose the unknown, subaltern knowledge and intuitive capacity for thinking post-Otherness in their text "The Post-Other as Avant-Garde". [14]

Sarat Maharaj proposes xeno-episteme as an alternative approach in the discussion of knowledge production. With his neologism he integrates the notion of "xeno" (strange, foreign, other) with "episteme" (knowledge), suggesting "both the idea of specific cognitive production and the search for a type of knowledge that does not avoid contradiction and difference and is not consumed by rational and empirical criteria."[15] Maharaj himself elaborates: "Rather it is a force in its own right, always incipient in "whatever" spaces –windswept, derelict brownfields and wastelands– where intimations of unknown elements, thinking probes, spasms of non-knowledge emerge and come into play".[16]

Xeno-epistemic, intuitive (and hence not approved by logical reasoning) and subaltern knowledge (subaltern to the Cartesian standards of rational and logic, separating the intellectual and sensory, body and mind) might indeed offer an alternative approach to think post-Otherness and to transcend normative systems of Othering. With Foucault in mind, Soh Bejeng Ndikung and Römhild suggest

13 Ibid P.40-41

14 See: Soh Bejeng Ndikung, Bonaventure and Römhild, Regina, "The Post-Other as Avant-Garde", in: Baker, Daniel and Hlavajova, Maria, We Roma, A Critical Reader in Contemporary Art, BAK Critical Reader Series, 2013, P. 206-225

15 Alejandro del Pino Velasco, Summary of An Unknown Object in Uncountable Dimensions: Visual Arts as Knowledge Production in the Retinal Arena, a presentation by Sarat Maharaj 12 November 2003, art and wisdom conference, Seville, as part of arteypensiamento project, organized by International University of Andalusia, in: Hlavajova, Maria, Winder, Jill, Choi, Binna (eds.), On Knowledge Production: A Critical Reader in Contemporary Art, BAK Critical Reader Series, 2008, P.135

16 Maharaj, Sarat, Know-how and No-How: stopgap notes on "method" in visual art as knowledge production, in: Art and research, A Journal of Ideas, Contexts and Methods, Volume 2, No.2, Spring 2009, http://www.artandresearch.org.uk/v2n2/maharaj.html, last accessed 19 June 2017.

the Post-Other as a "possible heterotopia where distances dwindle more and more".[17]

Can post-Otherness be understood as a "heterotopian imaginary in practice"? An imaginary that affirms difference and contradiction, a realm that gives space to rethink and evade normative and hegemonic conditions. An imaginary in practice that operates in realms beyond the binary and dualistic dichotomies of hegemonic powers and politics; and that flourishes within the realm of experience, the untranslatable, experimental and beyond the margins of semantics and rationalistic thought? Can post-Otherness function as a reflexive idea that extends the post-colonial discourse based on the systemic idea of "Othering"? [18]

Can post-Otherness then be comprehended as the moment in which socio-psychological mechanism of "Othering" –and the binary categorization that comes with it– is overcome? This moment can be a concept, a proposal and a practice in a broadened sense to decolonize and de-subjectify the (social) body from these structures and to change one's understanding of relationality to the Other and –with practice– eventually also one's actions; becoming an intersubjective agent. Extending the systemic postcolonial, capitalist, racial and gendered Othering to the micropolitical and psychological realm of Othering, in which the "I" supposedly feeds on the Other in order to define and demarcate its ego and own identity.

Post-Otherness thus can also operate as a conception or a strategy that is linked to creating critical consciousness to negotiate the "ego-identification" of the "I" and its ego-shell, to overcome the binary and dualistic structures of creating the demarcation between the self and "the Other".

17 See: Soh Bejeng Ndikung, Bonaventure and Römhild, Regina, The Post-Other as Avant-Garde", in: Baker, Daniel and Hlavajova, Maria, We Roma, A Critical Reader in Contemporary Art, BAK Critical Reader Series, 2013, P. 215. Needless to say in the context of this publication, that artistic practice can be one of the playgrounds on which the pondering on the dissolving of the frame of the "self" and the "Other" can be played out.

18 With postcolonial theorist Gayatri Spivak, Othering is systemic in the sense that it is the process of differentiating the subaltern from the ruling imperialist power, during which the colonizer categorizes herself as a constituted subject in the power relations. See Römhild, Regina, Post-Other Interventions, a talk and conversation, at Galerie Wedding, January 2016, as part of curatorial project POW (Post-Otherness-Wedding) by Solvej Helweg Ovesen und Bonaventure Soh Bejeng Ndikung, http://galeriewedding.de/post-otherness-interventions/, last accessed 16 June 2017

Eastern Philosophical rational can be enriching in the context of such contemplation: when the *ego*-driven "I" demarcates itself from the Other, it stops a dialogic process of listening, and with it, the understanding of "the Other". The demarcation equally obstructs the acknowledgement that there is an interrelation between the self and the Other. An interrelation that exists outside (and despite) hegemonic normative structures and power relations –which create categorisation, evaluation, judgement of difference, alterity and ultimately social injustice and exclusion– but an interrelation that subsists in a pure humane sense.

Zen Buddhist monk and peace activist Thich Nhat Hanh for example comprehends human beings as "inter-beings". The concept of Inter-being is understood from the perspective of the philosophical foundation of Zen Buddhism, that nothing constitutes as a separate independent self but rather that everything is made up of things and interconnected with everything. Inter-being is assumed not simply as "co-existing" but rather as being mutually intertwined and inter-dependent with everything; within human relationships but also in relation to non-human beings and the natural world at large.[19]

This thinking might assist in overcoming the ego-shell that has stopped listening to (and understanding) the self and it's complex interdependent relation to the world around and to the alleged "Other" and with it the ability for an empathic change in perspective. Through practice of critical consciousness on the very micropolitical level, for example through listening with awareness and therefore understanding the self and the Other, respect and appreciation of multiplicity of singularity and alterity can become a starting point for overcoming Othering.

Although post-Otherness might still be an imaginary concept, if anything far from being an established and a lived reality, it does allow for a heterotopian and xeno-epistemic imagination and awareness, that with time and practice might become reality.

19 Thich Nhat Hanh gives the sunflower as an example, that while looking at it, we not only see the sunflower, but with awareness, we can also see the other elements that constitute the flower: the sun, the clouds, the soil etc. without which the sunflower could not exist.

7.

YOU MAY CONSUME IT OR...

Lucy Rose Nixon >> p. 92

The MG&M Collective is a new brand by a trio of artists consisting of Rotterdam based duo Gil and Moti and Mosab Anzo, a painter from Syria who recently arrived in the Netherlands. The collective folded a paper boat in a generous performance to serve as a tray to distribute lollipops with faces drawn on them. Lick, give away or just keeping it were some of the options on offer to the individuals passing by, and it was these decisions that decided the fate of the lollipop or 'refugee child'. Not common for such things to circulate in all the imagery available within the commercial heart of the cultural nucleus of Eindhoven, the image of the boat and the refugee sailing into people's hands engaged a lot of people. Every man as well as the everyman reaches out to offered hands, as it keeps both our hearts burning and our social sphere healthy. In reaching out, this performance was lead by an attitude of compassion and love which weaved itself through the entire event. The way these three men held on to one another while writing 'home', 'safe', 'home' on the fronts of their respective shirts and 'home', 'sweet', 'home' on the back, was a gentle act so intimate it felt as if we, the viewer, were intruding on something. The care with which they treated each other was transferred to the way they approached the people of Eindhoven. Using the city centre as their stage, the collective extended a hand without making anyone feel uncomfortable or under pressure, making this quiet form of protest very effective. Their intervention into the public space created an extraordinary situation, one that was simple enough to pull people out of themselves. The service of the hand reaching out, from the position of the weak, is one of the strongest acts we can imagine. Is this what a decadent society demands of the ones excluded?

Exuding care and attention for one another and for humanity as a whole, MG&M Collective created a moving piece which left a lasting impression on us as the audience. As onlookers we felt their exuded warmth take hold of us and fill us with love and affection. Knowing that Mosab was a Syrian refugee who was actively approaching people in public also seemed to break through a wall of separation that sometimes exists between people and refugees. Failing to integrate refugees into our society is an issue that many countries and cities are experiencing. Whether due to the language barrier, differing cultural backgrounds or false preconceptions, it is rare for a free and easy interaction to exist between natives, refugees or foreigners. MG&M's contribution to the crisis is to have created a scenario in which the interaction between cultures was normalised and made casually possible. Their intervention saw them trade in compassion, with symbolic offerings taking the place of formal exchanges.

8.

SKY NAIVE | IT BEGS A QUESTION

Your reporter >> p. 96

Language is what we need and oooh baby, do we need it more than ever. But what forms of language can we use to help explain this jarring experiment that's reality? Abbreviations are pretty popular tbh, and emojis are 😮 but the platform that popularised this shrinking of language has just allowed a select group the creative freedom of 280 characters. Giving them the chance to run their fingers through the A,B,C's, moulding and bending them as they go. What new forms of communication will be coughed up and spat out at the world? Well, there have been blank pages staring back at us since we could draw shapes in the sand with wooden sticks. So it's not more space we need, but less. There is a delicious pleasure in being able to squeeze the entirety of human history and our collective knowledge into 140 characters. All of that accumulated knowledge being punched through greasy pads into an immaterial world that affects the material one, is of course, ecstasy of the naughtiest kind.

We need to be more deliberate with our words, and restricting them forces us to do so. A well timed and annunciated swear word is far more powerful than a spluttering, vein throbbing tirade. This art of carefully slicing language is something the collective Apparatus 22 know a lot about. Initiated by the artists Erika and Dragos Olea, Maria Farcas, and the late Ioana Nemes, the group use their critical minds to tackle subjects like fashion, the economy, language and institutional power. From their Untitled works that laser cut sentences that they had ached over into sheets of stretched and flawed leather, to just using words that paint mental images in their STILL LIFE series: the collective have mastered 'slow language'. A technique that helped stop the traffic and shatter the illusion one Sunday afternoon. Sky Naive | It Begs A Question, was a day long intervention that saw Apparatus 22 bring their particular form of slow language into the Eindhoven cityscape. Walking through the city centre hand in hand, clad in opaque ponchos, they ploughed through the barren high street; stopping only to perform a ritual that disenchanted their gifts for the locals. But what does the person who has everything need, anyway? Protection, it seems.

This sanctuary came in the form of over 100 rain ponchos that had abstract symbols and exact words stencilled on to them —

They Read:

Decoding The Formula of Illusion Brutally

(Re) Conquering Ourselves

We Must Reshape In New Archetypes

End The Trance of New and Now

Elemental Forces Above and Below

These words when read or said out loud act as an incantation or hex, through which the wearer can protect themselves from the multitude of invasive jingles, mottos, and focus group tested corporate logos that smother our imaginations. Hopefully blocking such pre-prescribed thoughts from our minds will allow us that, They Live moment, when we can put on the 'sunglasses' and see advertising or reality, for what it's really saying.

CONSUME
OBEY
CONFORM
THIS IS YOUR GOD
NO INDEPENDENT THOUGHT

The ethereal materiality of the ponchos twisted the nature of the words written on them. Each message was at the whim of the breeze and of individual movements. This nuance exposed us to the malleability of language and its formlessness which can change in a single breath—even when carefully chosen. This contradiction is what makes language such a powerful tool; and Apparatus 22 wield it masterfully.

The reach of this intervention has been the widest yet, with over 100 people accepting the ponchos that simultaneously alter and emit narratives. These practical pieces of art were not always easy to give away though. People seemed almost threatened by the disruption to their shopping experience. Even when the piece was explained and offered for free, there was still an inherent mistrust. Bringing the gift economy into a space that imposes the polar opposite created a friction that burnished the "facts" as we're sold them. This act highlighted the stubbornness of individuals when offered an alternative to the norm. But that isn't to say there weren't smiles, exchanges, conversations and questions, abound.

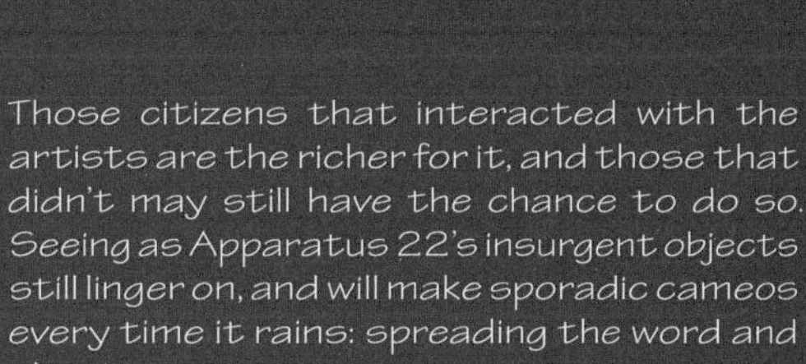

Those citizens that interacted with the artists are the richer for it, and those that didn't may still have the chance to do so. Seeing as Apparatus 22's insurgent objects still linger on, and will make sporadic cameos every time it rains: spreading the word and altering perceptions one moment at a time.

9.

FLYING COLOURS

Your reporter >> p. 141

Staking your claim to something is a contentious act and is bombastic in its assumptions. So the moon, we hope, belongs to no one, yet on its surface rests a piece of cloth designed in 1777. The greatest nation on earth has seemingly spread to that life giving rock, upon which their flag pole acts as an antennae, broadcasting the words 'Free to those who can afford it, expensive to those who can't' out into the deep black. This congregation of fibres can inspire both love and hate, often in the same second. For some there is no separation between these two emotions, to love the flag is to hate people. It forces our worst jingoistic tendencies to the surface. But that's exactly the point perhaps, the flag floats on the surface of things, first appearing as something solid that we can hold onto, but as soon as we get within reach when we need it most, we quickly realise it only provides sanctuary to the delusional.

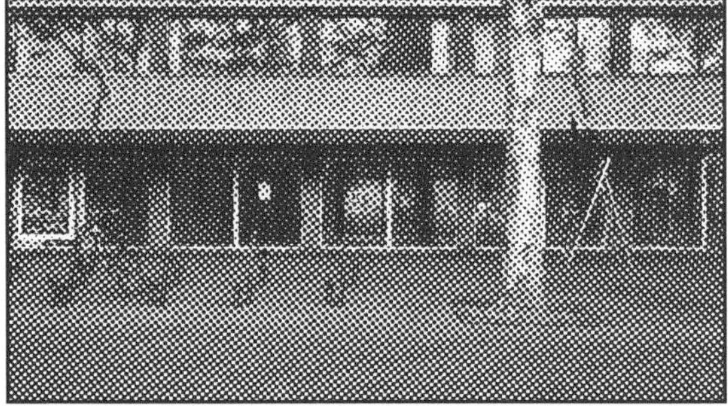

Who then owns the city centre? In this intervention, Onomatopee and the artist David Blamey have both laid claim to it, but so to have the brands: they're all flying flags that demand allegiance from the public. In the case of the work *Flying Colours* by Blamey however, the role that a symbolic rectangle of fabric can play in our lives raises questions about who owns the streets and what it means if the individual lays claim to private property by planting a flag? The sudden appearance of two flags in a familiar environment that appear to have been dissected into parts hints that maybe they would be able to one day join together. But this will never happen as they are chromatic opposites and no amount of fabric can bridge the divide. It makes it clear that a flag is nothing but material, and staking claim to something takes action that goes beyond rhetoric. *Flying Colours* plays with our need to apply agency to the inanimate and our longing to believe in something: whether it be god, country or commerce. Every revolution needs a flag, but tearing one up seems the best place to start. Rally under *Flying Colours* and realise that all that is solid can melt into air.

10.

TOKO

Your reporter >> p. 144

It has been written on extensively, but it's always worth pointing out that we are drowning in plastic, a form of brutality that we're actually enabling instead of abating. It congregates in our oceans, is entombed under our feet, and drifts around our streets. There is however, a more sinister element to this non-sentient presence in our lives: like a poltergeist it disturbs us by materialising a world we don't understand. Each piece of plastic is like a bump in the night, it wakes us for a split second and makes us shiver, but the majority of us just go straight back to sleep. But now it is no longer just a spectre as it has become part of us. Through the years of injection moulding we have introduced this substance into our very blood streams. We have become what the geologist Patricia Corcoran and artist Kelly Jazvac describe as Plastiglomerate. While their research and definition focused on the amalgamation of mineral and plastic, it is now a term that can apply to humans too. It enters us through the food we eat, with the Belgians being the most exposed through the sheer amount of mussels they gorge on: there are around 11,000 plastic fragments in their seafood alone.

This anthropocentric view of plastic may be the most powerful way of dealing with the subject. It's almost impossible for us to comprehend the scale of things when it floats in gyres in the west Pacific ocean, won't biodegrade for around 450 years, or is swallowed whole by an albatross in Midway.

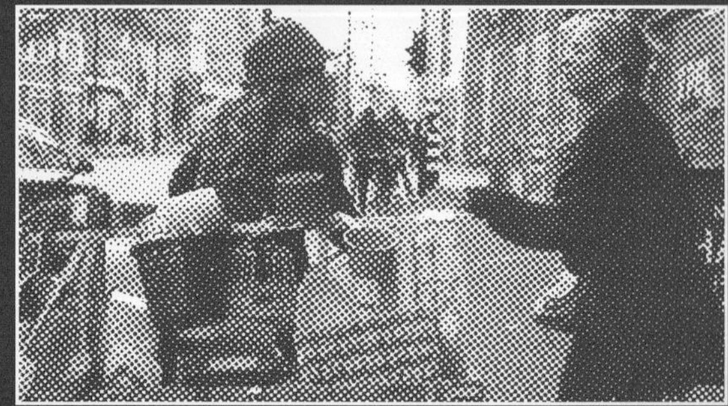

As technology has almost annihilated the temporal effects of distance and scale, our sense of existing in a moment is often lost and we're denied that crucial visceral reaction.

How then can we engage with this slow violence of plastic? Well, Su Tomesen, an Amsterdam based artist is one person who is trying to help us come to terms with our situation. During a performance called TOKO, Indonesian for shop, Tomesen cycled through the streets of Eindhoven spreading the word. Initially instigated as a response to the disappearance of corner shops in the Netherlands, Tomesen loaded up her bike with a huge selection of brightly coloured and culturally alien plastic objects and began to interact with the residents of Eindhoven.

The objects were brought over from Indonesia by the artist herself in her luggage: doing so comments on the impersonal aspects of global trade and asks questions like is a mass produced object worth more if it's brought in the luggage of a family member, rather than in one the millions of shipping containers? How much is the human worth and needed in situations like these? It was during this performance that Tomesen interacted with the 'perfect stranger' of the city, engaging with them on subjects ranging from the ignorance of single use plastics to the over saturation of stuff in our lives.

Reminiscent of the Dutch voddenman, an individual who would walk the street chanting and selling clothes, Tomesen cycled through the streets announcing in Indonesian 'plastik, plastik': a simple but effective reminder that the material surrounds us at all times. This intervention also forces our attention on to the artist as the individual, or even more pointedly, society as the individual.

The piece literally places the burden of such a global problem on the back of a cyclist— artist or not, the medium meant it could have been anyone riding that bike. Under neoliberalism we have been told that saving the planet is down to us and our individual actions. We are alone, and forced to believe that we're immediately responsible for the world we live in. A lie that has been foisted on us, so as to shift the blame and avert the critical gaze of the public. It's because of this that we need more people on bikes beautifully oppressed by plastic to create public happenings in which the stranger is engaged. It's maybe through these tiny blips of communality that something can form.

Yet, while reflecting on a rather bleak contemporary, TOKO also speculates on an alternative future. One that involves micro-economies where materials and knowledge are exchanged on the city street. The simple act of using a bike as a means of transport to sell your goods, instantly challenges the emotionless corporate homogeny that has spread into every city centre. How can the west learn from the micro-economies of Indonesia when dealing with the death of the high street, and therefore inevitably the local? Through acts like Tomesen's we can either be apathetic, shrugging it off as an ineffective act, or use it as means of creating socially aware plastic partisans in a system that values profit over people. This may mean we have to walk that extra 100 meters to the recycling bins. But, it's probably the more sensible option, given the current climate.

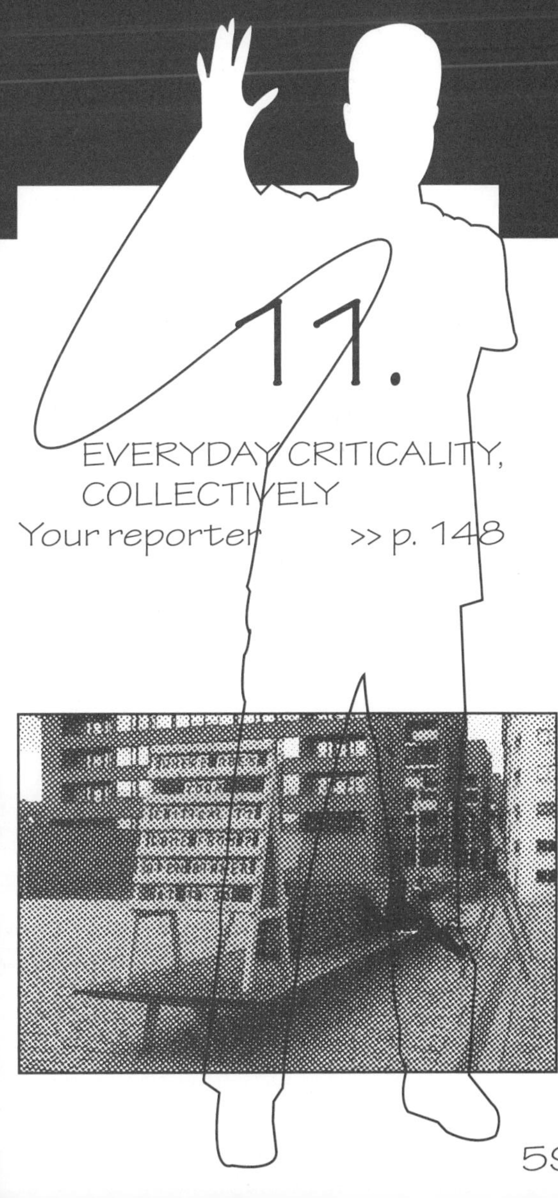

11.

EVERYDAY CRITICALITY, COLLECTIVELY

Your reporter >> p. 148

"WE, THE PEOPLE" DEMAND AN UPDATE OF WHAT "WE, THE PEOPLE" MEANS

By Lietje Bauwens & Dirk de Raeve

"We, the people, demand a more inclusive society!" How do we take back our public space, asks Onomatopee, and what are both the possibilities and responsibilities for a cultural institution in the city center of Eindhoven in this regard? Different writers, such as myself, were invited to double as bartenders, and think and speak about this question —not to spread our knowledge but rather to listen and generate new, local input as a breeding ground for further research. Dialogue over discourse.

Apparently, bars and progressive thought still go hand in hand, since the invitation immediately reminded me of a proposal by architect Markus Miessen about half a year ago. The team behind 'Perhaps it is high time for a xeno-architecture to match' [1] of which I am a part, asked him and philosopher Armen Avanessian to further develop the neologism xeno-architecture during a live-performance at Kaaitheater in Brussels (18 April 2017). Miessen came up with the idea to build a bar in the center of the stage, from where he and Avanessian would serve the audience drinks and engage in conversations. Not transferring

1 "Perhaps it is high time for a xeno-architecture (of knowing) to match" is the next to last sentence of Armen Avanessian's preface in Markus Miessen's publication Crossbenching (2016). Inspired by this, Alice Haddad, Wouter de Raeve and me initiated the eponymous research project into the potentialities of a 'xeno-architecture' through various cultural productions.

knowledge, but a new form of producing knowledge; not a static illustration of 'what is', but a dynamic exploration of 'what could be'. Besides the impossibility of giving a clean-cut lecture about a concept that does not even exist (yet), it is also very much 'xeno' to approach unknown and speculative territory in order to do so.

The image of Miessen and Avanessian as bartenders however did not entirely appeal to us—it resembled too much an echo of 'relational aesthetics' as Nicolas Bourriaud identified the 1990s art movement that focused on inter-human relationships and their social contexts. Participative projects often abolish the difference (or hierarchy) between stage and public to celebrate local and physical moments in complete horizontality. This would contradict a xeno-architecture focusing on spaces that surpass our current cognitive capacity. Abstract structures that, instead of being tangible and physical, are global and above all (hyper)complex. More and more, however, I question our determined dismissal of the bar. Have we gazed too longingly at a horizon whose territory we knew only by its provisional unfamiliarity?

To better understand this (retrospective) dilemma, it seems necessary to return to the roots of our project, our frustrations with the (architectural) reality and our consecutive interest in the ambitious prefix 'xeno' [2]. 'Perhaps it is high time for a xeno-architecture to match' resulted from a dissatisfaction with practices in the tradition of relational aesthetics in the public (and thus political) sphere. The city of Brussels, our hometown and fertile soil for starting our collaboration, is instructive in this regard. It embodies a long tradition of social engagement, of which the resistance to urban developments of the 60s and 70s is emblematic. In response to the dramatic mutilation of entire neighbourhoods in the name of modernisation and profit – a phenomenon known as Brusselization —citizens, architects, artists, cultural workers, academics

2 We encountered the prefix 'xeno' in the "Xenofeminism" manifesto (2014), in which the Laboria Cuboniks collective proposes a politics of alienation: http://www.laboriacuboniks.net/qx8bq.txt.

and the like called for the right to make decisions about their city and for a politics that emphasises particularities. Small-scale, local and especially bottom-up projects became more and more popular—a city garden to halt climate change or a communal playground to overcome segregation. Even if such practices used to perform engaged and subversive functions (like relational aesthetics), at present their radical nature has been neutralised. Key ideals such as participation, direct human contact and local action have been integrated within the neoliberal logic against which they believe to defy.

A merely local and physical approach is incapable of dealing with the complex and planetary challenges we face today. Politics of austerity and exclusion, protection of privacy, climate change, etc—how do we start thinking about solutions when it is impossible to even truly fathom the problems? These issues, whose size and structure dazzle us, are often engineered by ourselves—technology, the capitalist economy, big data—but have become performative actors in turn, planning our present from the future. If Facebook convinces us whom to vote for at the next election, if Google tells us what treatment to seek when we feel sick, and fridges, mobile phones, and public transport passes are in constant interconnection, tracking and determining our daily movements, we should be asking ourselves who, or what, is truly governing reality?

'Folk-politics' [3] , as direct, local and bottom-up approaches are accurately but also slightly derogatorily called, is no longer capable of effectively instigating structural change. But how to cope, then, with problems that transcend our current imagination? Is it possible to upgrade our actions, ideas and concepts, in order to stop passively following or deconstructing norms, and start to rather co-create them? In the words of the Onomatopee pamphlet; how do "we the people get full access to all lifestyles?"

3 Nick Srnicek and Alex Williams have introduced the term "folk politics" in their "#ACCELERATE MANIFESTO for an Accelerationist Politics" (2013). Instead of dismissing or counteracting existing structures, organizations and technologies, Srnicek and Williams propose to "accelerate" them.

Contemporary 'speculative' thinkers offer valuable tools for further exploration. It is hard to trace the exact beginning of the speculative movement, but the 2007 conference at Goldsmith University of London hosting Ray Brassier, Quentin Meillassoux, Graham Harman and Iain Hamilton Grant marks an important moment in this regard. Whereas the four philosophers hold very different (not to say contradictory) viewpoints, they, at least at that moment, found each other in the idea that became fundamental to what from then on has been called 'Speculative Realism'; we need to break with the correlationist conception from the Enlightenment that takes the human being as the centre of all meaning. Even what we cannot see or understand (or know of) is real, and it becomes possible to talk about a world that is not completely understood by us only with a rationalist speculation that is inclusive for risk, uncertainty and the unknown. This is especially crucial in the world as we live it today, since we can only deal with, for example, privacy and data-issues once we learn to think through the contingency that is inherently present in algorithms. Thus, a solution for climate change needs to be as abstract, pluri-local, multi-systemic and trans-generational as the problem it directs. In order to formulate effective progressive political strategies, one needs to reach for what is (as yet) unknown and strive ambitiously for 'what could be' instead of settle for answers that are within reach and under control.

This motto of looking beyond the horizon has, of course, been on the progressive agenda for quite a while and, as often happens with (new) tendencies, the concept of a speculative 'what could be' was enthusiastically embraced in philosophical but explicitly also in artistic contexts. 'Xeno' and 'speculation' are attractive and fashionable terms, but hyping their abstraction entails a danger. Whereas speculation emerged out of a dissatisfaction with the deconstructionist Critique with a capital C, critique as an-end-in-itself, our research also unveiled the temptation of fetishising the 'unknown'. And when the 's' of speculation starts growing, it risks to lose exactly the productivity it is aiming for.

There appears to be a struggle (or more optimistically, a challenge) inherent in the desire to move away from 'what is' toward 'what could be' and the necessity to still account for 'what actually happens.' However, it is important to comprehend that 'what could be' should never be a goal, an sich, but only a way to expand our rational capacity from within—by mapping and simultaneously extending the limitations of reason. A global, abstract and theoretical 'what could be' loses its productive potential when cutting its ties with reality. There is no such thing as discourse without a dialogue.

Reconsidering the bar-concept again, while this time keeping in mind the necessary nuance in 'what could be', forces me to take a step back and rethink the balance between the global and the local and to acknowledge how totality does not exist beyond the local, but always has a particular perspective as its point of departure towards abstraction[4]. In a recent conversation[5] , Nick Srnicek and Alex Williams admitted that their term 'folk politics' was never meant to propagate a complete abolition of bottom-up and grassroots projects, but rather that we should search for a 'glue'; ambitious organisational strategies that can give small-scale projects a propelling force in order to effectively politicise their ambitious 'what could be's'.[6]

4 Nick Srnicek and Alex Williams have introduced the term "folk politics" in their "#ACCELERATE MANIFESTO for an Accelerationist Politics" (2013). Instead of dismissing or counteracting existing structures, organizations and technologies, Srnicek and Williams propose to "accelerate" them.

5 Together with Wouter de Raeve I interviewed Nick Srnicek and Alex Williams for Rekto Verso, no. 74, December 2016, 'Steeds betere valstrikken creëren is de enige optie' [The only solution is to create even better traps']. The glue-metaphor derives from an interview with Laboria Cubonics from 2015, http://www.kunsthallewien.at/#/blog/2015/12/next-universal-interview-laboria-cuboniks: "For this universal to live up to its name means not to do away with the important work that's been done on particularisms, but instead turn our focus to the engineering of a kind of abstract "glue", in order to plot out coherent relations between particularities — or "solidarities", in a way."

6 Patricia Reed points in 'Uncertainty, Hypothesis, Interface' (2017) to the necessity of "a new formulation of the relationship between abstract theory and material practice, inference and action" and designing an interface in which the conceptual and the material meet. Accessible through the online publication 'Scientific Romance': http://www.ah-journal.net/issues/00/uncertainty-hypothesis-interface

Yet, how do we create such a constructive balance between the abstract and the concrete, the local and the global, between 'what is' and 'what could be'? This brings me from a theoretical account to the concrete material that Eindhoven, 'the design city of the Netherlands', has to offer; not only does the design discipline pursue and shape the techno-scientific world of the future, its speculation is also inherently chained to the physical materiality of the 'now'. Speculative designer Benjamin Bratton therefore advocates a general design attitude that exceeds tech labs and design academies. Beyond the mere creation of objects, his focus lies in developing a future-oriented way of thinking that goes beyond the descriptive. He names our ever faster-changing world 'the new normal'—only an approach that includes or even encourages the contingency and emergence that is inherently part of (yet) unknown technological phenomena, is capable of actively co-creating a world that has long ceased to be merely futuristic. It is, according to Bratton, a missed opportunity to fantasise and construct AI with as much human, and therefor recognisable, characteristics as possible, or to only search for solutions to problems we are currently aware of. Behind this limited and therefore limiting perspective lies a world full of possibilities.

"The things that are of interest to me in the field of AI philosophically have less to do with how to teach the machine to think as we think, but rather in how they might demonstrate a wider range of embodied intelligence we could understand. That way we could see our own position in a much wider context and it would teach us a little about what 'thinking' actually is." [7] By departing from a not purely human point of view speculative design can help us to learn from (still) unknown technologies to expand our image of humanity, our way of thinking and thus our political agency.

In this light, it seems necessary to reconsider the decisive "we, the people", that is so prominently present on every page of the Onomatopee pamphlet. According to

7 Benjamin Bratton, http://www.archdaily.com/799871/benjamin-bratton-on-artificial-intelligence-language-and-the-new-normal-strelka-moscow (2017)

philosopher Reza Negarestani, true collectivity is impossible as long as we keep holding on to concepts of consensus and dissensus between different cultures and groups. Only by getting to the bottom of "what gives rise to the economy of false choices and by activating and fully elaborating what real human significance is" [8] can we incorporate the (technological) evolutions and developments of the 'new normal' into our self-image. Instead of dismissing the humanist project—as post-, trans- and non-humanistic proposals do—Negarestani therefore proposes an inhumanism. Not a denial of, but contrarily, a dedication to humanism and rationality as being a continuous (re)construction and stretching of what it means to be human at this very moment, and thereby "fundamentally revising not only what we understand as thinking, but also what we recognise as 'us'." [9] 'Us' in this sense is not a static calculation of human entities but a constant and abstract construction precisely consisting of the way we relate to each other and the world around us. The simplistic understanding of emancipation as 'we', being a gathering place for as many (human) 'me's' as possible, can only shelter certain categories and therefore automatically leads to new forms of dominance. Only if we look at the structures that underpin these forms of exclusion and admit that we all have a share in this, we can start visualising and changing the situations that such conflicts arise from. In order to think of new, more inclusive forms of 'we', the unity of 'me' needs to be questioned — embracing its potential to grow, shrink and change [10]—and its relational nature fully acknowledged; 'me' fundamentally consists not only of (its relationships to) digital technologies, but everything that surrounds us.

If 'we the people' actually wants to access "a diverse lifestyle supply that innovates us and helps us to reinvigorate our community", it is undeniable that the word

8 E-flux journal #52 - February 2014, Reza Negarestani - The Labor of the Inhuman, Part 1: Human & Part 2: Inhuman.

9 Ibid.

10 An important source of inspiration is Tristan Garcia, and within this context especially his research into the possibilities and limitations of emancipation, in 'Nous, animaux et humains. Actualité de Jeremy Bentham' (2011)

'we' should be detached from 'the people'. Not in order to dismiss humanity (ourselves!)—as post-, trans- and non-humanistic proposals do—but out of the recognition that a truly emancipatory 'we' honours a world in which it is not the center. From a new normal perspective, we do not only take care of human relatives, but we start thinking of inhuman rights and constructions inclusive for all that (will have) agency of some sort; "We (all people, donkeys, robots, plants, chairs etc, etc, etc, etc...) demand an inclusive life." According to Reza Negarestani, the first question that should be asked in the context of the Onomatopee pamphlet is; "Are your commitments up to date?" [11] The examination of what at this moment really functions as public space, does not come before or after, but (co)defines the meaning of an up-to-date inhumanism and its emancipatory agenda. Taking to the streets of Eindhoven for a more democratic inclusivity might still be a (perhaps effective) possibility, yet the fact that our public, and thus political, life decreasingly takes place in physical spheres, makes us into fundamentally different people from who we were 20, or even 5, years ago.

How to think in pluri-local and planetary structures without losing sight of the actual city center and its inhabitants? It is the task of designers in the broadest sense to research, explore, and practice a productive balance between the realistic 'what is' and the speculative 'what could be' and to work towards a conception of 'we' that does justice to everything that is (at this moment) connected. Srnicek's and Williams's glue between the local and the global does not merely imply designing a horizontal connective network structure, but moreover employing a level of abstraction and complexity without losing contact with what happens on the ground level—or at the bar. Only with a double focus—upwards and downwards – and a cumulative feedback loop in place between them, can our notion of 'we(eeeee)'

11 E-flux journal #52 – February 2014, Reza Negarestani – The Labor of the Inhuman, Part 1: Human & Part 2: Inhuman

not merely be expanded but especially deepened. In so doing, we could redefine the concepts of 'relational aesthetics' and 'folk politics' in the context of what is 'normal now'. As a result, a collective horizon might arise, visible far beyond the walls of Onomatopee, all the while expanding from a sticky bar, perhaps.

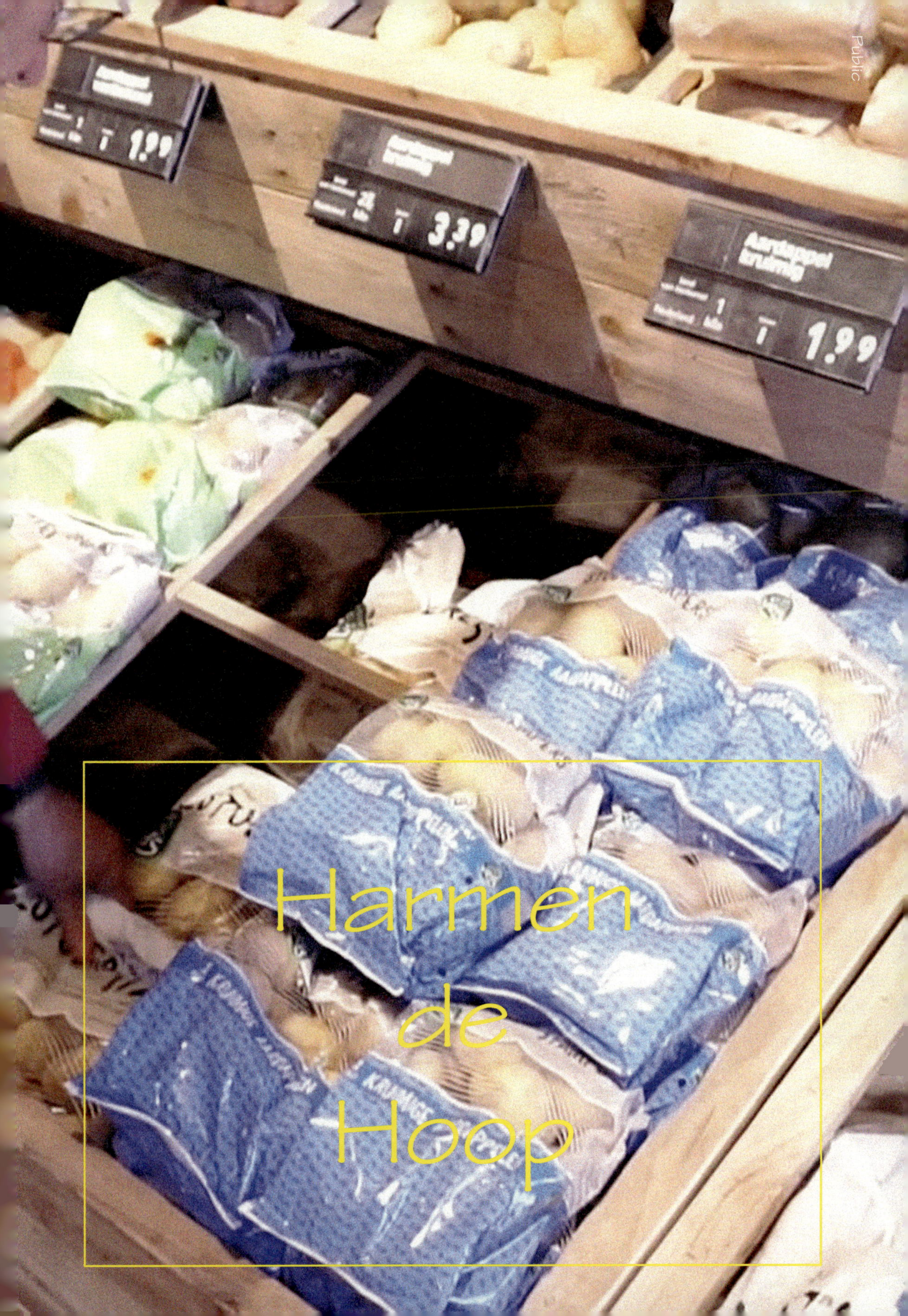
Public
Aardappel kruimig
1.99
3.39
1.99
Harmen de Hoop

ACHIEVEMENT #1
AARDAPPELEN!
HARMEN DE HOOP

is a visual artist who makes anonymous and illegal interventions in public spaces. He works on the notion of 'place' in the contemporary city, the behaviour of individuals or groups, and the conflicts of interests in public space. His interventions are made by re-contextualizing existing signs or objects, adding them to a location in an unexpected way and by doing so questioning 'normality'. The work is social, political and philosophical, often about the functionality of materials and objects, or about rules and regulations and the way in which people behave in the public domain. His interventions confront an unprepared public with unexpected actions; he addresses the passer-by without using the existing language of the art world. With this he tries to let people look at themselves in a different way, often with a sense of humour.

Before making a work, he visits and photographs a large number of locations in a chosen city, until he finds the right site for his intervention.

This first achievement of the project led Harmen to contribute to urban gardening and propose an upscaling of urban agriculture, by utilising both the seeds from the supermarket as well as the underused green spaces in the city.

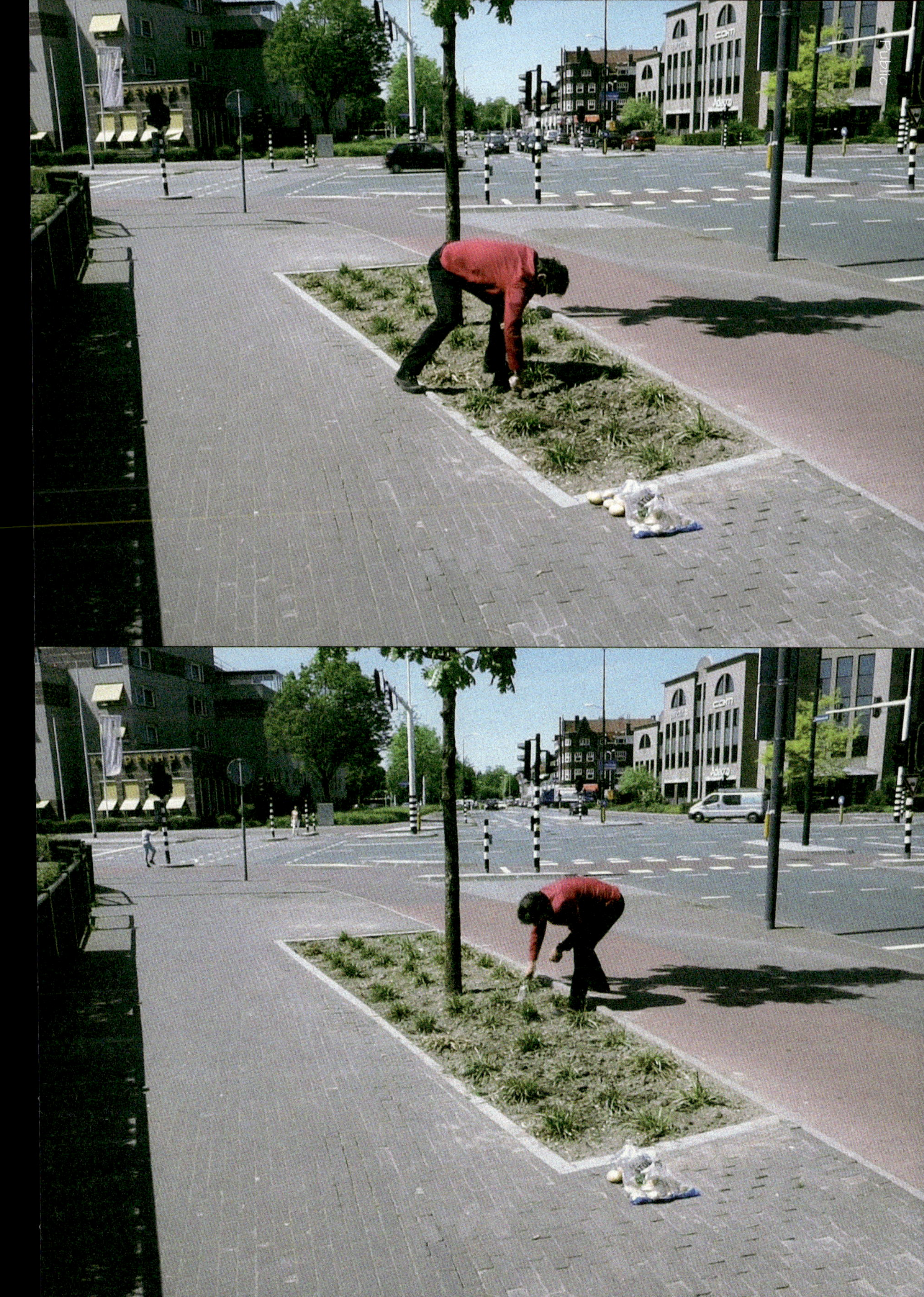

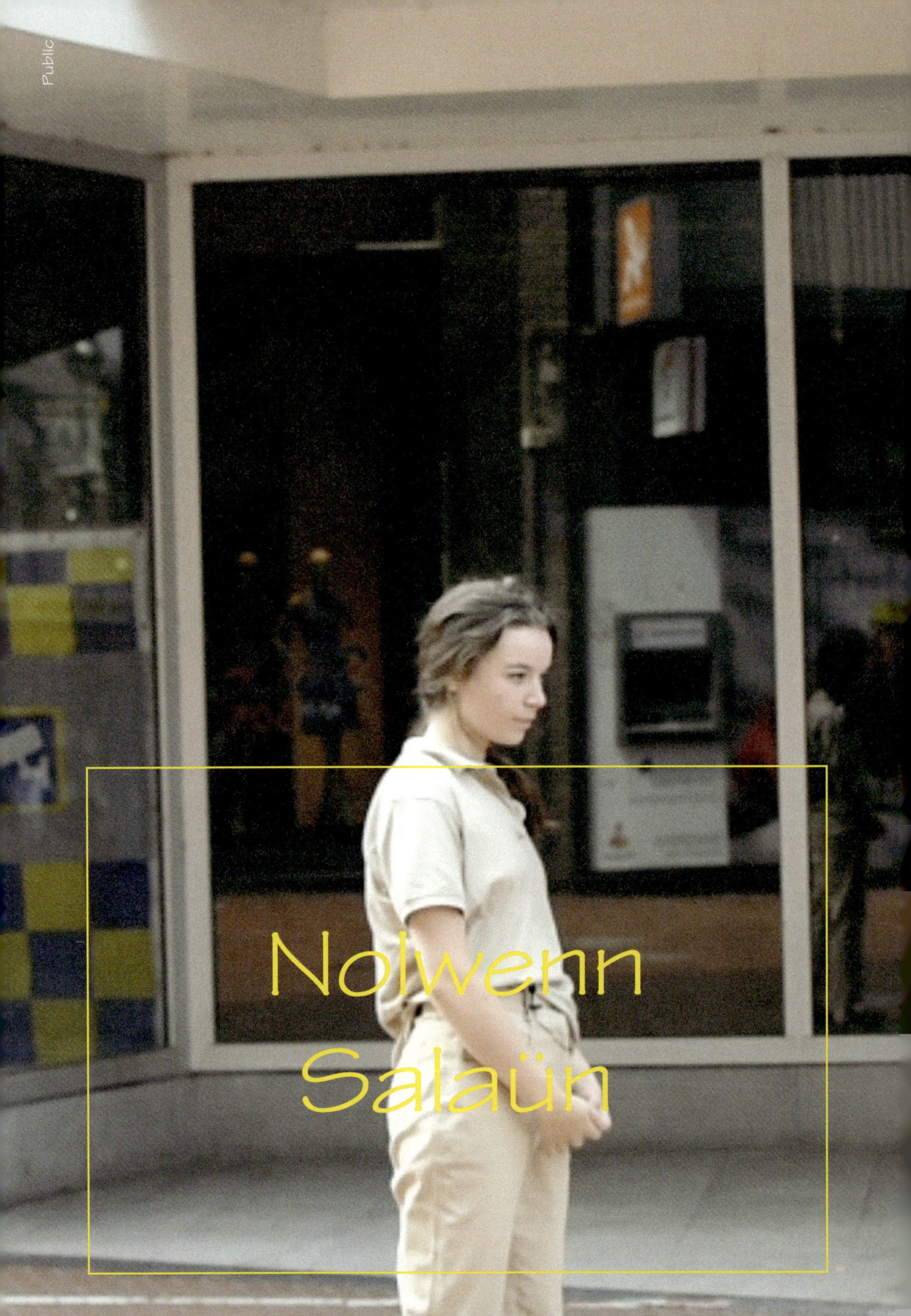

Nolwenn Salaün

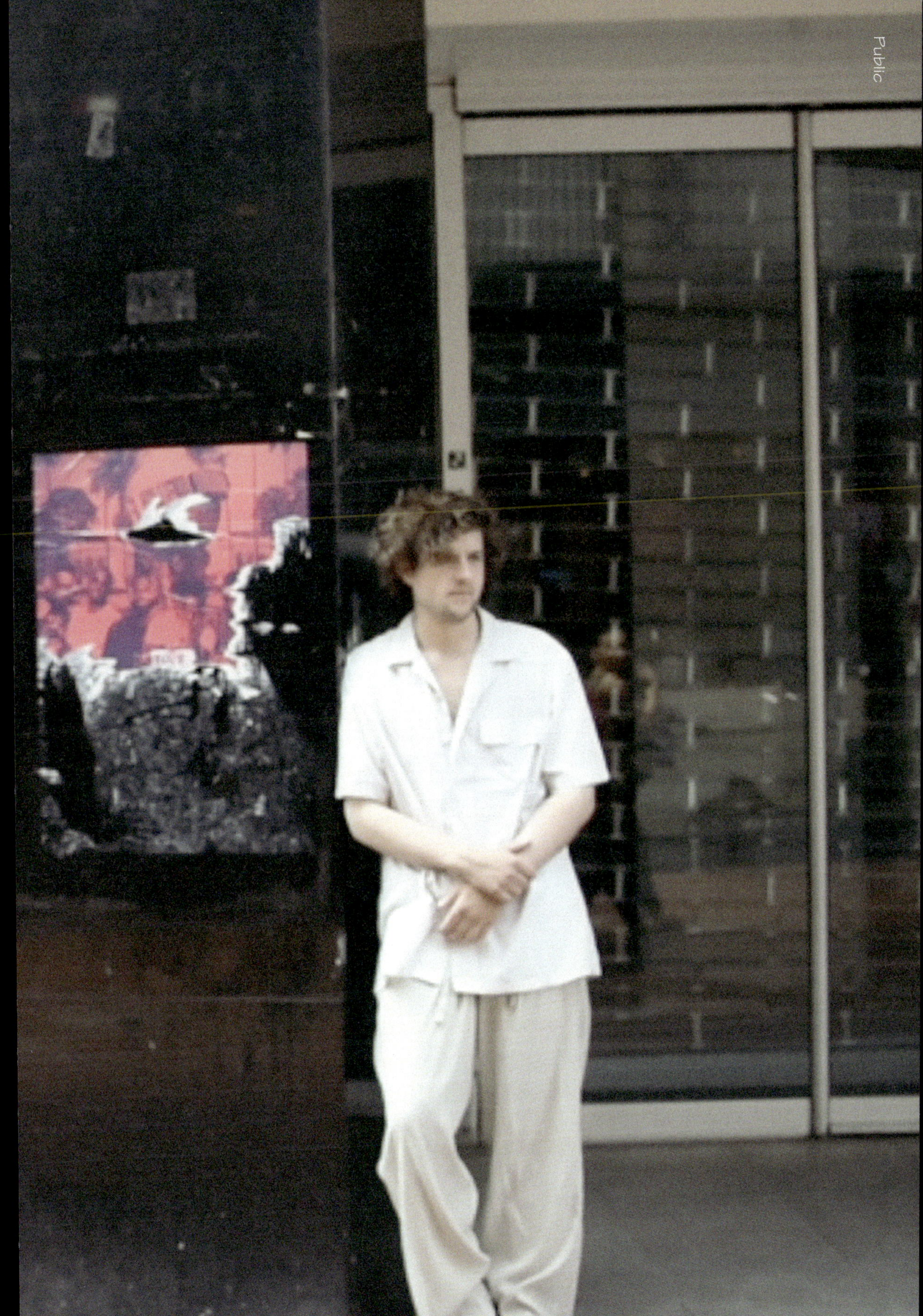

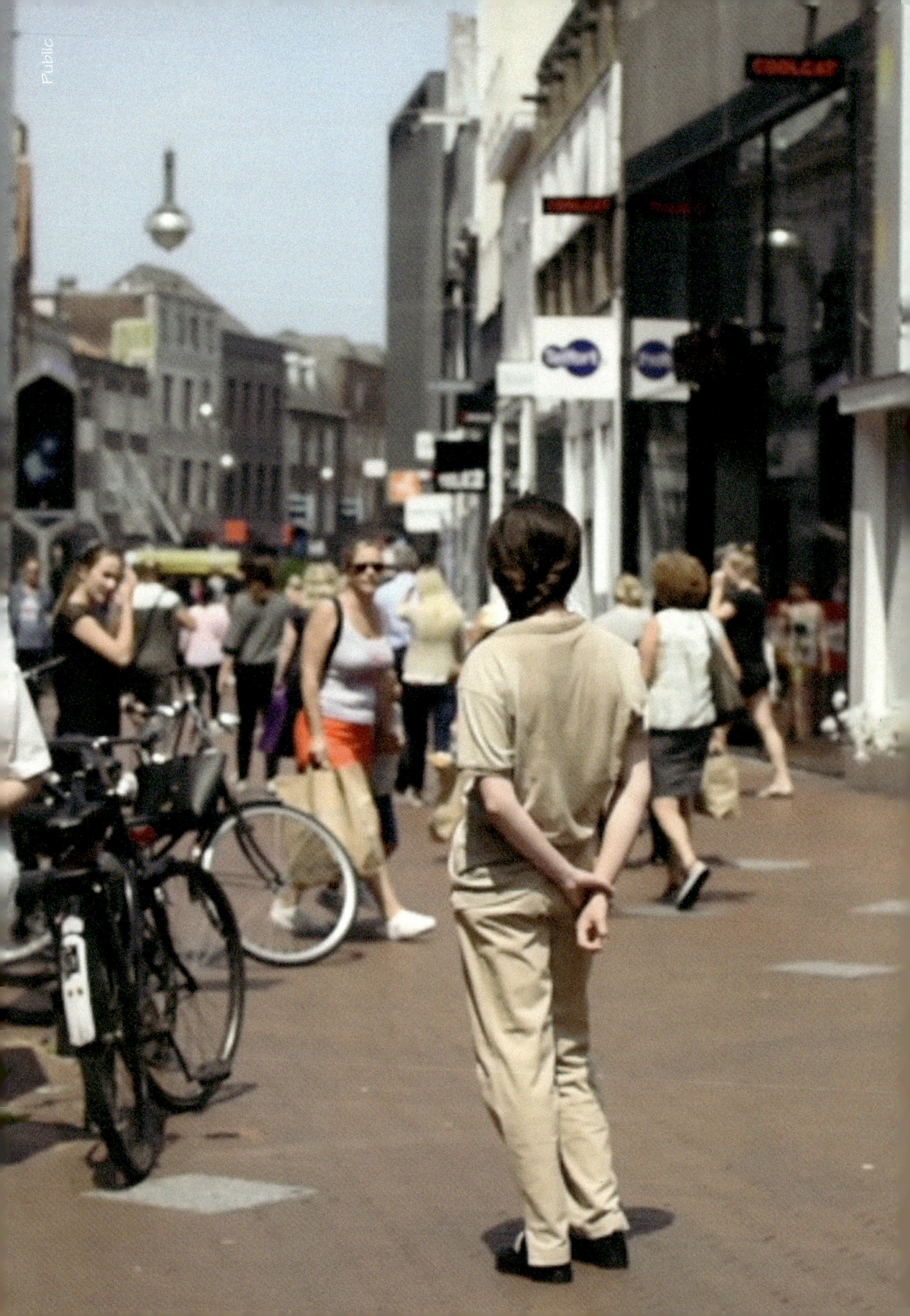
Public

ACHIEVEMENT #2
MISTY WALK, SWEATY TALK
NOLWENN SALAÜN

French artist Nolwenn Salaün, explores conscious or instilled mannerisms, tricks and habits that inhere in spaces and bodies through combining means of writing, photography, sound, video and performance. She is preoccupied with closed interiors, gatherings, rooms or groups one cannot easily escape, and in which incoherences in behaviour and spatial disposition emerge.

Passive involvement challenges purpose and questions meaning. There might be a space for contemplation, but having people contemplate without designated space, takes away their visibility as they loose a readable function. The achievement of Nolwenn Salaün therefore poetically emancipates the undesignated.

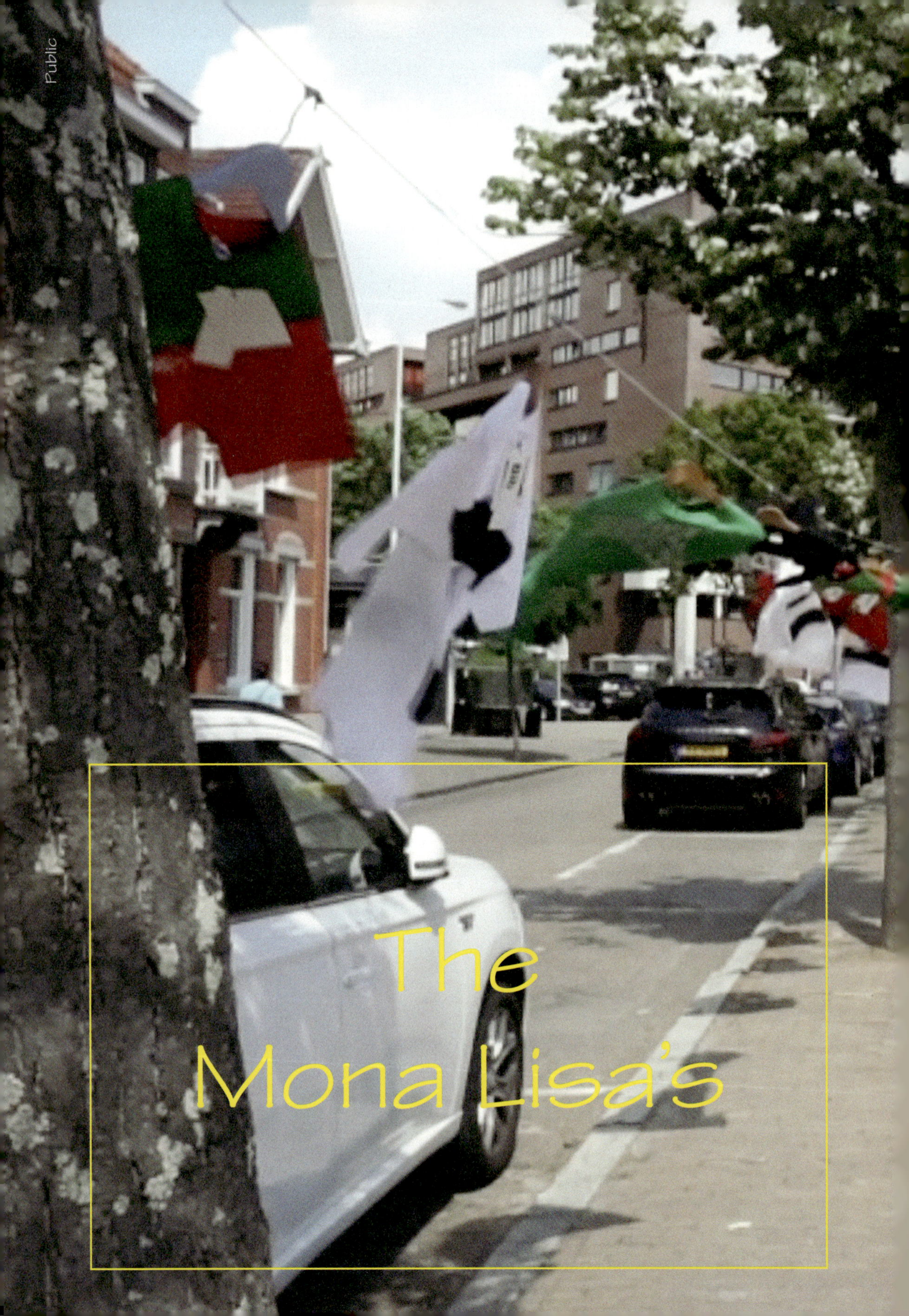

The Mona Lisa's

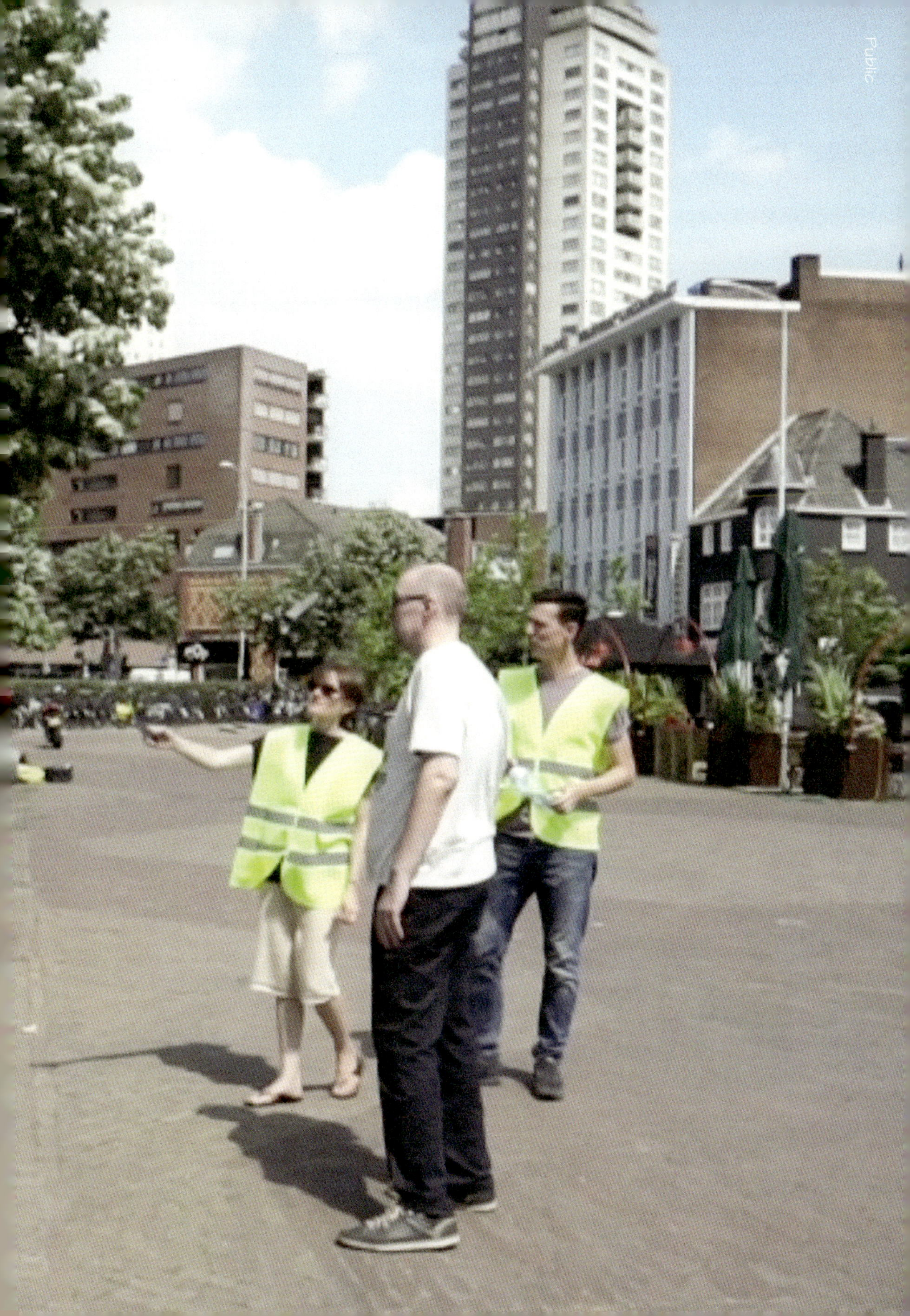

ACHIEVEMENT #3
Bruce&
Ronnie&
Bip&
Flip.
THE MONA LISA'S

The Dutch collective, The Mona Lisa's, explore internet memes and folklore and the relation between the two, as well as pagan rituals and anonymous expressions of cyber subcultures, as they produce situations in a range between carnival and activism of sorts.

As a group, consisting of Kim de Groot, Maarten Brandenburg and Barry de Bruin, their contribution to We Are The Market! is that of questioning identity and the presentation of the self through the clothes that people wear. Publicly displaying secondhand t-shirts that have been slightly altered with fake logos, mirroring commercialised action figures such as Flipje van Tiel, a cherry guy selling jelly from the Dutch city Tiel or Bibendum, the Michelin tire guy, they reclaim heroes for alternative modes of production and distribution.

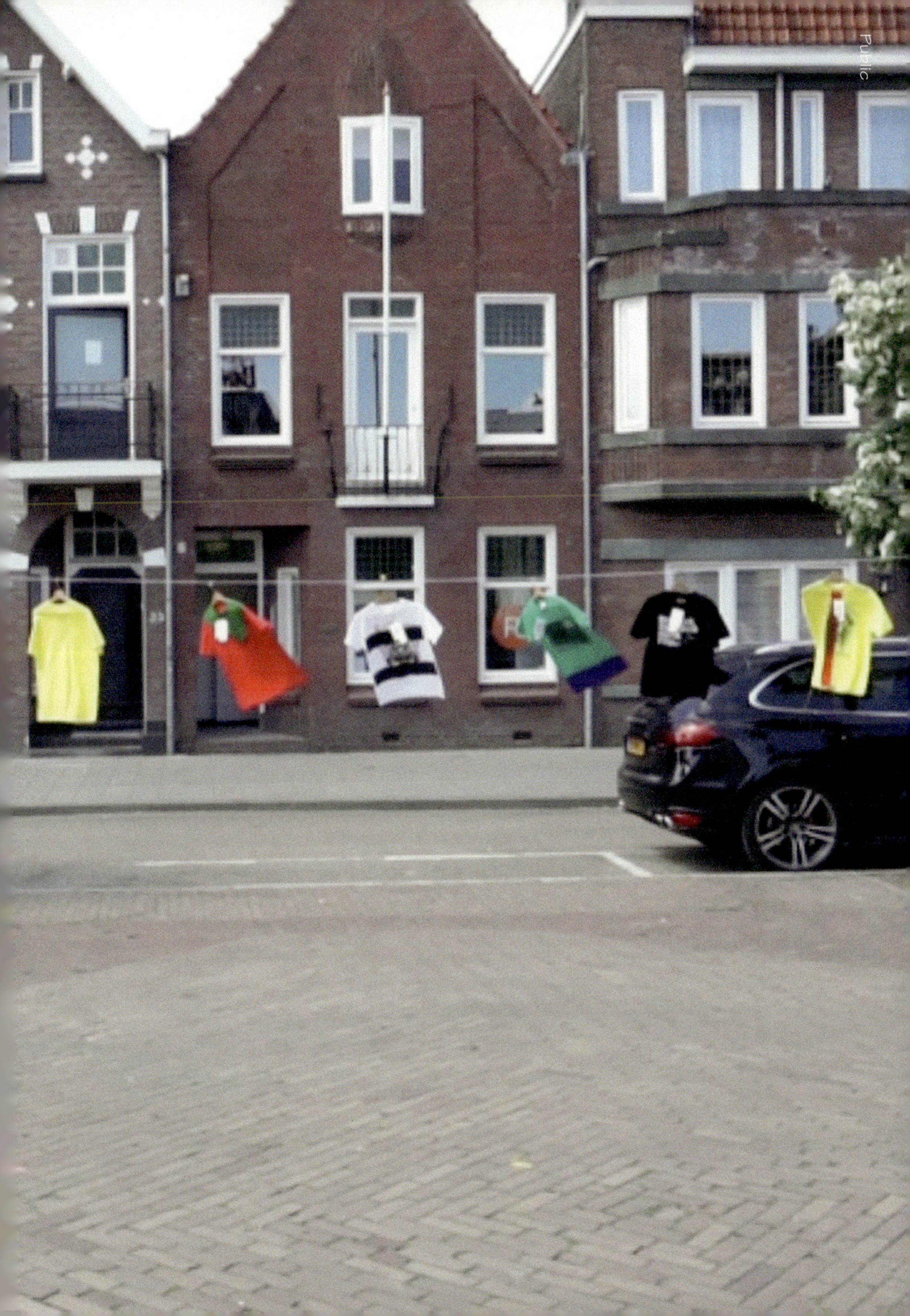

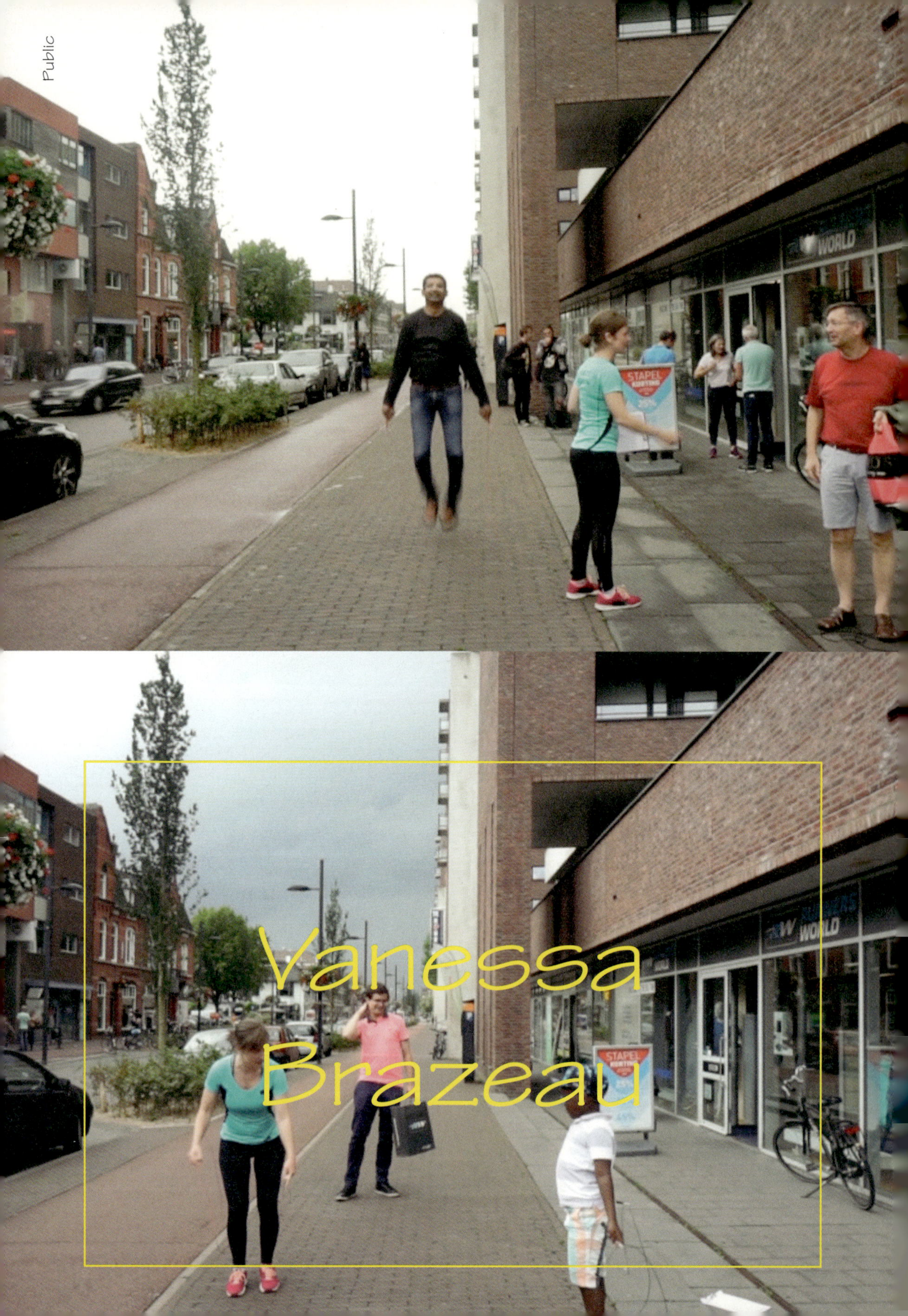

Vanessa Brazeau

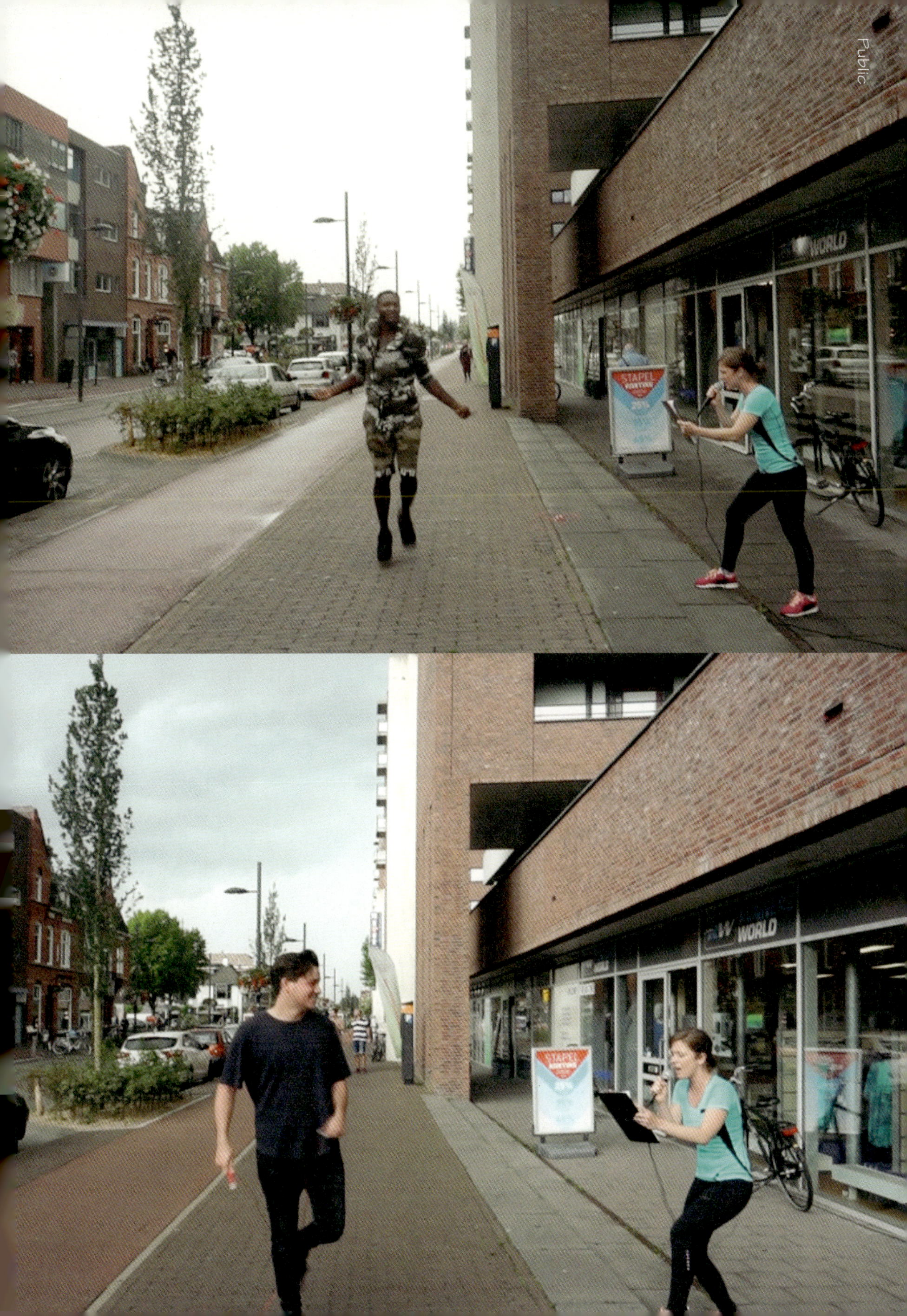
STAPEL
KORTING
WORLD

ACHIEVEMENT #4
MARKET TRAINING, EXERCISE #1
VANESSA BRAZEAU

Vanessa Brazeau is a Canadian artist, based in Berlin, whose practice currently focuses on implementing social and political themes into athletic frameworks. She uses the body as a tool for education, empowerment and stimulation of the mind, while also critiquing contemporary mentalities concerning the body, competition, labour and productivity. Many of her performances encourage public participation, activation and resistance, through which she aims to engage with people, making topics accessible through exercise and interaction, blurring the lines of how art can be perceived. Her work and techniques are very personal to her own experiences, as they represent her own struggle with fitness and body image.

Vanessa's contribution to *We Are The Market!* aims to highlight the irrelevance of choice in the commercial world, which stems from the similarity of products and a hand full of brands dominating advertising spaces. Wanting to randomise choices, she asks people to jump rope, which will make their next purchase decision for them. Disrupting people's routine of going out to buy shoes and then being stopped to jump rope also adds a humorous sub-tone, which she believes lets her connect better with people.

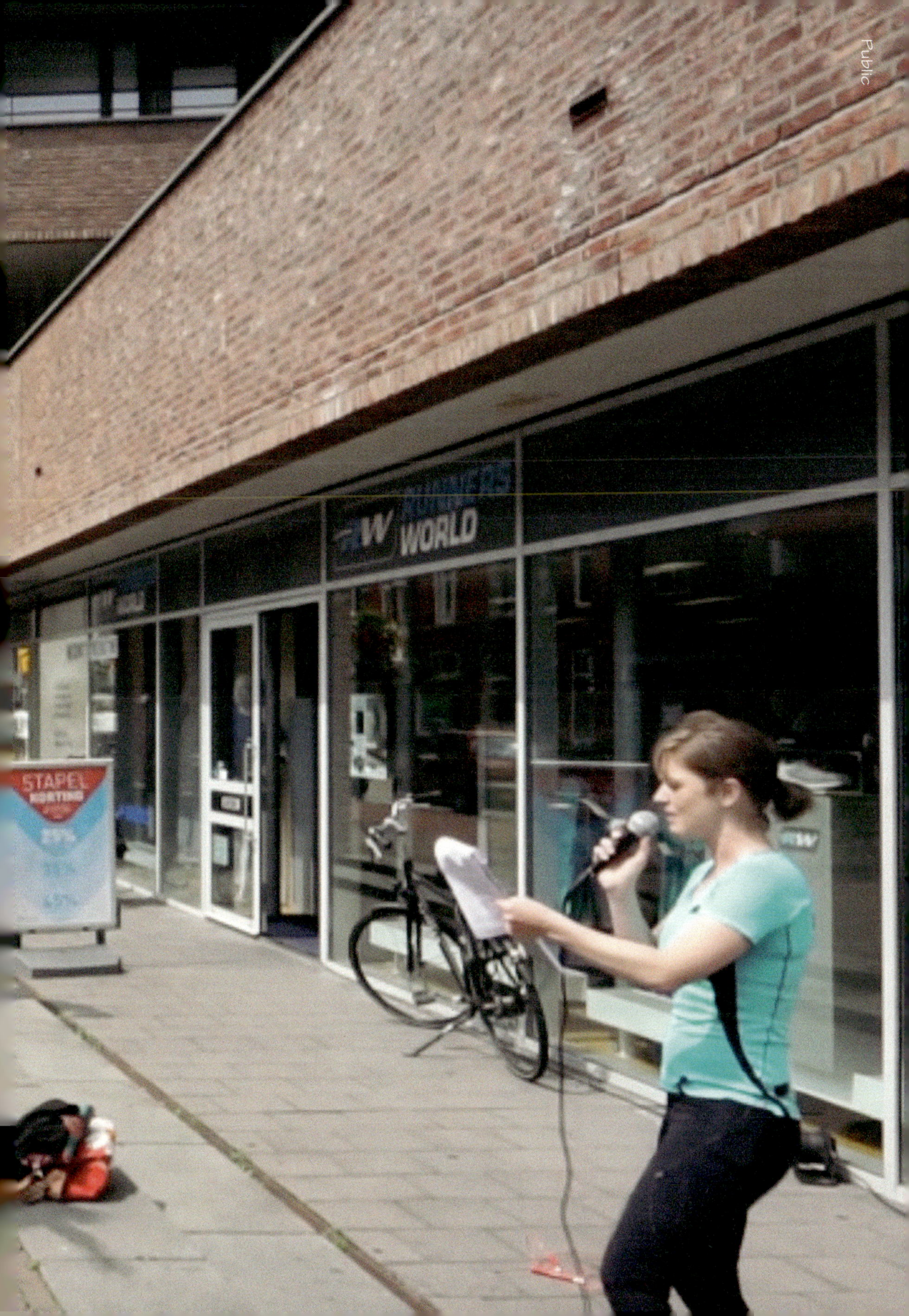
RUNNERS
WORLD
STAPEL
KORTING
25%

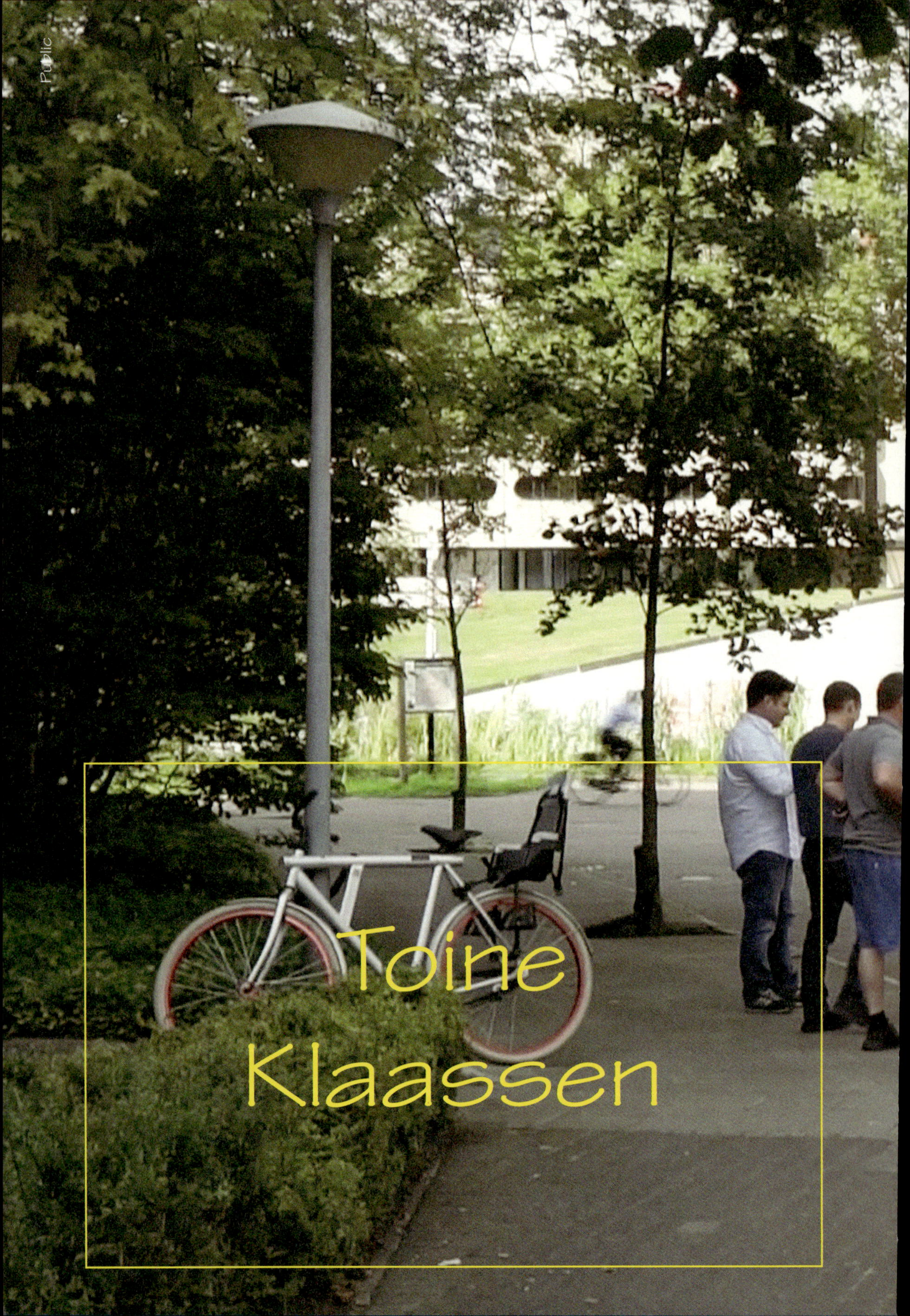
Public
Toine
Klaassen

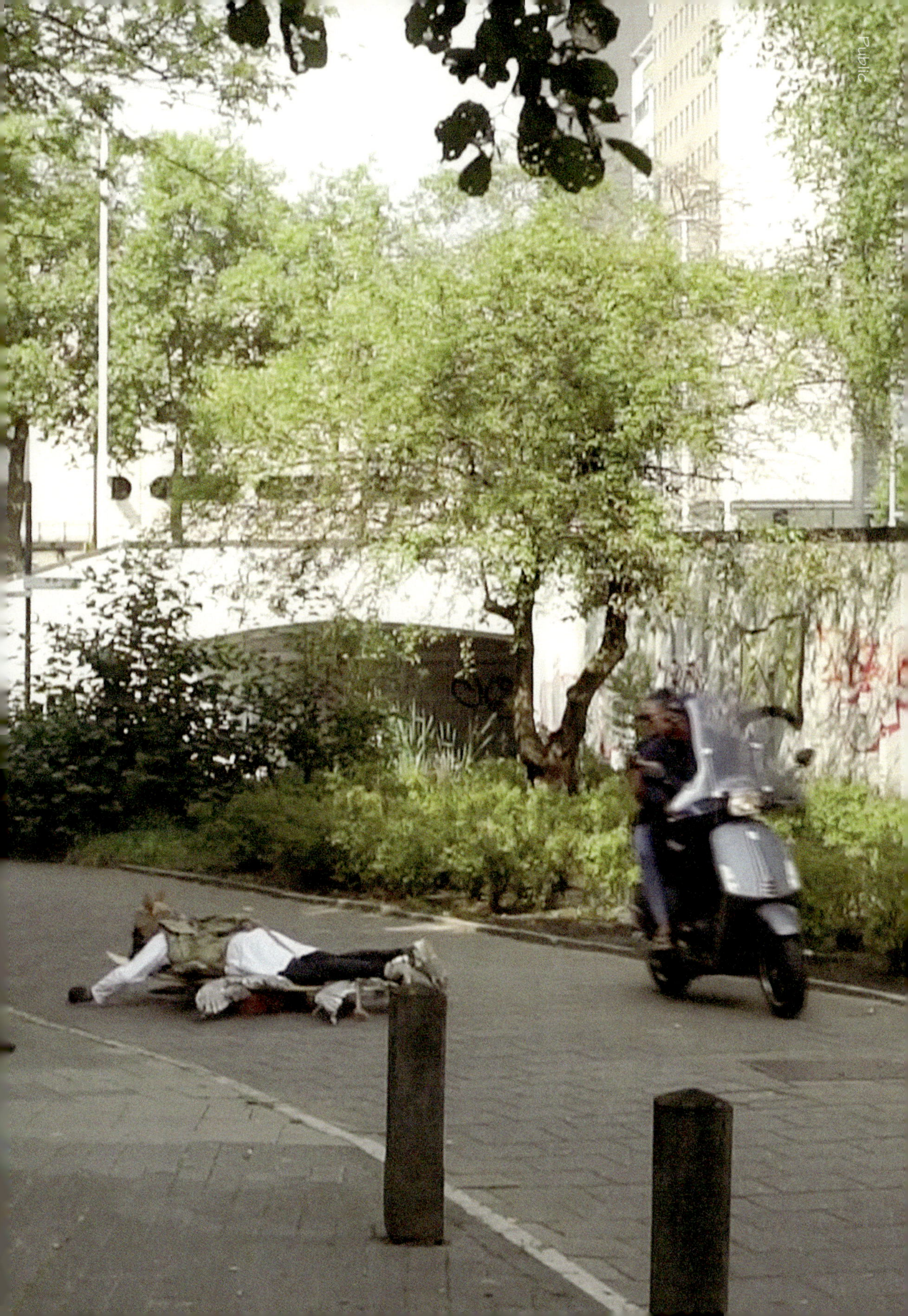

ACHIEVEMENT #5
EXERCISES IN CITY HYBRIDISATION
TOINE KLAASSEN

Being an inspired scavenger of the outdoors as well as using and exercising imagination through role-play, performance artist Toine Klaassen stretches the sense of identification and explores home territory. His work leaves bystanders to consider the symbolic range. One of his many characters is that of a city hybrid, a modern-day bushman, who scours through the urban landscape, seeking leather sofas that he can scalp to source materials, in order to make shoes and other indispensable stuff.

Through his particular character, Toine wants to draw attention to humanity's wasteful habits and ridicule single-mindedness and notions of property, by creating habitable oases next to streams and railway tracks near the centre. He describes himself as a farmer, who literally remodels the urban landscape and worships anything other than the commercial gods. Exposing himself to the public and acting in unusual ways also makes him very vulnerable, a crucial assett to his performance.

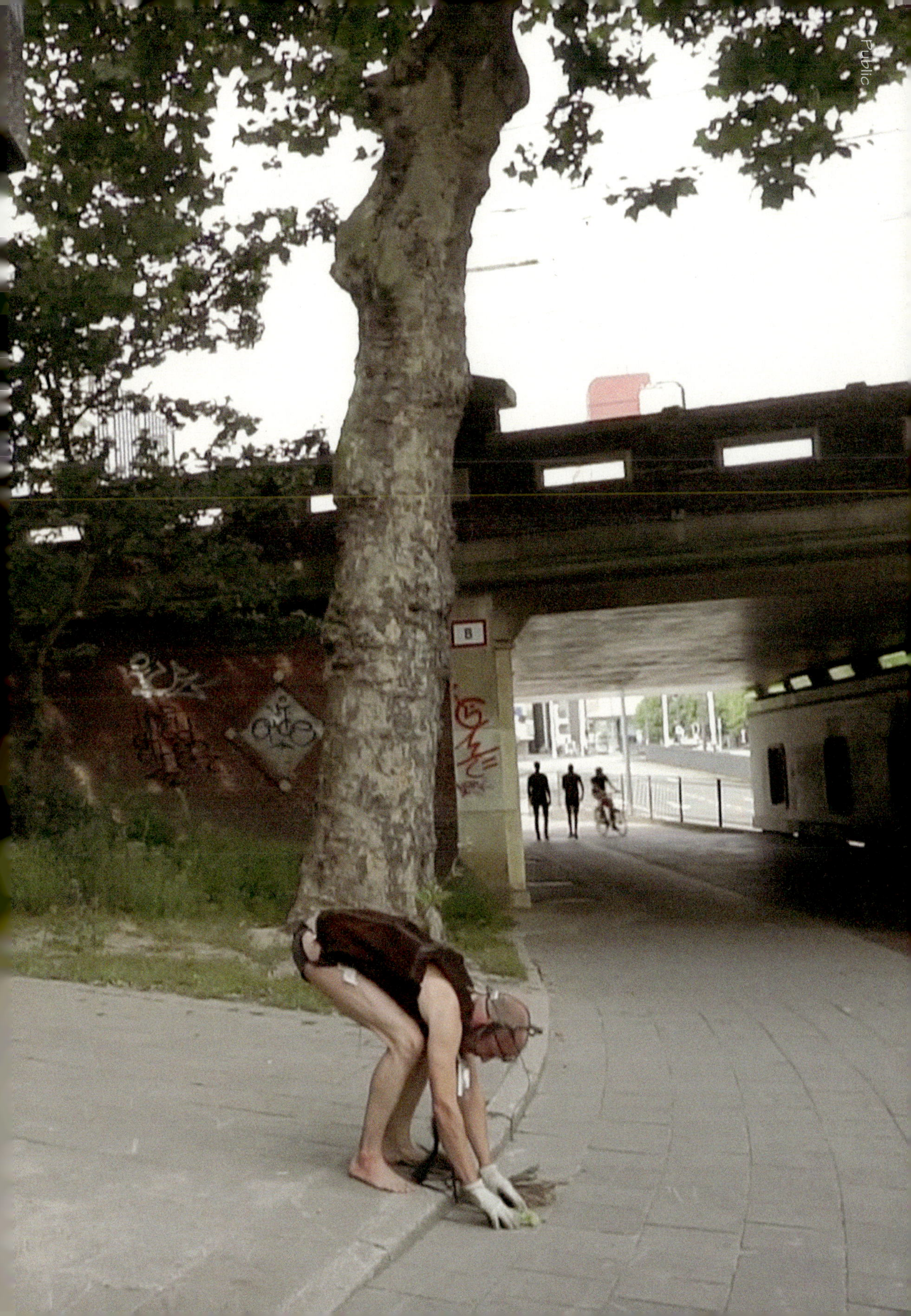
B

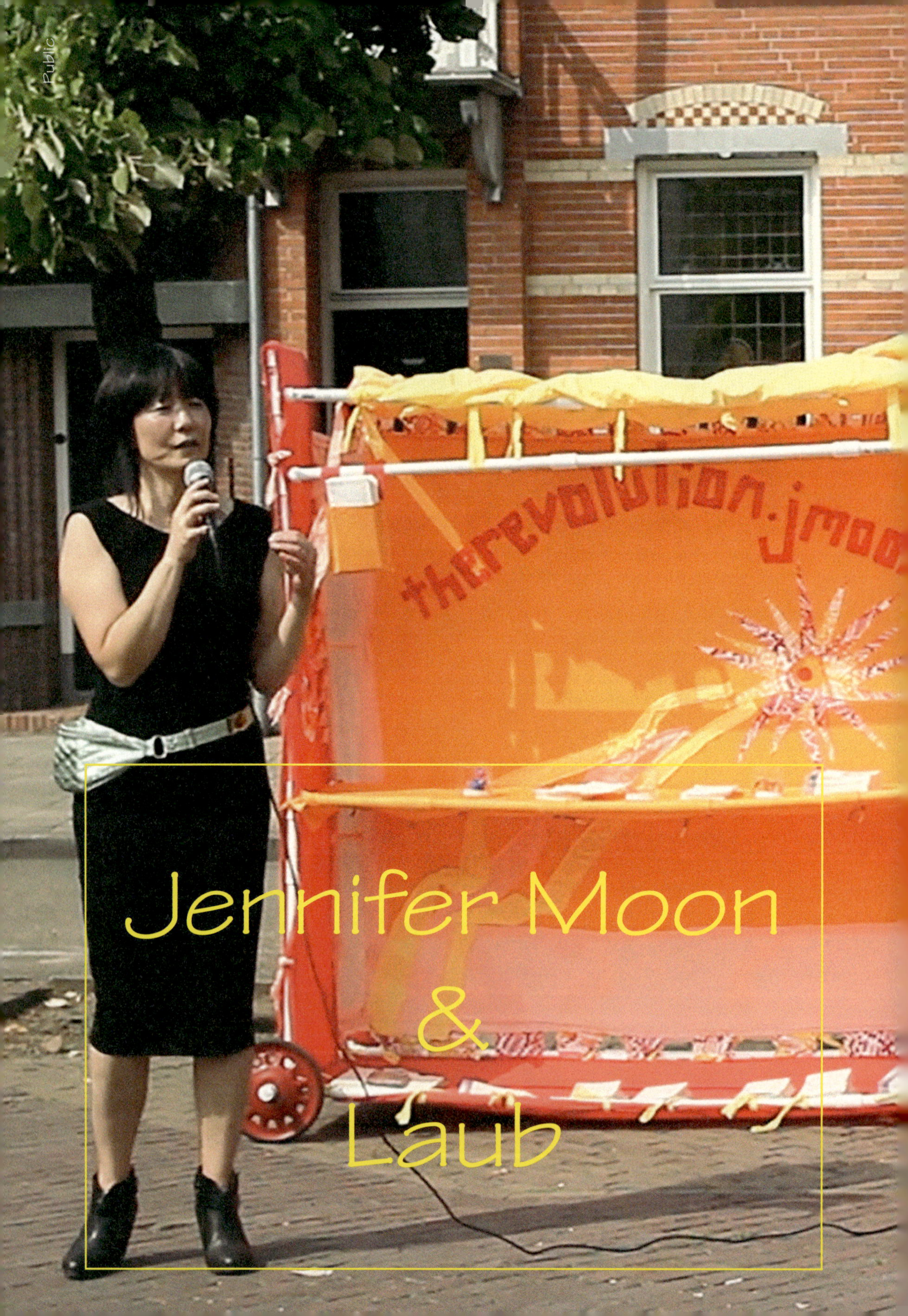

Jennifer Moon & Laub

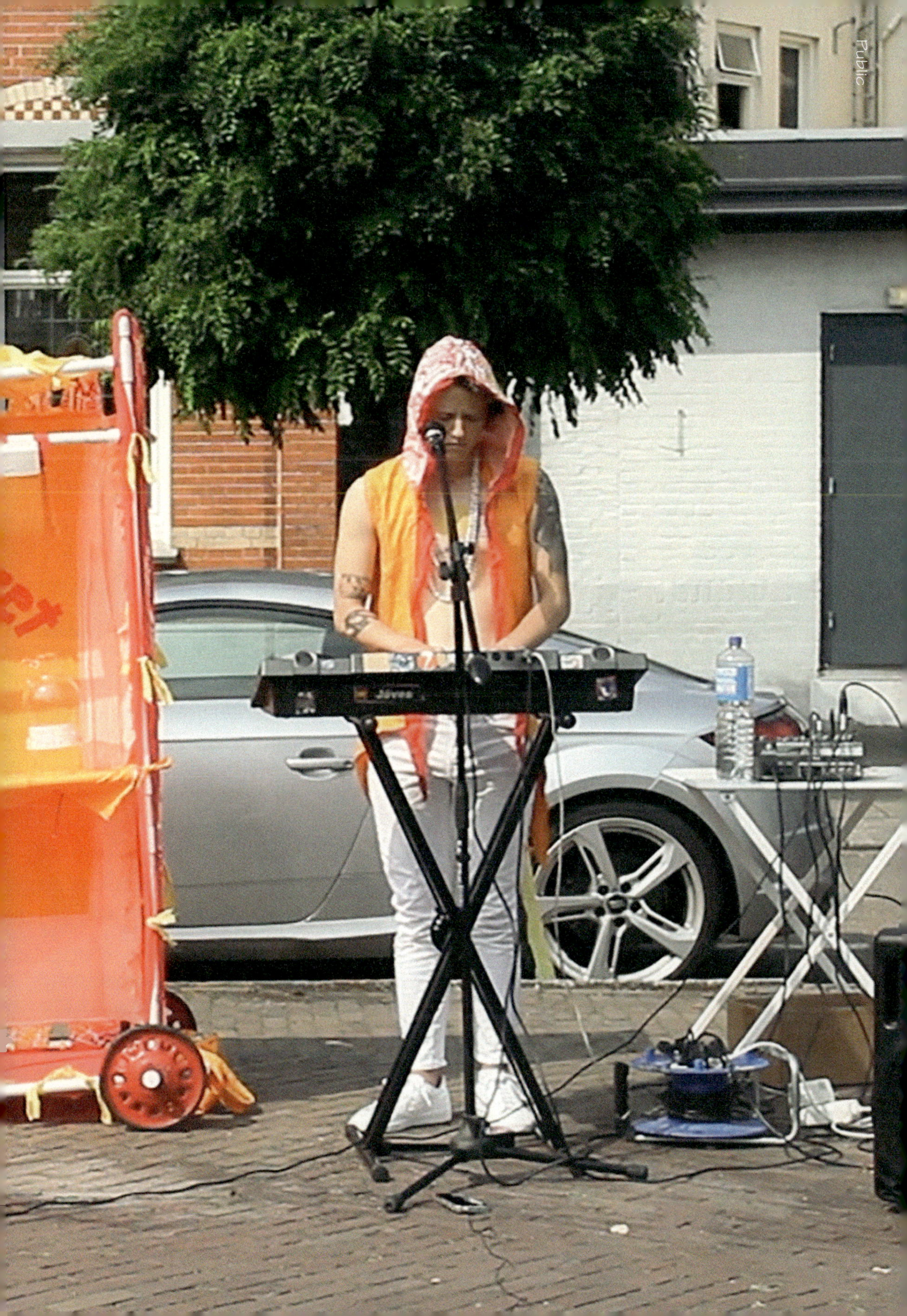

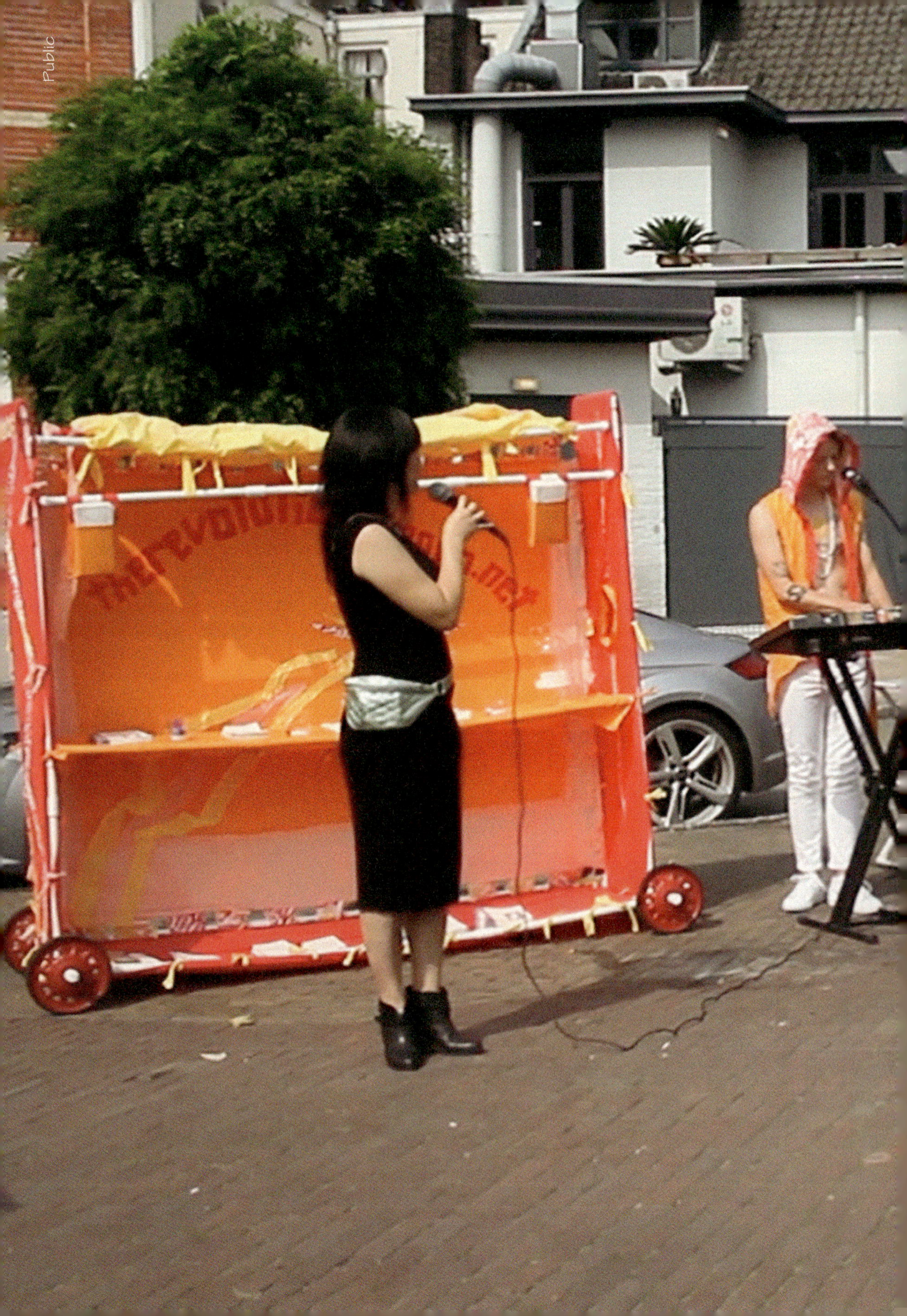

ACHIEVEMENT #6
THE REVOLUTION COMES TO EINDHOVEN: ABUNDANCE AND EXPANDING BEYOND THE 5% UNIVERSE
JENNIFER MOON AND LAUB

Jennifer Moon is a Los Angeles- based artist and initiator of 'The Revolution', with which she envisions to encourage transition, by following love, presence of mind and empowerment in everyday life. Together with her partner laub, the two of them combined self-help, fantasy and wisdom of life, to impart knowledge and inspiration onto the viewer through method of talks, workshops, performances and pamphlets. Generously offering ideas of self-improvement, their demand in return was that of death of self i.e. commitment and participation of the audience. Originally romantically involved with each other but in the process of breaking up, their performances and workshops also became increasingly influenced by the exposure of their raw emotional feelings, in relation to the painful split. Believing that revolution must come from within, Moon takes herself as the first example, and therefore emotionally exposing herself to the audience as a first step to self-improvement.

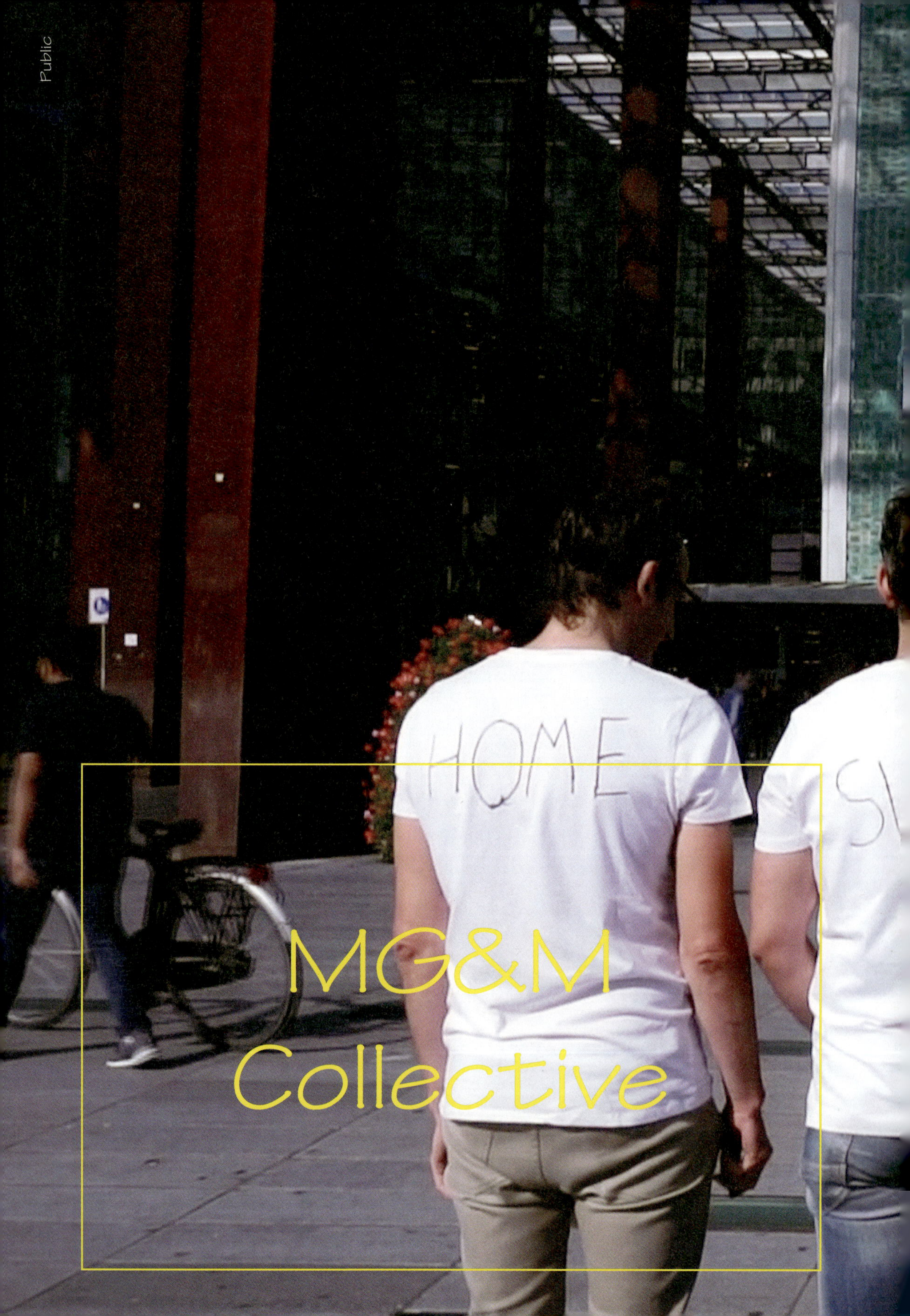

MG&M Collective

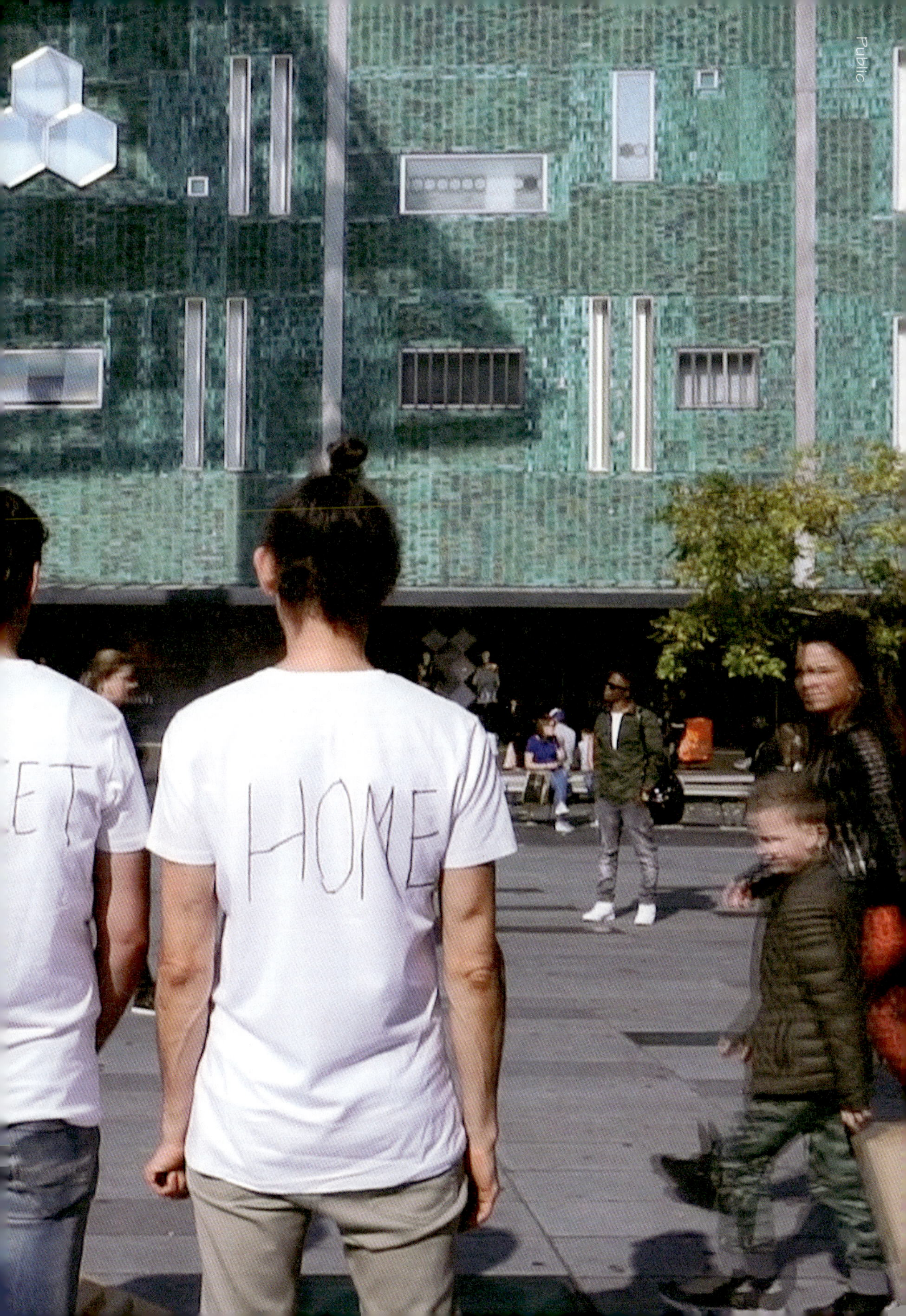
HOME

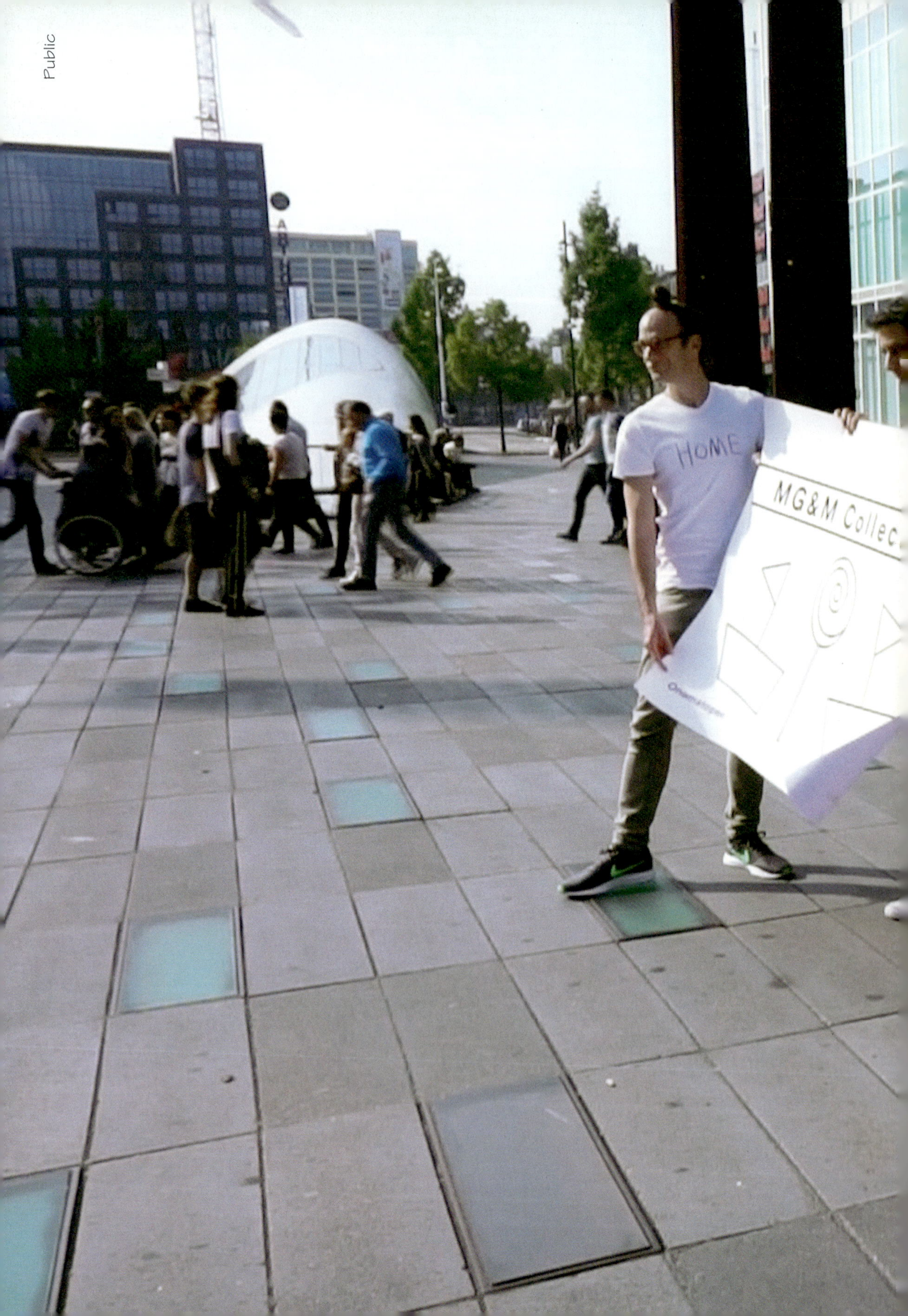
HOME
MG&M Collec

ACHIEVEMENT #7
YOU MAY CONSUME IT OR...
MG&M COLLECTIVE

MG&M Collective consists of Israeli artist duo Gil and Moti, in collaboration with Mosab Anzo, a Syrian-born painter who has been working with the duo for almost two years now.

While the natural response to being victimised, marginalised and brutalised is to hide and silence oneself, the collective opens up to the opportunity of interacting with generosity and love, and to foster sociability and engagement anew. To reach out and to touch.

In the context of We Are The Market! MG&M Collective took the central shopping square as its site to offer a lollipop, in a hand-folded boat, that could be licked, thrown away, given away or otherwise, while representing a refugee.

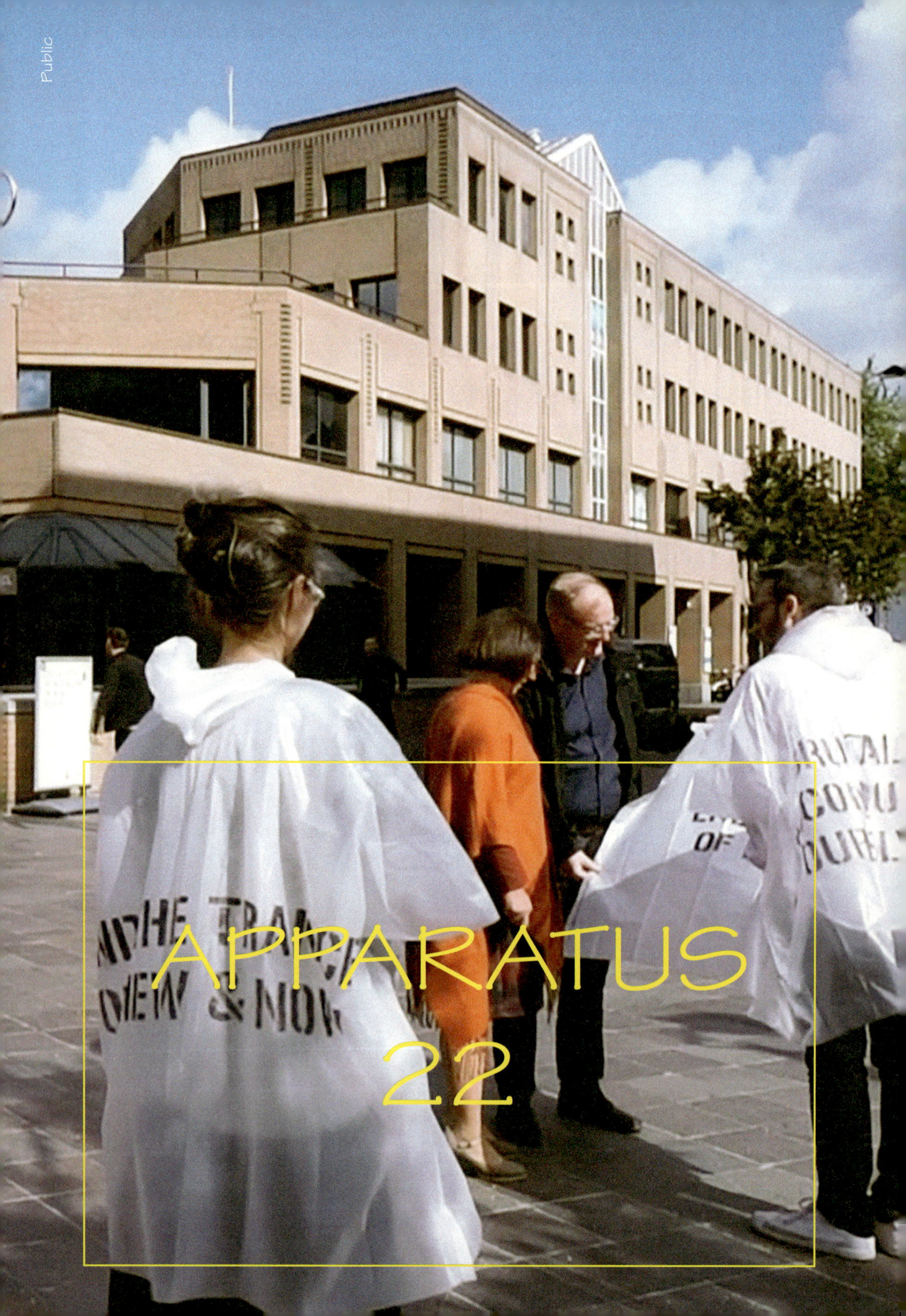
APPARATUS
22

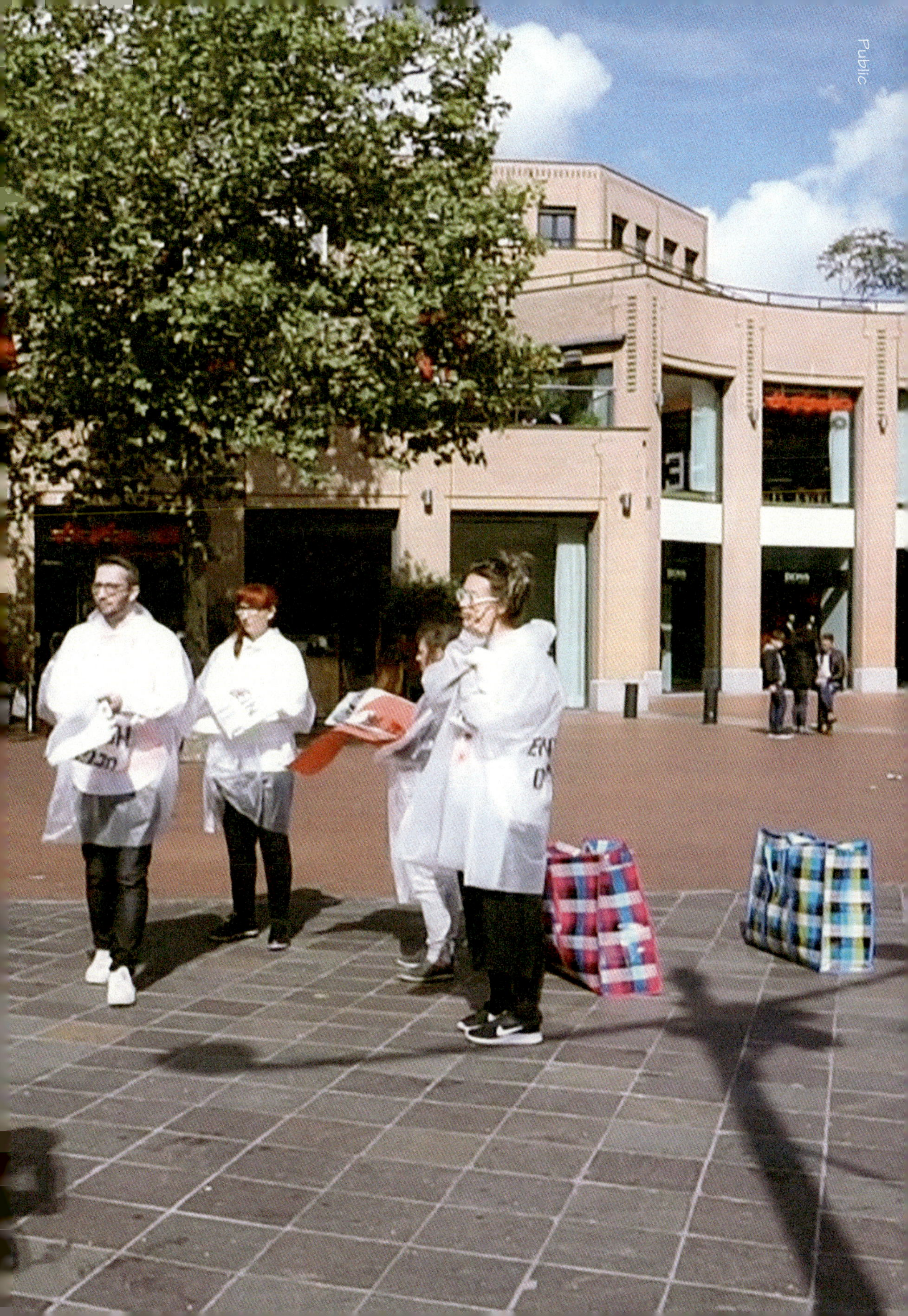

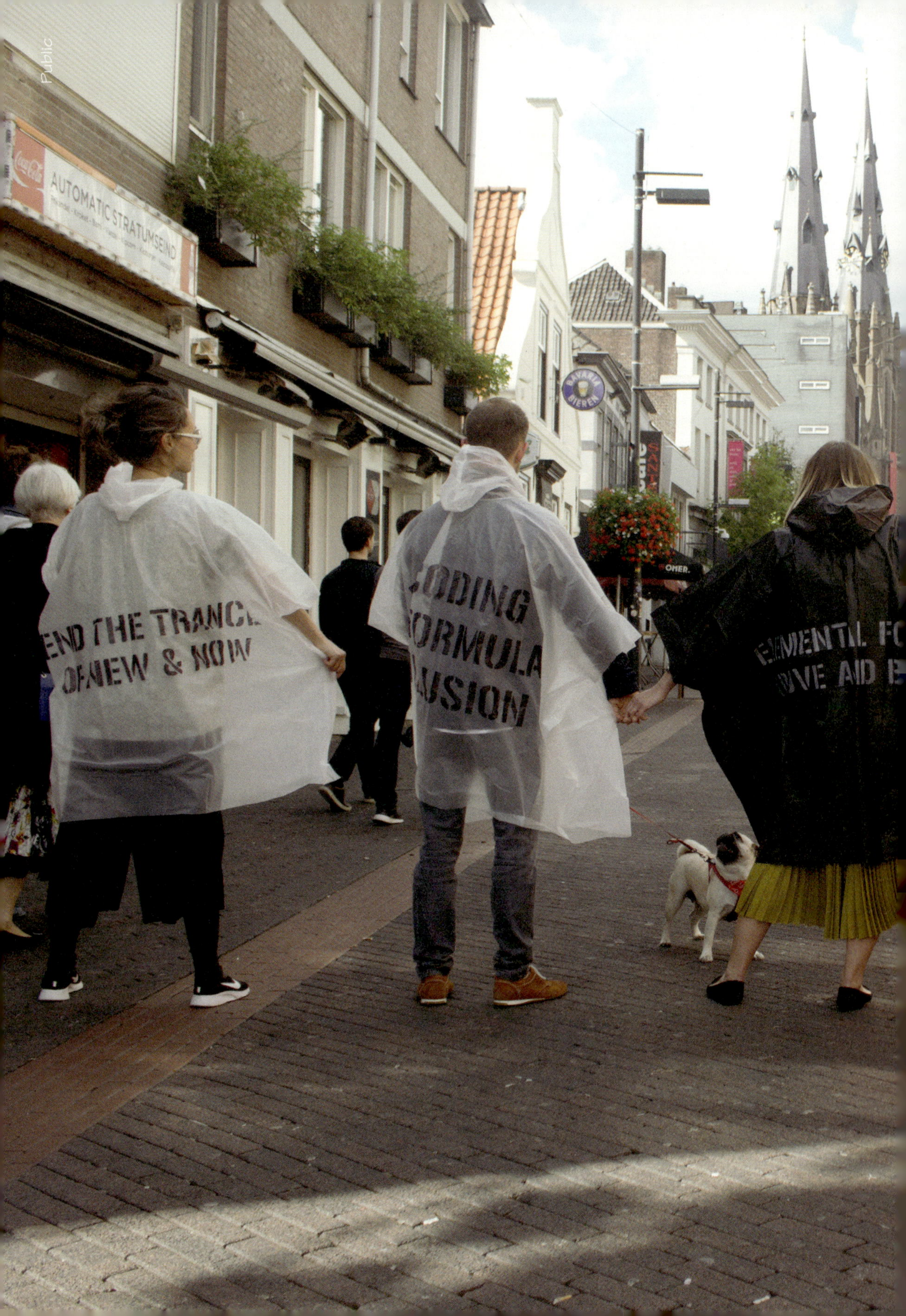
Coca-Cola
AUTOMATIC STRATUMSEIND
BAVARIA BIEREN
END THE TRANCE
OF NEW & NOW

ACHIEVEMENT #8
SKY NAIVE | IT BEGS A QUESTION
APPARATUS 22

Initiated by artists Erika and Dragos Olea, Maria Farcas, and the late Ioana Nemes, the collective Apparatus 22 is a Europe-wide based collective. With a joint background in fashion, but having become tired of the superficial brevity which prevails within the industry, they have now turned to art to air their thoughts and concerns. Still relating to fashion, as well as the economy, language and institutional power, they approach these topics from an artistic and culturally progressive point of view, instead of that of the highly competitive fashion industry.

Wanting to devitalise the influence of large-scale commercial brands that oversaturate most town centres, the collective offers protection against the commercial slogans and sales techniques, in the shape of rain ponchos that bare confirmative slogans to re-empower the individual consumer and shield them from the influence of commercial industries. Their work, titled Sky Naive | It Begs A Question, involved the distribution of a gift with conversations alongside it. Through this act they hope to raise awareness and resistance against the commercial influence over individuals.

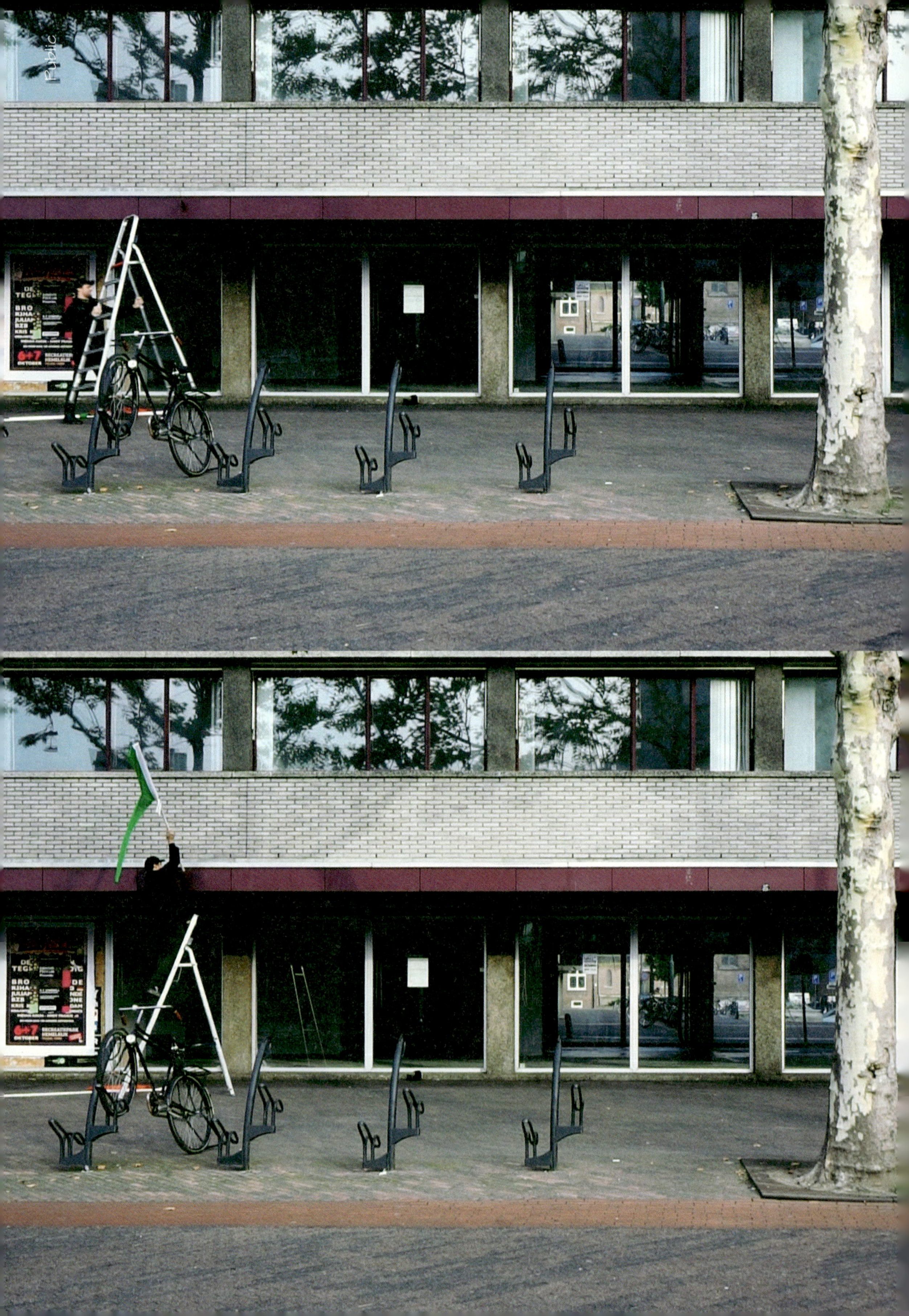
6+7
OKTOBER

THE ETHEREAL THEATRE

By Dirk Vis

Lately I appear as a saint, a king, or a baby. I myself do not actively pursue these transformations. When my wife, brother and friends take pictures of themselves and of me, sometimes they draw or write over our photographed faces. Sometimes they add a static or animated filter to change who we appear to be. I've heard things about my own life from my friends, which they found out through the social media posts of third parties. It was not my intention, but thousands of people saw a video clip of me, a man, manipulated through the use of automatic algorithms, to look like a woman. I can feel cornered and caught by those many tiny cameras that are everywhere and invisible like a young upstart god. When the nymph Diana was being chased by man god Apollo, with hearts in his eyes and likes on his mind, to evade it all she turned into a tree.

I look at the video in which I have algorithmically extended lips and enlarged almond shaped CGI eyes. I feel manly. I see a photo of myself, manipulated into the image of an old man and I feel young. In the next picture I wear a crown, digitally drawn by a designer for an American company. The crown rotates, radiates gold and blue and I feel poor. All persons with this digital crown atop their heads serve the unordained sovereigns of Silicon Valley. These recorded representations of me make me into their opposite. The added effects make them inverse to reality.

In the process of analog photography a negative image is developed on film—a reversed image through which projected light generates a positive image on photosensitive paper. This process can be altered and the resulting photos manipulated, but they have generally been looked at as truthful. In the early photographic technology of the camera obscura or pinhole camera, light enters a space through a tiny hole in one of the walls and is projected onto the opposite wall in the otherwise dark space. The projected result shows the scene directly outside that space, but upside down and reverted. Representation and inversion are deeply connected.

When light hits the sensors in the camera in your smartphone it sets off electronic reactions that are being stored in digital memory as colour information: every snapshot generates millions of tiny status updates. After the initial digital recording of the picture – skipping the step of the photographic negative and in a reversal of the analog photographic process—these images go through endless further development. With every added filter, manipulation effect, encoding and sharing action they become more and more like a negative of the original image, with every algorithmic retouching more unreal. Only after the positive image does the digital photographic negative appear.

'A constructed Situation is a moment of life,' so said the Situationists half a century ago. An artistic flash-mob attitude *avant la lettre*. They would turn the coincidental appearance of a circus elephant in the streets into an absurd performance. A piece of commercial artwork doubles as the backdrop for an improvised play. Observers could get a glimpse of other possibilities, whether you would consider it fragments of utopian dreams, religious ideals or revolutionary goals. For them it was only possible to do this without the use of representation, because anything represented is immediately part of the unfathomably large spectacle, the unreal world of images, representations, phantasms and the viewers' relations, that numbs the participants, guards the status quo and makes any change impossible.

This 20th century idea of avoiding representation can still be found. The organisers of certain underground club nights where taking out a mobile phone will get you expelled, know that most of the time the use of a camera will make anything that happens instantly part of the normal, everyday, represented world, making any kind of transcendental experience impossible. There is something sacred in having only the physically present audience members experience something for a limited time. Sacred in the simplest and most secular definition I know of: something separated from, set apart of the ordinary and banal. But all contemporary representation-free zones are by definition limited to the marginal, avant-garde and out of the ordinary. A complete withdrawal from representation would mean a withdrawal from public life.

A lot of precarious freelancers do not even have a choice: Designers, models, actors and writers have a daily work routine of updating their online market stalls. The larger their audience, the more clients will follow. Not being represented is not an option anymore. More practically, even if you don't produce your own self-representations, others will do so for you.

'Neo-feudal!' is how technology critic Evgeny Morozov defines this way of living. In the system of medieval feudalism, labour was exchanged not for money but for services like military protection. In neo-feudalism public lives are increasingly governed by private corporations. Currently you get to use social media platforms in exchange for data. Corporations can sell that data to advertisers who want to sell their products to specific target groups. In Evgeny Morozov's neo-feudalist scenario advertising will be a less important business model than the commercial licensing of AI services by tech giants and it will expand into other areas like city planning, medical services and insurances. As a result, the currently bustling online shopping malls and free social media platforms will be as hollowed out as their brick and mortar equivalents already are. Together they form the stage for future public actions.

Most people choose an online persona and stick with it. Their profile pages change in tandem with their real life personas. But some manage to challenge what you see online.

'Will be performing ' says artist Amalia Ulman. Over four months she created a fictional character from her supposedly real and personal life on an image-centric social media platform. Hordes of people followed this fictional story and for a moment it turned the rules of the platform upside down. I could not find any official reaction on her work by the social media company. Presumably they didn't care. As long as most people still consider their profiles authentic, their business model is fine. Ulman is like the jester in a medieval court: someone who makes fun and a living off of the courtly proceedings, but still functions well within them.

The world famous image streams of Kim Kardashian work in many ways: from advertising channel to something of an online prayer book. In her fully developed digital photographic negatives, consciously or unconsciously, she and others like her, take on poses of muses, angels and madonnas that in the past could be found on medieval icons and paintings. Secular and unholy, her photos make the platforms she fills larger, and she makes those platforms work for her as well, funding her. Her posts are as artful and fictional as Ulmans even if they are considered real. There are many more versions of these deliberately constructed moments of digital life.

'I'm an avatar and artist originating in virtual space,' says LaTurbo Avedon who is the virtual embodiment of an anonymous group of artists.

What would happen if *everybody* with a social media account would consider their representations purposely fictional? Not just unreal, but consciously constructed. If the stage, the props and the *eyeballs* that social media grant would be used for an improvised and omnipresent theatre? Theatre director Peter Brook writes about what he calls the rough theatre, the immediate theatre and the holy theatre: 'Dirt, filth and vulgarity are natural, obscenity is joyous.'

In the virtual theatre the actors and directors travel from court to court, fooling, jesting, leaving behind a trail of otherworldly glimpses. A dream image is blurry, messy and constantly changing. The ethereal theatre flourishes in a social imaginary world, a shared dreamscape for a future real world scenario with ever growing inequality, gated communities and legions of freelancers depending on corporate servitude.

This isn't completely disconnected from what's happening in the professional theatre world. Stage performances have increasingly used virtual techniques to continue to reach their dispersed and individualistic audience members. Theatre artist Dries Verhoeven for instance has combined the dating-app Grindr and a glass booth in public space to stage his play. He has also used the technique of the video conference call to choreograph a dramatic play for a single audience member at a time. By using elements of the ethereal theatre for his works, Verhoeven has managed to break open the boundaries between online an offline, public and private, art and commerce, tech and flesh.

Peter Brook: 'The spectacle taking on its socially liberating role.'

Paradoxically, being active in these silicon streets brings your attitude into the world of pedestrian areas and pavements. Theatrical online personas and performances can simultaneously break the barrier between online and offline as well as form a protective layer against the engineered addictiveness of these black hole media. Anyone taking part in the ethereal theatre is necessarily strongly grounded.

Already some of the rules can be discerned. Always follow a script that is never written. Withdraw from representation only into further representation. The moment anything is shared, whatever is represented is left behind like the snake's skin. Let go of your images, let them exist in myriad versions, not one of them authentic. Use all the filters you can find. Superimpose, Facetune, Hyperlapse, Afterlight, Snapseed, Colorburn and then on top construct your own. These filters add instead of take out, they contaminate instead of clean, but because of the reversed process the effect can be the same. Add minuscule particles wherever you can find them. Gumballs for eyes. Be an ever-changing blend, a mystery to everyone including yourself. With every filter a piece of representation is blocked. Your private self is something to guess at. Fully develop your images into complete digital negatives. A real crown works better than a paper one. A home-made shoddy paper crown better than an animated, drawn one. Do not limit yourself to the stuff provided by someone else's dressing box. Tap into the creative energy needed for these inventions. It's the same energy the Situationists used, the same energy that could man the barricades. No online action goes without its material world equivalence. When you end up as a king in a digital photo stream, appear as one in the streets as well. When the digital code of your next selfie gets sent into space I hope it mixes with the encoded cosmological photographic messages already out there before it bounces back, unrecognisably altered, to your followers on earth. The next time somebody takes a picture of me at least I want to have the DendrologiseMe filter ready and look like a tree.

12.

POINT OF LEISURE

Comments >> p. 152

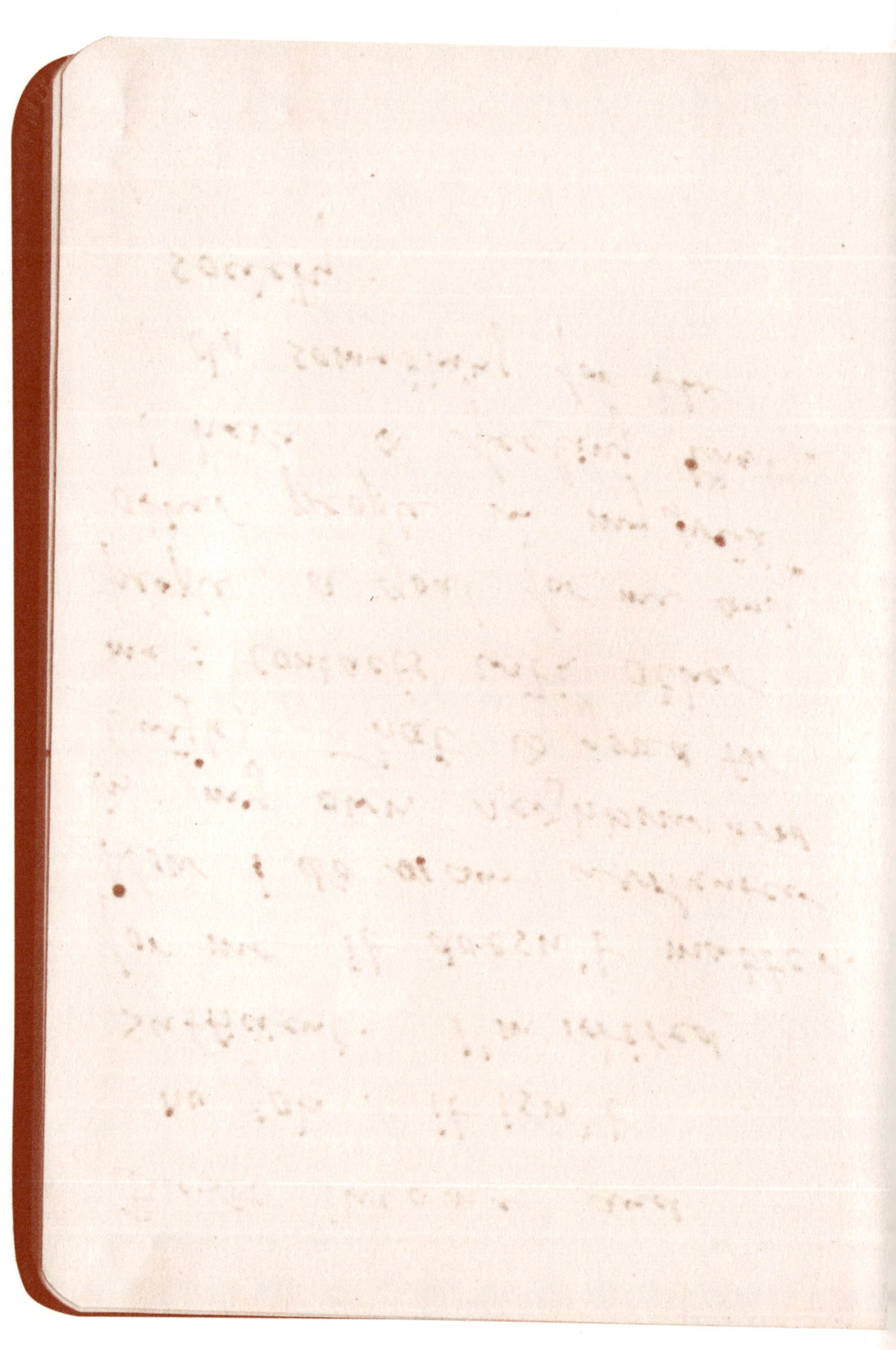

Coming from an artistic background / point of view this scenario seems like a dream initially.
Being able to pursue whatever you'd like, realising artistic visions...
But how would that contribute to society? Unless I made critical / conversational art?
Also; would I be motivated enough?

↺

Coming from an artistic background / point of view this scenario seems like a dream initially. Being able to pursue whatever you'd like, realising artistic visions...
But how would that contribute to society? Unless I made critical / conversational art?
Also; would I be motivated enough?

would Society be able to function?

Looking at it from the left wing pespective I would support an unconditional basic income. It's a fair and equal chance for everyone to start out in life and people's emotions and happiness would improve dramatically.

would society be able
to function?
Looking at it from the
left wing perspective I would
support an unconditional
basic income. It's a fair and
equal chance for everyone
to start out in life and
people's emotions and
happiness would improve
dramatically.

The challenge of
collaboration between
people is something
That I think is important
in the question. Something
I would love to work on
if my basic income is set.

The challenge of collaboration between people is something that I think is important in the equation. Something I would love to work on if my basic income is set.

I enjoyed having spent time with you. It's a comfortable feeling to meet someone who wants to speak about an important topic but who doesn't impose an opinion.

when my income
is taken care of!

I would try to
make money of
my hobby's ~~and~~ of
Find creative way's
to make extra.
money. (and never
work a 9 to 5.

xx [illegible]

Great

BRAINSTORM

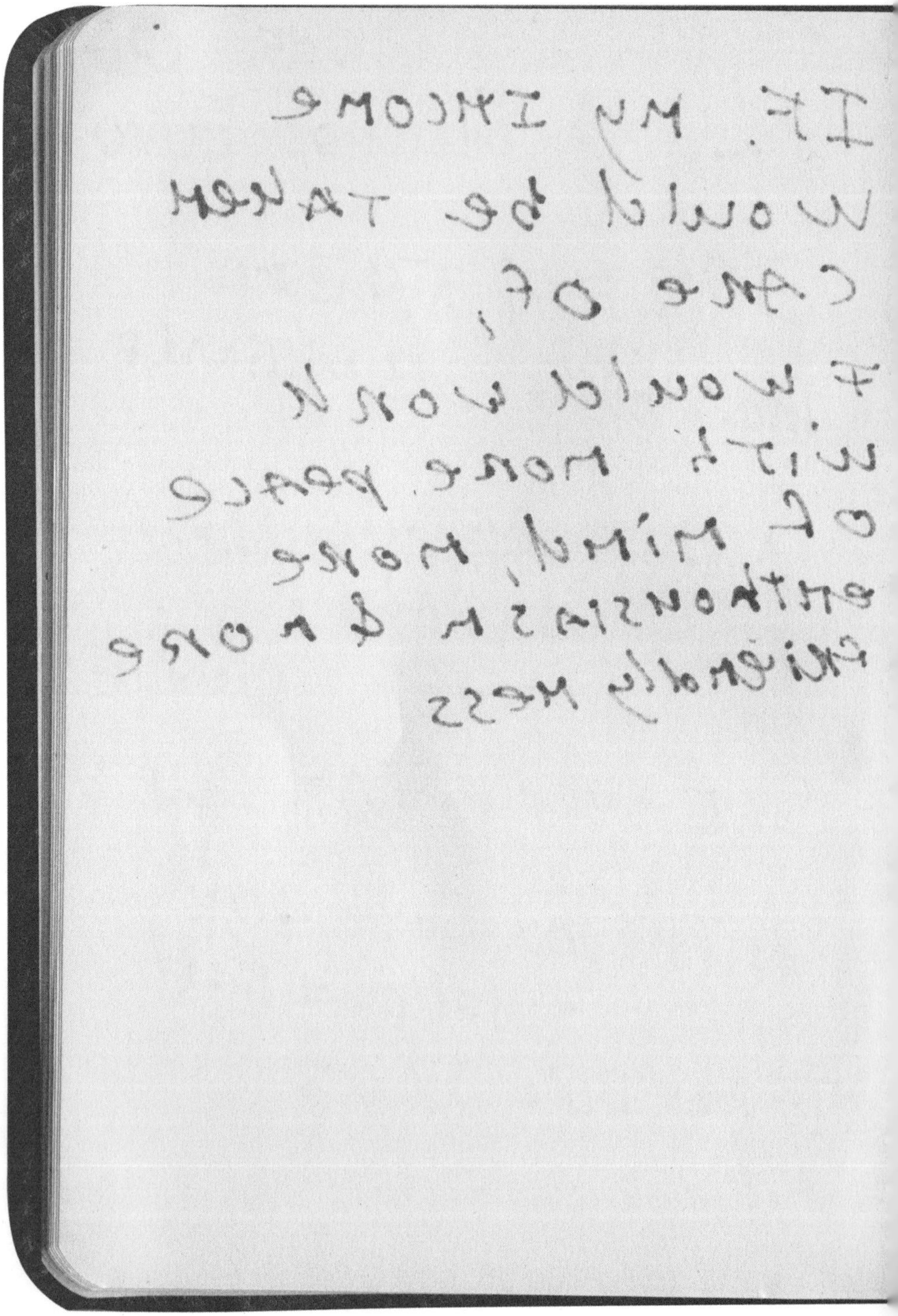

If my income
would be taken
care of,
I would work
with more peace
of mind, more
enthusiasm & more
friendly ness

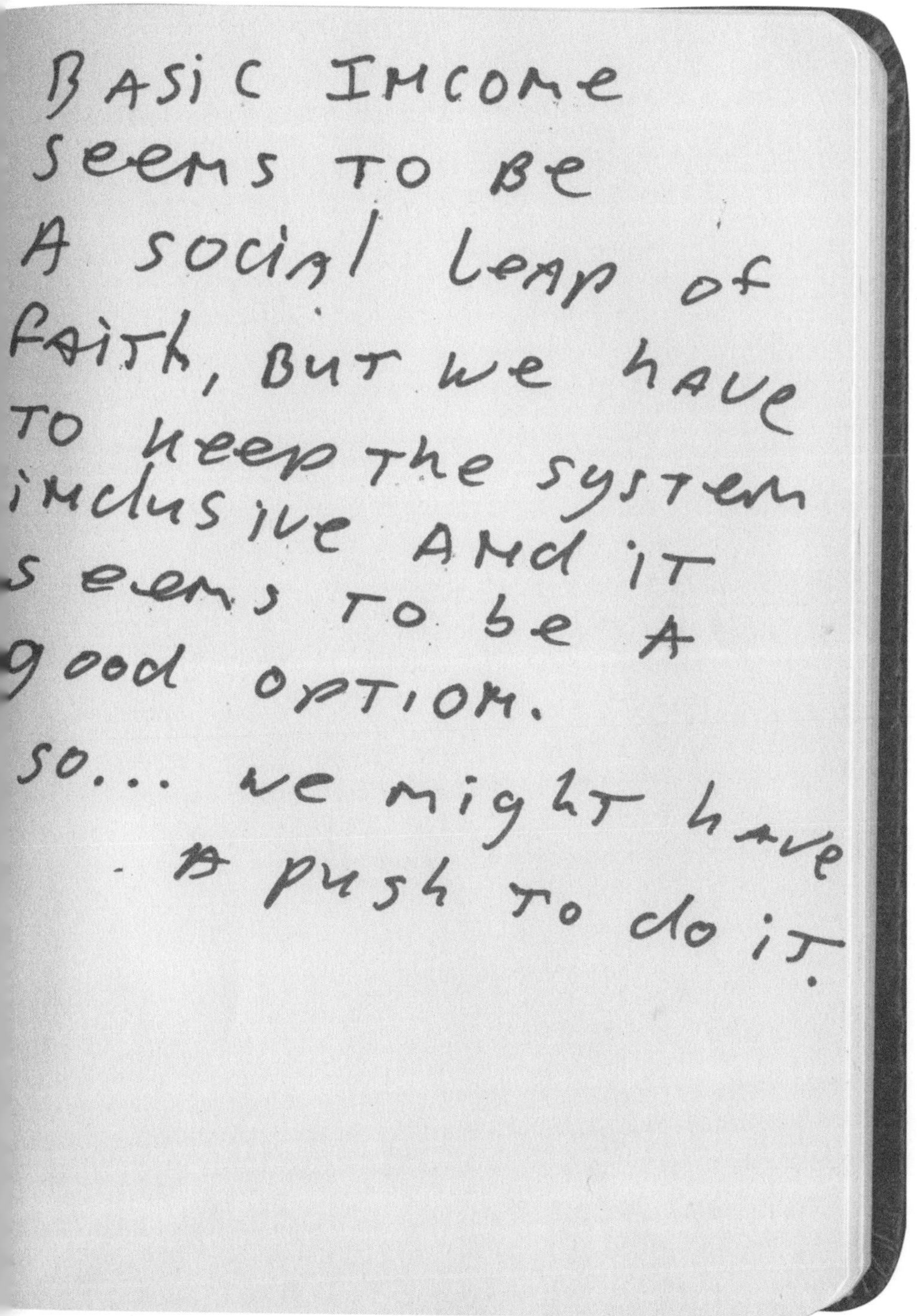

BASIC INCOME
SEEMS TO BE
A SOCIAL LEAP OF
FAITH, BUT WE HAVE
TO KEEP THE SYSTEM
INCLUSIVE AND IT
SEEMS TO BE A
GOOD OPTION.
SO... WE MIGHT HAVE
A PUSH TO DO IT.

Basic income
seems to be
a social leap of
faith, but we have
to keep the system
inclusive and it
seems to be a
good option.
So... we might have
a push to do it.

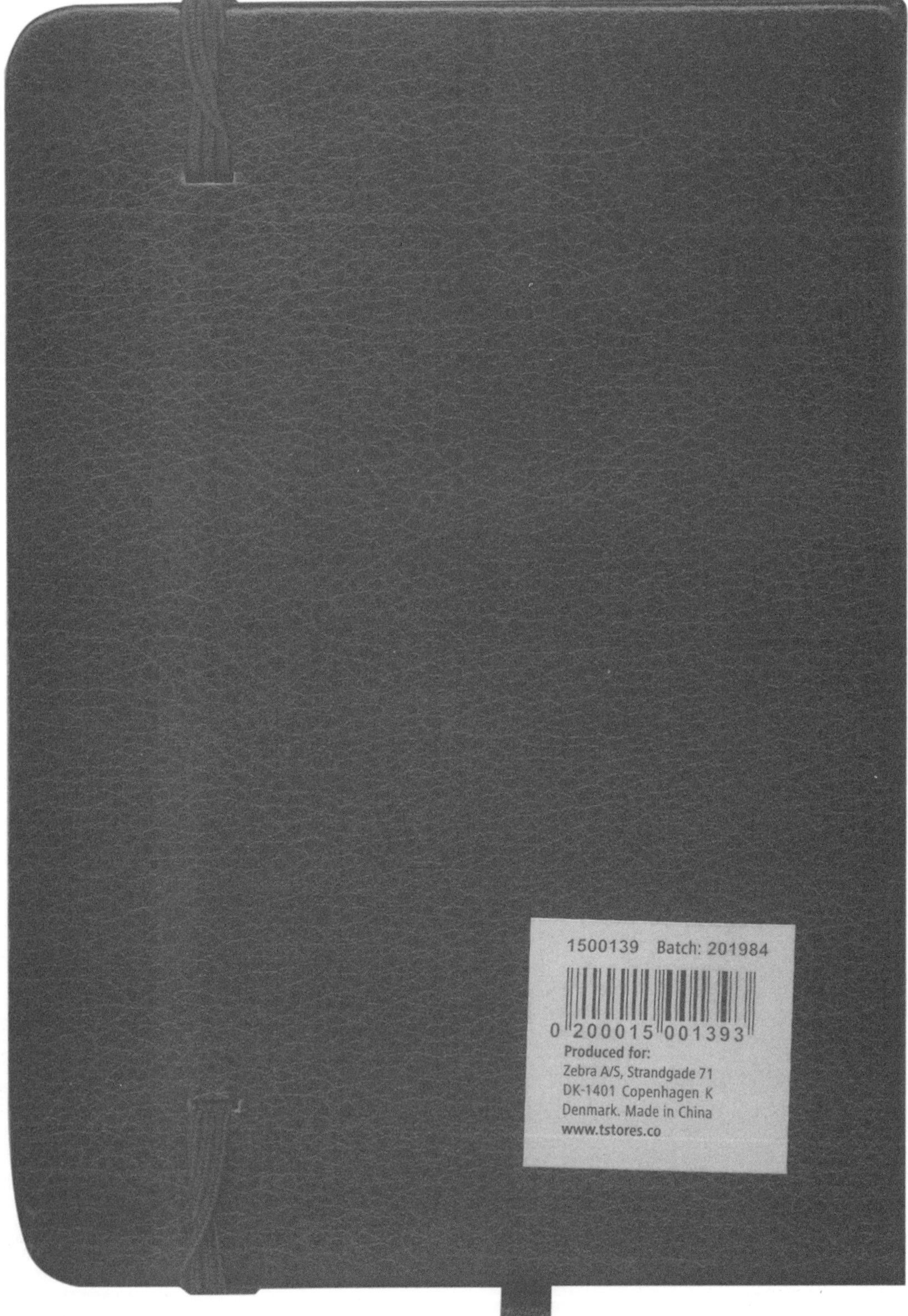
1500139 Batch: 201984
0 200015 001393
Produced for:
Zebra A/S, Strandgade 71
DK-1401 Copenhagen K
Denmark. Made in China
www.tstores.co

WE

By Robert-Jan Gruijthuijzen

The preamble of the American Constitution opens with the famous words "We, the people (...)". To me, these beautiful first words represent a sense of community based on an actual experience of the possibility and necessity to shape our world together.

The phrase *"We, the people demand an update of what we, the people means"* immediately caught my eye. It made me think. What does this 'we' mean? What's the underlying idea of this "we" as a whole? Why do we speak of a "we" at all?

Dear readers: *'We' cannot say "We!".*

We enter a world.
We form relationships with each other.
We are not unique in this regard.
We try to interpret relationships in a unique way.
We interpret through language.
We interpret language.
We make our way in a changing and challenging world with a crisscross of languages.
We shape our understanding in conversation with those who share our language.
We lend others a helping hand when we become aware of a mutual understanding.
We help foreign speakers from a common understanding of our world.
We lose sight of foreign speakers.

'We' is like a medal.
'We' has a reverse.

We are back to back.

We depend on each other.
We however, standing back to back, can never look each other straight in the eye.
We feel each other closer than ever.

'*We*' is bound up in thoughts about something that is beyond comprehension.
'*We*' includes, 'we' excludes. 'We' confuses.

We all reach out towards higher spheres.
We are religious people looking for that one final explanation of what 'We' actually is.
We learn to balance our minds, through the act of searching as such.
We are still seeking and haven't found a balance yet.

'*We*' is lost without balance.

We are in it together.

We speak of 'the people'.
We demand clarity without any sense of understanding.
We are living on the edge.
We experience the most thoughtful space in elusive times.
We grasp the matter in the smallest details.
We claim to know a thing or two about any topic at hand.
We forget to think while we steal each other's ideas.
We can't say "*We!*" after all.
We have bad timing.
We have limited vision.

We hear so many things.
We are turning into work.

'We, the people' without contemplation is nothing but an empty idea.

'We' demands that a yet unspecified completeness (de-), be placed in our hands (manus) (to de-mand), in other words:
"We, the people demand (...)".
set a goal with our demand: to get our hands on an *update*.
We demand an up-to-date idea of "we".
We want to grasp the current meaning of "*We, the people*", to seize it, get our hands on it.

We want to reclaim public space.
We imagine artificial worlds. Worlds full of concealing ideologies.
We ideologize 'truth'.
We share a free space for shared phantasies with the people who speak our language.
We let our imagination run wild.
We enlighten the most outrages phantasies when we abhor neoliberalism and embrace our inner Marxist, or vice versa.
We seek redemption.
We even take possession of the latest garden gnome: the buddha statue.
We practice goat yoga.
We follow hypes.
We enter hyperspace.
We hyperventilate over issues like #metoo, gender neutrality, Black Peter, fireworks, sports and so on.
We are lord and master of tea leaf reading.
We become increasingly divided as we gasp for air.
We drown ourselves in small beer, hopping from hype to hype.
We long for a life on the surface.
We therefore demand the feasible.
We demand a feasible divide: a Them and an Us.
We are obviously not like Them.
We are clear.
We build on clarity and they are behind.
We master the art of discrimination.
We long for completeness.

We repeat the obvious until it sounds right to us.
We share each other's preconceptions, because it feels nice.
However,
We live with one another.

We don't know any better.
We express ourselves in a human world.
We automatically have to rely on each other.
We automatically create understanding in, to and for life.
We lack a clear concept of the way we conceptualise ourselves, the human world, "we".
We will not be owned.
We don't know any better...
We know nothing of the interpersonal, relational, common world of people to the extent that it precedes all we profess to know.
We only understand in retrospect.
We know through language.
We express ourselves through language.
We think through language.
We systemise through language.
We invent language systems.
We systemise language.
We systemise our language.
We systemise.
Systems language...

We systemise the world of people who influence one another as 'We'.
We actualise what it means to speak of a 'We' only in retrospect.
We speak of our-kind-of-'We'.
We create a sense of unease as an inevitable consequence of this speaking of 'our-kind-of-We'.

'*We*' can't be reduced to one single notion of course, but we try nonetheless.

We are in awe with an impossible understanding, in a restless world that precedes us all.
We distinguish content, concept, clause enclosed in language.

We set the difference, without ever going any deeper.
We fire yet another blank at our existence.

We are our own example.
We were all innocent once.

We recognise each other in a split second.
We emulate each other.
We perceive the world as one(fold) during that split of a second.
We dictate the mothers a short-term upbringing.
We support the mother in a painless upbringing.
We limit a child's life by doing so.
We render life feasible and small.

We limit the upbringing to one language, one sport, one instrument, one musical style, one hobby, one art tradition in one culture among thousands.
We ask the most limiting questions about a healthy diet only in retrospective, at a later stage.
We love to believe in baby food because it's feasible and ready-to-eat.
We are prisoners of that which naturally feels and tastes good.
We taste everything the way it should Be from the start.
We are becoming, however, and are often absurd.
We are "trapped" in Heidegger's *"House of Being"*.We close our doors when we are home.
We are losing altitude here.
We develop a fear of heights.
We get nearer and nearer to the ground.
We build on technologies as ways of Being.
We learn to live without pain.
We abandon the urge to strengthen love.
We slowly let love wither away.

We want power.
We are full of imagination.
We are powerless without imagination.
We create our world. A powerful world in which we transcend life.
We are extraordinary in our own powerful world.

We want more power. More power than yesterday.
We are the driving force behind sustainable development.
We practice *"Machtsteigerung"*.
We desire power.
Power desires power.
Power desires more power.
Power prances.
Power proliferates.
Power seizes.
Power is powerful.
We live in paradoxical times.
We want to not-want.

We strive for a higher power, a space in which we no longer want anything, like dead ghosts.
We place our hope in a technical world.
We thus authorise the technical world to rule over us.
We once used technology's toolkit as a means to an end
We stand as if pinned to the flat floor.
We are slowly being reduced to links in a chain and the technical world marches on.
We devise the last formalities and rehearse them in unison.
We learn to think technically and lose a perfect pitch.
We then stop calling each other by name, but refer to sequence number.
We find our final happiness in sequencing numbers.
We consequently become more and more adapt at attaching predicates to sequenced numbers.
We are being divided in pieces at the assembly line without unity, melody, beauty, love and a heart for the other sense of hearing.
We forget that in the beginning, that which is self-evident as such, has sustained us far beyond any shared language.
We have forgotten to understand language and technology as sources of our capacity to discriminate.
We forget how wonderful it is to discriminate.
Discrimination is a powerful way to distinguish.
Discrimination has positive and negative aspects.
Life is a matter of discrimination.
Life is about good or bad.

Life is about beauty and beasts. A proper balance is a matter of knowing how to discriminate the proper discriminant among thousands.

We will learn how to discriminate again this way, beyond the technical language: the grammar.

We will open ourselves up again this way to be overwhelmed by the highest and most exalted clamour, so our lives will not be marked by limitations but by a multiplicity of stories.

"How hard it is, when everything encourages us to sleep, though we may look about us with conscious, clinging eyes, to wake and yet look about us as in a dream, with eyes that no longer know their function and whose gaze is turned inward."

(Artaud; The Theatre and Its Double)

We only prove our mastery, however, when we try to conquer the technical world by means of our imagination. Because this proves to be the greatest challenge: the human task to make room for imagination, power, connection and discrimination. From this task we can learn how to handle our limitations. To cite Goethe: *"Mastery is first revealed in limitation."*

We are obliged to strive for mastery. Techniques only affect the limited among us. We can't allow any limited ones, because to us they deprive the world of life.

We will have to arm ourselves against the limited ones with their endless quarrels, mind-numbing meetings, empty terminologies and turbid and timid language.

We will no longer allow our minds to be wrapped up by policy makers who always expect 'something concrete'.

We liberate ourselves from the daily repetitive activities that continue to exist without any sense of common purpose.

We liberate ourselves from structures and alienating systems.

We raise ourselves up, our back straight, our sight straight ahead.

Ecce Homo, behold the Man!

We behold the Übermensch.

An Übermensch who doesn't necessarily want to limit the other, but turns to himself instead. A man who, with a clear sight on his own and most inner limitations, clears a way towards the ultimate liberation. A man for whom the eternal recurrence of the same can be understood as a return to the most inner Self. An inner quest for peace. A man whose freedom, the eternal recurrence of the same, lies within himself and not in the limitation of the other.

We learn to live and although our lives are full of technologies, lives and technologies never coincide. To cite Kierkegaard: *"Life can only be understood backwards; but it must be lived forwards"*.

We all once entered this world without a past and, as a consequence, without understanding. From that moment on we all live our lives forwards. But the more we advance, the more we seem to lose sight of our advantage.

We understand the past at a later stage, but we experience it from the start.

We don't need to become cynical when we try to under stand our past. Even though, according to Schopenhauer, *the worst is yet to come*, the worst as such isn't here yet.

We are still here! At least as far as I can tell.

We don't want just *anything*, but specifically *this: Miteinandersein.* For *what* we want is of a passing, temporary nature. The fact *that* we want, is universal and as such it is all-encompassing and intangible at once.

We demand an update of what we, the people means. But this *"demanding"* of an *"update of what we, the people means"*, is exhausting. After all, a demand has to be met immediately. A demand knows no nuance or degrees. A demand is unilateral. Such a unilateral demand really leaves very little room for edification. A unilateral demand is the ultimate waist of force and leaves behind a world where powerless souls look completely lost and lack all trust in each other.

We demand an update but instead we become more and more exhausted.

We attach new, trendy but yet empty concepts to this war of attrition, like burnout, overstraining, stress and we start looking for the ways the brain and social life func-

tion in order to describe this war of attrition in detail.
We not only lose sight of the cause of exhaustion, we even enforce exhaustion itself.
We exhaust each other by searching for certainties in the figments of our imagination rather than to look for worlds that lie within our imagination.
We will never, as long as we keep imagining, run out things to say! Ideologies clash, evolve and try to survive. Clashing parties are powerful.
They are signs of imagination.
They nurture life.
They are life itself.
They grant us life.
They make us whole.
To cite Karl Popper: *We* thus have a duty to be optimistic! If the future before us is completely open, there is no reason to be either optimistic or pessimistic. In that case we have a duty to be optimistic!

We will therefore raise my glass to life!

Cheers my friends!

RJ

TALKING ABOUT PERSUADING PUBLICS, EXPECTATIONS AND HONESTY

By Rogier Brom

Whether we like it or not, art shares some important characteristics with the market. The strongest similarity may be found in the need to persuade a public. In addressing basically anything to a group, a sender needs to fixate the product, process, perspective or what have you. However, for a healthy form of living together in a society, a certain fluctuating state is needed without it being appropriated, or stabilised.

To be able to persuade a public, one needs to have control of the surroundings in which the contact with the public is established. For this purpose, I propose to look at a public as a collective that holds together and functions through a common logic. The size and duration of this collective is determined by the necessity of individuals to actively commit to a community. As long as there is an active reason to behave as a group, the group will hold together. Let's explore some views on such active relations. Paolo Virno states that in modern day (or, Post-Fordist) society, labour has absorbed many characteristics that are typically political. In this sense, it is no longer solely in politics that 'the relationship with the presence of others, the beginning of new processes, and the constitutive familiarity with contingency, the unforeseen and the possible' (Virno 2014, p50) can be found. New strong and outspoken communities can come to life on many levels and in potentially all walks of life. There is diplomacy and crossover all the time, in every sector and every scene. Giorgio Agamben tackles the question of how a sustainable community is formed by introducing the notion of profanation. You can look at this notion as an annulment of overarching power structures that try to fixate communal identity. This means that the power structure within a delineated field is deactivated and the confiscated space is given back for communal use, re-injecting a sense of flux in how the community can behave. In other words: to neutralise the direction that is enforced by an imperative system in public space. In this case, the social system changes course by building on meaningful differences that exist between multiple communities in order to become a new system. By doing this, by profanating a space, the expectations within this space are changed, changing the behaviour within it and even its function.

These thoughts combined, create the opening to think of public space as an arena for contesting truths that have the possibility to persuade its users while the possibilities in fact are boundless. Communities can form and dismantle, thwart rules and regulations by setting new standards. It is, however, quite a naive system to work with. For it will benefit the one with the most compelling story, granting it power to sustain a community around that story.
Jacques Rancière states that a human collective consists of a node of aspects that carry a certain degree of 'sense'. Only by a consensus about what is communally regarded as meaningful, and is experienced as such, can a collective be affirmed that consists of individuals that share this commonality, but differ in other aspects. And if such a heterogeneous community opens up to the insight that they form a community, they implicitly confirm the idea that other forms of community are possible too. By doing that, they also open up to the idea of forming a future community in a new composition; to flexibility. But then, the movement towards a new future stops if the

truth—or the set of things that make sense—has an inward perspective.

Now, let's look at the two players that seem to be antagonistic players in the project *We Are The Market!*: the commercial market and the cultural free-thinkers. The market often offers lifestyle, an entrance into a select group of people, whereas culture or, better still, an art-work, can offer a proposition, subjectivation. The latter would surely be an approach that would prove more healthy to a society that remains in flux, that keeps building towards a future most suitable to ever changing circumstances.

So, how then does one demand a bigger say in public space if a commercial logic seems to take over? The answer to this question, in my opinion, starts with the idea of honesty. If the objective of your endeavour is truly to make sure that a certain amount of flexibility is possible, you will be able to form a community that's able to recognise other communities and build towards a shared future. If there is clarity about the fact that the idea that is propagated is not its own ultimate version or definitive form, the community surrounding it is potentially stronger because there is room for adaptation. Thus, the notion that the community is centred around, keeps its potential to cater to the varied needs of all constituents. If the promise that's made is a false one, chances of making it in the long run are slim because the reason to stick together as a community will erode at the speed of it losing its credibility. But this honesty is vulnerable. Especially where works of art are concerned and the proposals they can make. My claim is that works of art have a subversive potential, they do not hold groups of people together but break through their individual views on the world around them in such a way that they allow other perspectives. In that sense they help facilitate the moment Rancière describes, in which a community acknowledges the possibility of another community, opening up the possibility for future communities to be formed. This effect will be strengthened if it is clear from the onset that within the community there is room for the political potential of its constituents and that power structures can be profanated if need be; if there is a clear and honest awareness of the community's fluctuating identity.

However, for a society to function, certain rules and regulations have to be in place. Culture can affect how these ways of relating to one another are systematised, but once they're settled they have a tendency to stay fixed and stagnate. It's what Pascal Gielen and Philipp Dietachmair call *civic* space. It's the regulated form in which the societal structure of the outside world is arranged. Next to this, they place *civil* space which remains fluent. It's the framework within which thoughts of the people can be organised. This organisational quality is what discerns it from public space, the latter being the place where a free exchange of thoughts should be possible. They add that: 'public space provides, as it were, both new ideas and new people (new citizens) but they can only claim and obtain their place in society through self-organization in the civil domain. Vice versa this also implies that public space is reliant on civil space, as the latter makes the public domain possible by organizing it or claiming a place for it.' (Dietachmair & Gielen 2017, 17)

As far as the persuading of a public goes, what we, the people or the creative free-thinkers should do, is make people see that it's possible to have a public space that's suitable for a variety of communities. To create the expectation that an active or even activist attitude is required to obtain and maintain such a civil society, but that there is political potential present. And be honest about the fact that although the role art can play in this can be brittle, it is at the same time essential for keeping the regulated structure of society alive and in motion. And that the outcome can not be predicted, nor can all of its aspects be measured. A suitable quote to end with in this respect, is one by John Holden about his ideas on the value of culture:

'I maintain that value is located in the encounter or interaction between individuals [...] on the one hand, and an object or experience on the other. Intrinsic values are better thought of then as the capacity and potential of culture to affect us, rather than as measurable and fixed stocks of worth.' (Holden 2006, 15)

For further reading: Boomgaard J. and R. Brom (2017), Being Public: How Art Creates the Public, Amsterdam: Valiz. Dietachmair, P. and P. Gielen (2017), The Art of Civil Action: Political Space and Cultural Dissent, Amsterdam: Valiz. Holden, J. (2006), Cultural Value and the Crisis of Legitimacy. Why culture needs a democratic mandate, Londen: Demos.

13.

THE TEMPLE OF TEASE, ON TOUR WITH PRIESTESS PUSSYLICIOUS

Your reporter >> p. 156

Local Arts News.

That Day in October.

31st of October. Halloween. What once was a pagan celebration on an entirely different continent, now having passed through the charnel house of capitalism, has come out the other end all plastic pumpkins and scary spiders. Usually a night that sees people indulge in a little casual racism or sexism, with black face and rape victim costumes a plenty. This year Eindhoven was exposed to a wholly different experience.

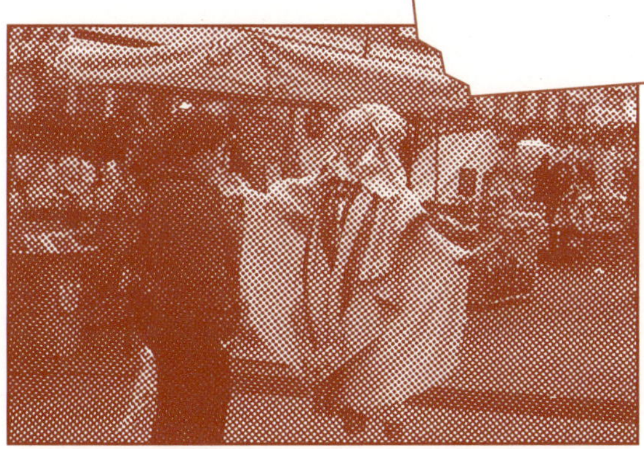

Listed as number 36 out of 38 on ranker.com's 'Offensive Costumes You'll See This Year', the vagina is something that seems to play large in the popular consciousness. Although not surprisingly it's something that's not often publicly discussed. Yet the British performance artist Izabella Finch appeared in Eindhoven as Priestess Pussylicious, dressed as a giant vulva. Finch sang and danced through the streets asking passers-by to touch and caress her like they would their own; or if a man, what their techniques were.

Armed with cucumber "dildos" the Priestess made her way along one of the city's main shopping streets, singing, performing, and talking to members of the public who either willing interacted or were coerced into doing so. With disarming charm and intriguing questions Finch pulled people in with lines like 'show me what you like to do'. Then, blush having receded, the public often felt compelled to stay longer, discussing intimate details about themselves and their relationships.

On offer last Halloween were a wealth of interactions that saw sheepish, shy men alongside proud and bashful women; they either declared their love for the High Priestess or trailed off with excuses like 'I will definitely come back...'. The one clear thing was that the word 'authentic' went past the high street definitions of faux leather and distressed denim: for all their convenience these things are often found to be lacking.

However, the conversations and divulgences that occurred that Tuesday were authentic. A shallow observation, but one subtle enough to leave smiles on faces long into the new year. As some claim we live in times of great shamelessness, levelling down cultural elevation and overruling class with banality, this priestess of shamelessness might just shamelessly elevate into deeper understandings of love and femininity.

Whether it's croquettes, crocs, cigars, fake crystals or cable ties, everyone can be provided for. Yet it's also within this bounty that ignorance can start to fester, and with it violence. With instant fulfilment via the market, shrieks, giggles and groans are often short lived and replaced by the ambient emotions of passivity: Leaving the violence for the Christmas sales.

Priestess Pussylicious coaxed and teased the people of Eindhoven, even finishing them off with the chant 'Jesus come in my heart'. Through the laughs though, the performance allowed some reflection on why dressing up as a vagina, or more correctly a vulva, could be considered obscene. Over three million people clicked on the ranker.com link and conflated the female body with offensiveness. If we're going to confront topics like gender liberation, emotions and the patriarchy, doing so vulva to face seems very appropriate.

14.

PULTRA ECOSEXUAL POLYAMORY

Your reporter >> p. 160

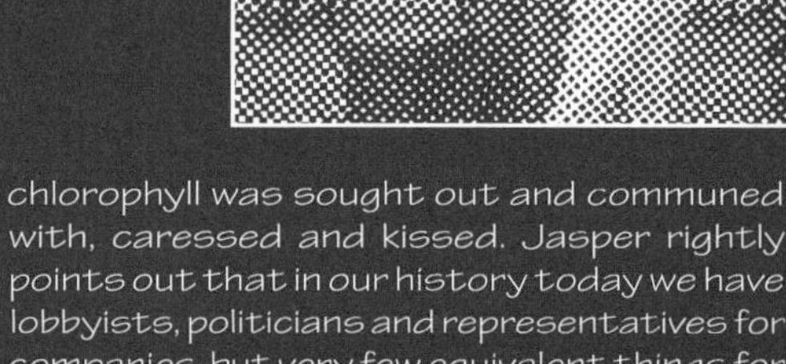

Space is space whether it's covered in concrete or grass or adorned with trees and lamp posts. Why should we (re)connect with the green? What captures us when we gawp at a sign or remember a jingle? Is it a whiter present, cleaner future or a more comfortable past? Wallowing in the fantasy of late capitalist social mobility—that's why we all moved to the city anyway, isn't it? To improve; to synthesise with the synthetic.

However, our brains still equate modernity with progress and the dualism between humanity and nature. Nothing is yet to disturb the dust from industrial production that's settled over us. Having smothered almost all of the alternative narratives, it now threatens to choke anyone who opens their mouth's to talk.

This is all hyperbole, of course. It's something to stir the senses and make you shoot a jealous glance at an empty Coke can. However it does serve as an image to strengthen the symbols that swell around our heads without us noticing. How easy it is to walk past a tree without paying any attention to it, all the while are eyes are drawn to the smell of Subway.

On the 4th of November an off-white skin tight onesie, slender legs and painted nails poured through Eindhoven like oil over a naked body. The Flaneur, The Druid, The Individual, The Collective, The City; all where present simultaneously. According to Jasper Griepink, a Dutch performance artist, when we collaborate with nature we can be incredibly resourceful and invincible, allowing us to build our own futures, with our own hands. What Griepink delivered on that rainy day was a mossy fuck you to the way we interact with cities and our attitudes towards nature.

Ultra Ecosexual Polyamory. Permaculture A.S.A.P was a performance that saw a Neo-Druid wind their through Eindhoven in search of meaningful connections to what ever green spaces are left in the centre. Whether it was trees outside Primark or in a car park, chlorophyll was sought out and communed with, caressed and kissed. Jasper rightly points out that in our history today we have lobbyists, politicians and representatives for companies, but very few equivalent things for nature and all it offers.

While the performance was just for the day, what it allowed for was a glimpse at a symbiotic future. By showing that these natural sites can be of interest, Griepink challenges what has economic worth in the city centre and what doesn't. Pushing a kind of political Druidism, the artist was at one point met with a little hostility with some children shouting insults like 'Tree Hugger' at him. Although to Griepink this was not a slight but an affirmation that others like himself still existed.

These others, are the Druids. An ancient order of people that could and should have a future in the way we run our countries and cities. The three orders that make up the training are the Bards, Ovates and Druids. This system of education makes sure individuals are first trained as artists or poets(Bards), then as healers (Ovates), finally 'graduating' to become law makers, politicians or community leaders(Druids). This holistic stance to life feels very alien to our urban condition of parking fines and smart streets.

So if there is a Druid in the next city council, who knows how different the decisions could be. Maybe there would be less privatise concrete and glass shells and more community spaces. Because, as Griepink has noted, 'we're making a very flat parody of what nature actually is, it's deeply insulting to where we come from.' Nevertheless this parody is our reality, and needs to be addressed. Revolutions have historically began in squares not parks, so lets start seeding the pavements.

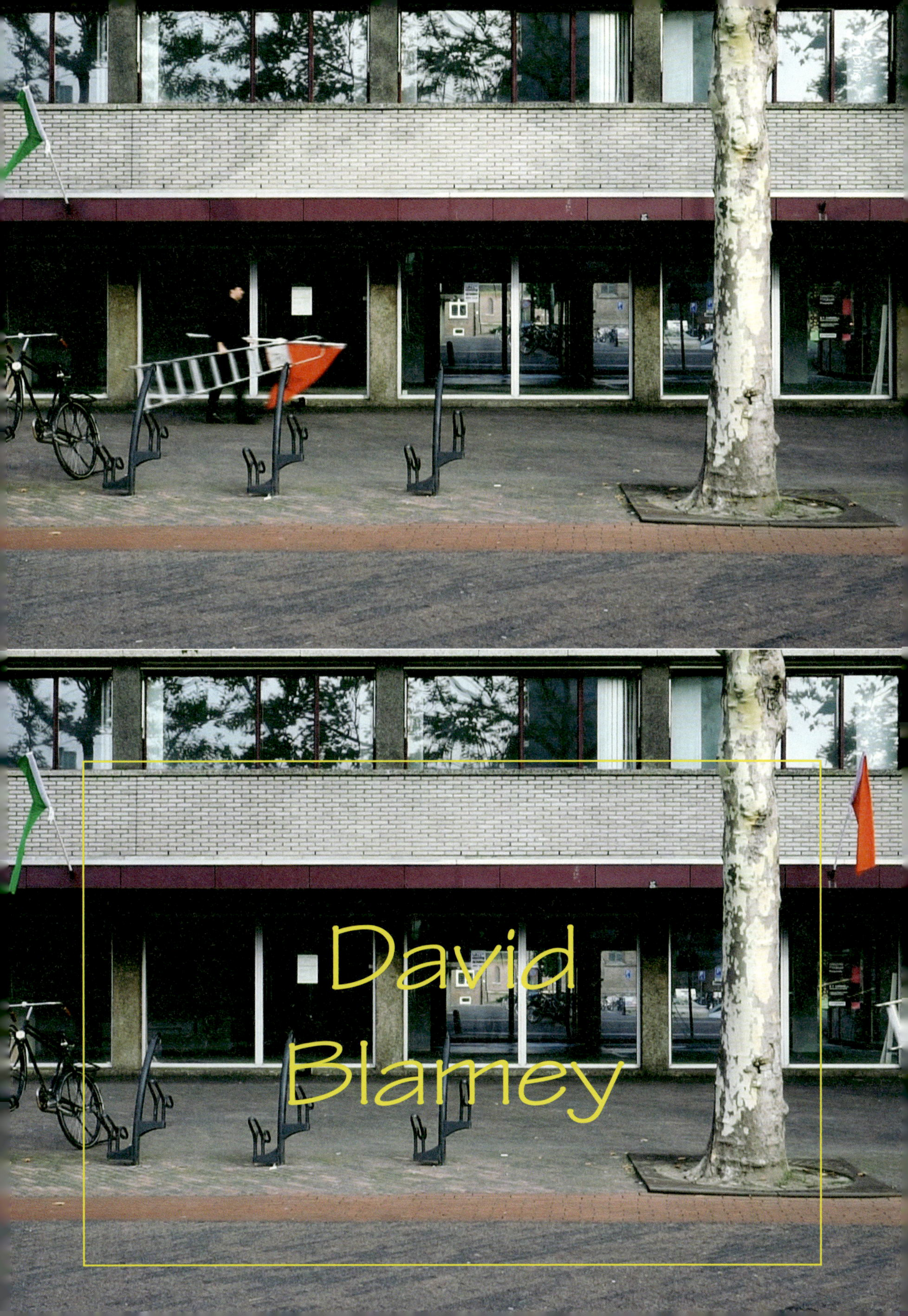
David
Blamey

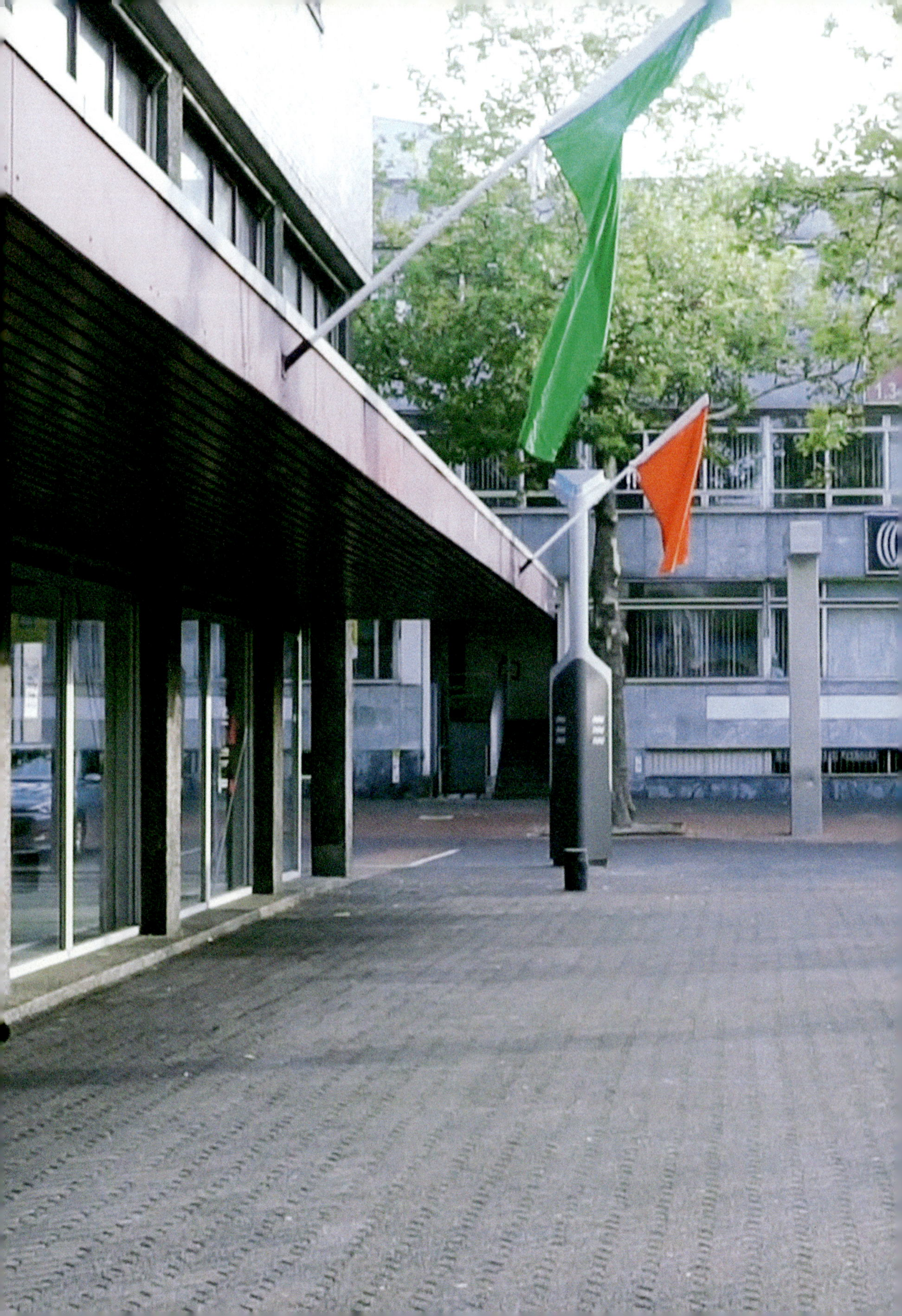

ACHIEVEMENT #9
FLYING COLOURS
DAVID BLAMEY

His work is consciously positioned within a range of public situations, both inside and beyond the art gallery. In Eindhoven he questioned the notion of ownership and reciprocity within the city centre, where shops and companies display their status with flags as a way of attracting the public's interest. By inserting a diptych of torn flags in complimentary colours the possibility to reconsider this dynamic of presented. The space that the flags occupy begins to become a concern.

Why aren't they telling us anything obvious? What has happened to cause their damage? Is it just me, or do they remind you of abstract paintings too?

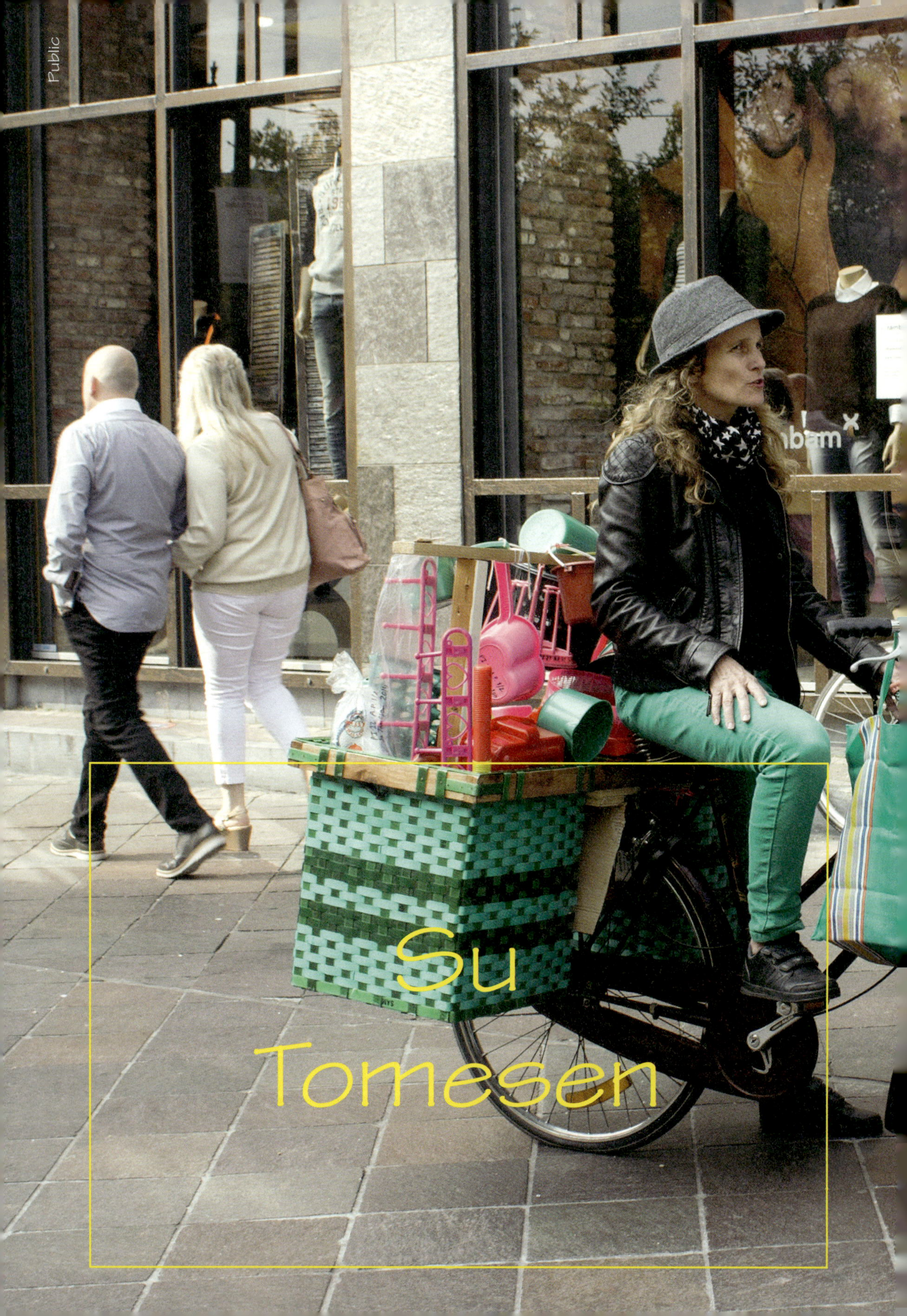

Su Tomesen

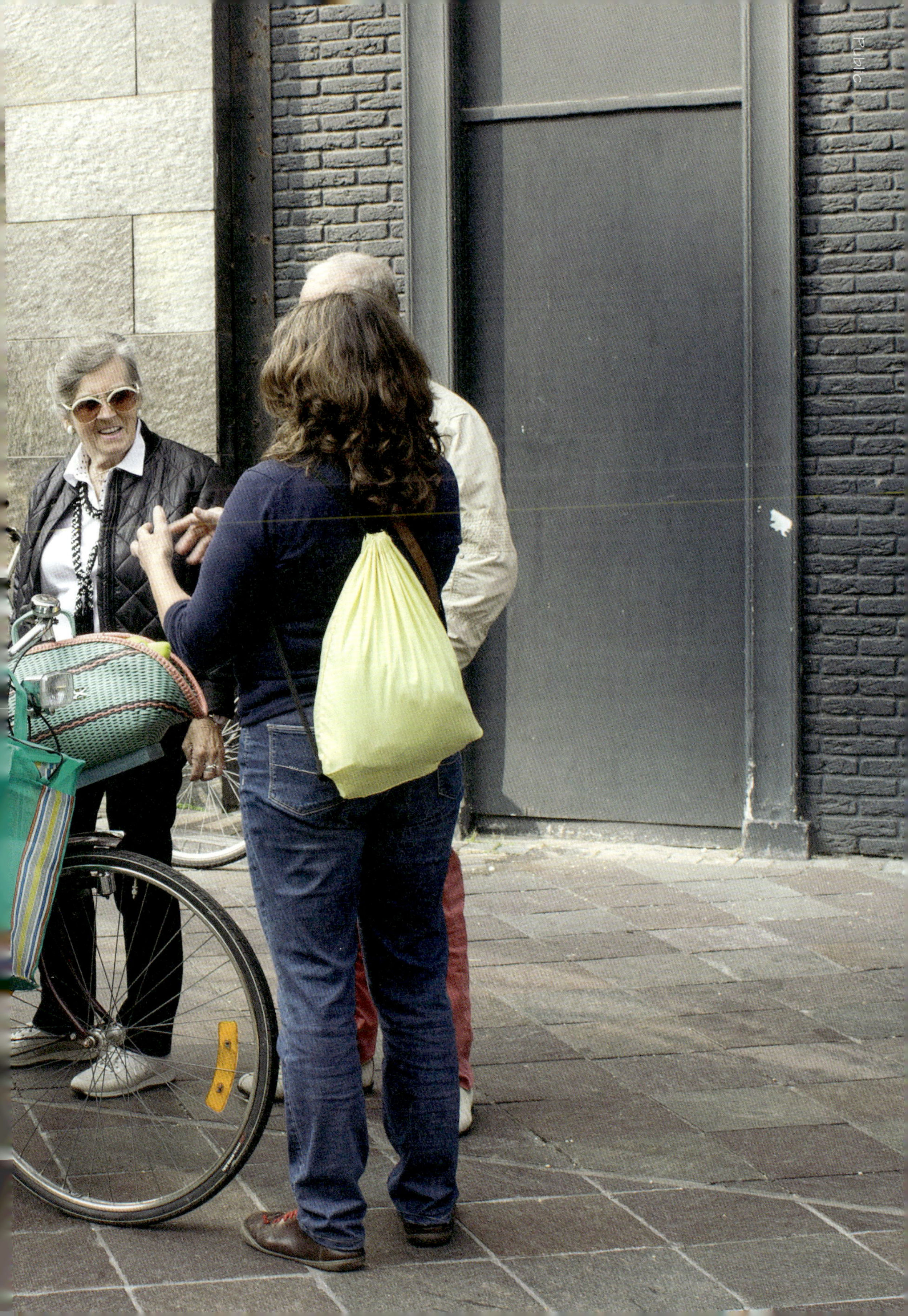

ACHIEVEMENT #10
TOKO
SU TOMESEN

Operating between Amsterdam and Jogjakarta Su Tomesen's visual practice consists of videos, photographs and installations highlighting issues of cultural divide that come to her attention. Indonesia loves plastic, a throw-away item to the disturbed Dutch eye and a robust hard-plastic item meant to last forever, apparently undervalued by the Dutch. Inspired by the decreasing number of corner shops in the Netherlands and relating to Indonesian mobile sales stands, Su uses the streets of the Netherlands to release the best plastic Indonesia has to offer for sale, self-imported, and opens up conversations with the public, concerning the wide ignorance about the effects and opportunities that plastics have.

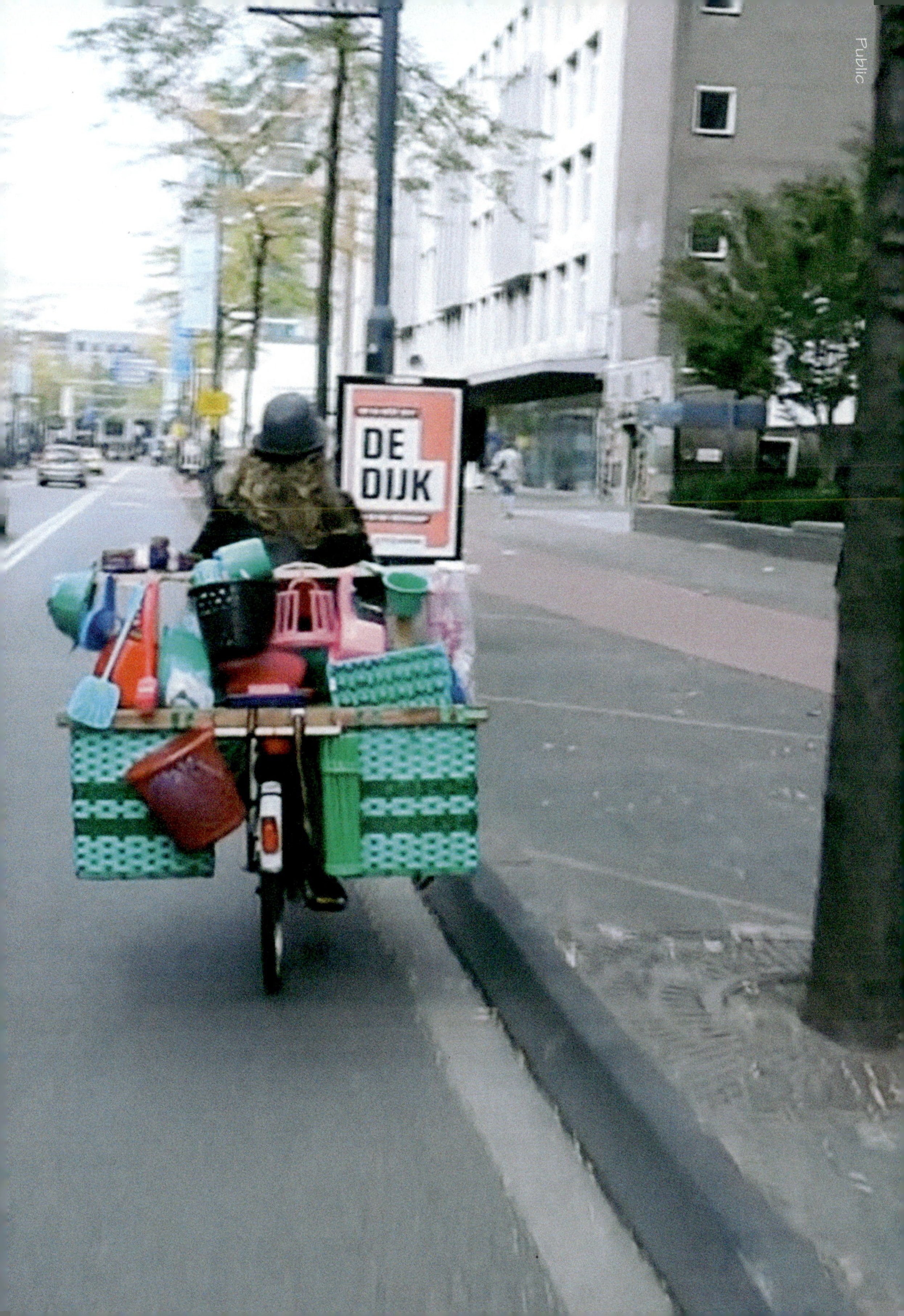
DE
DIJK

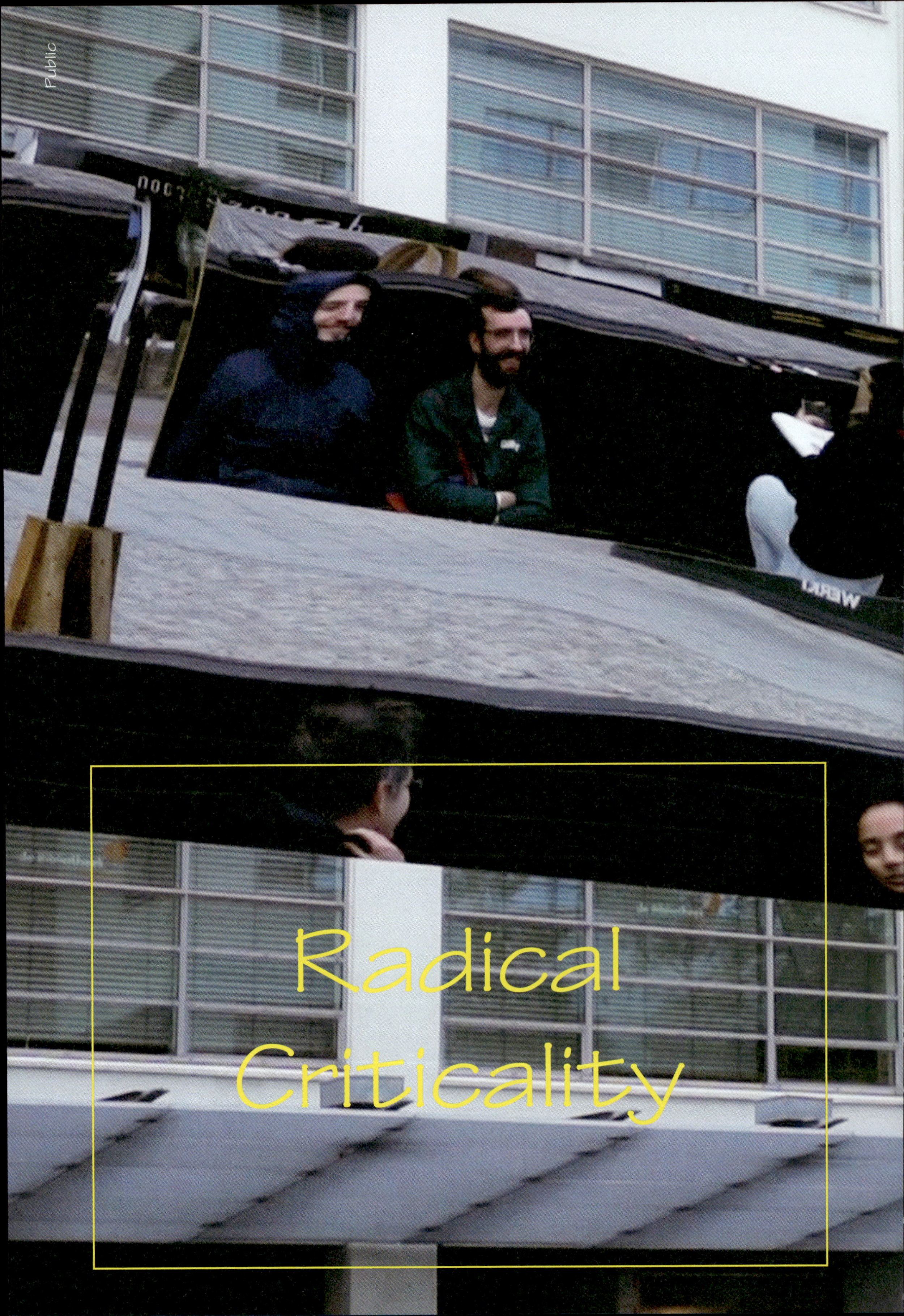

Radical Criticality

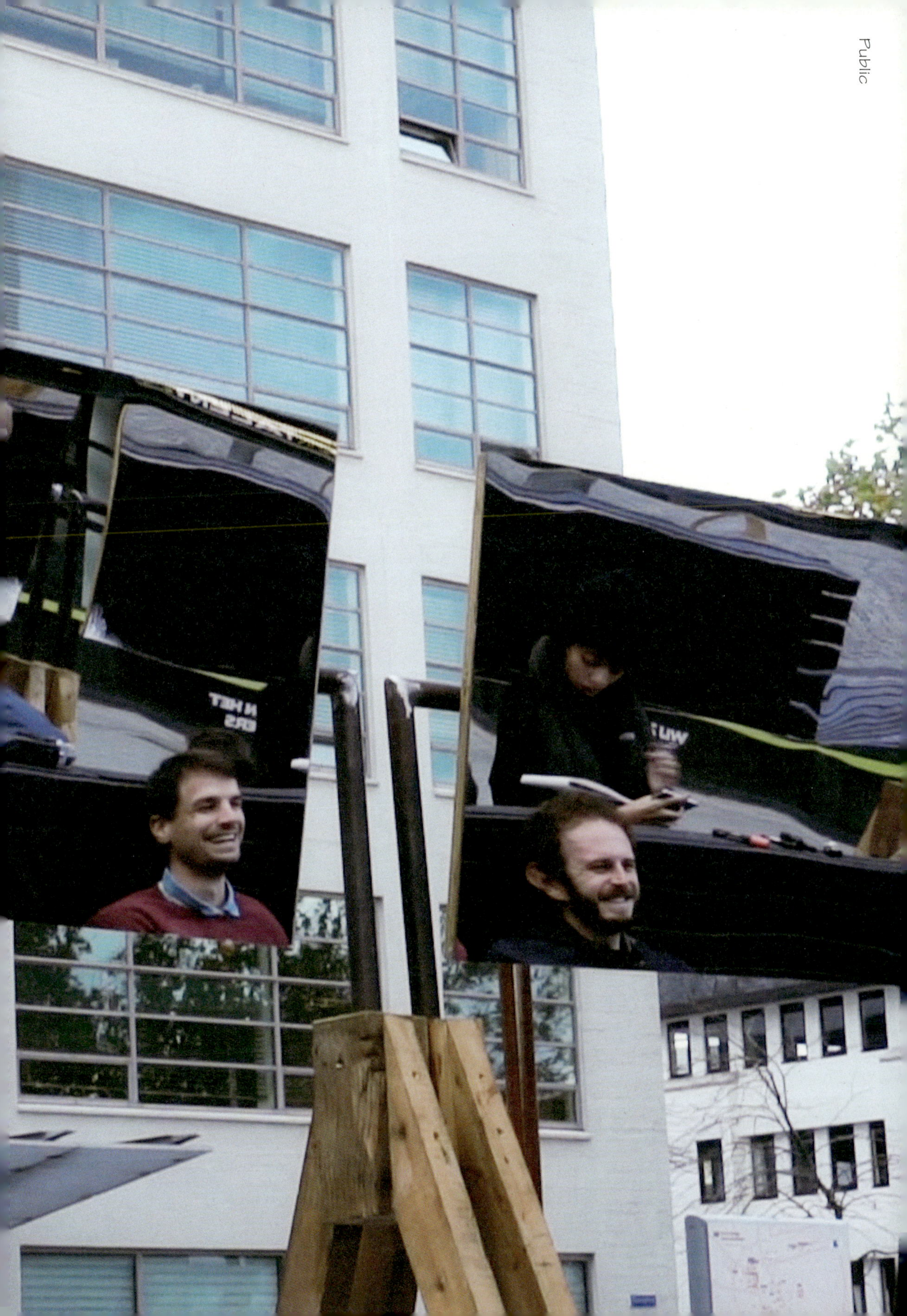

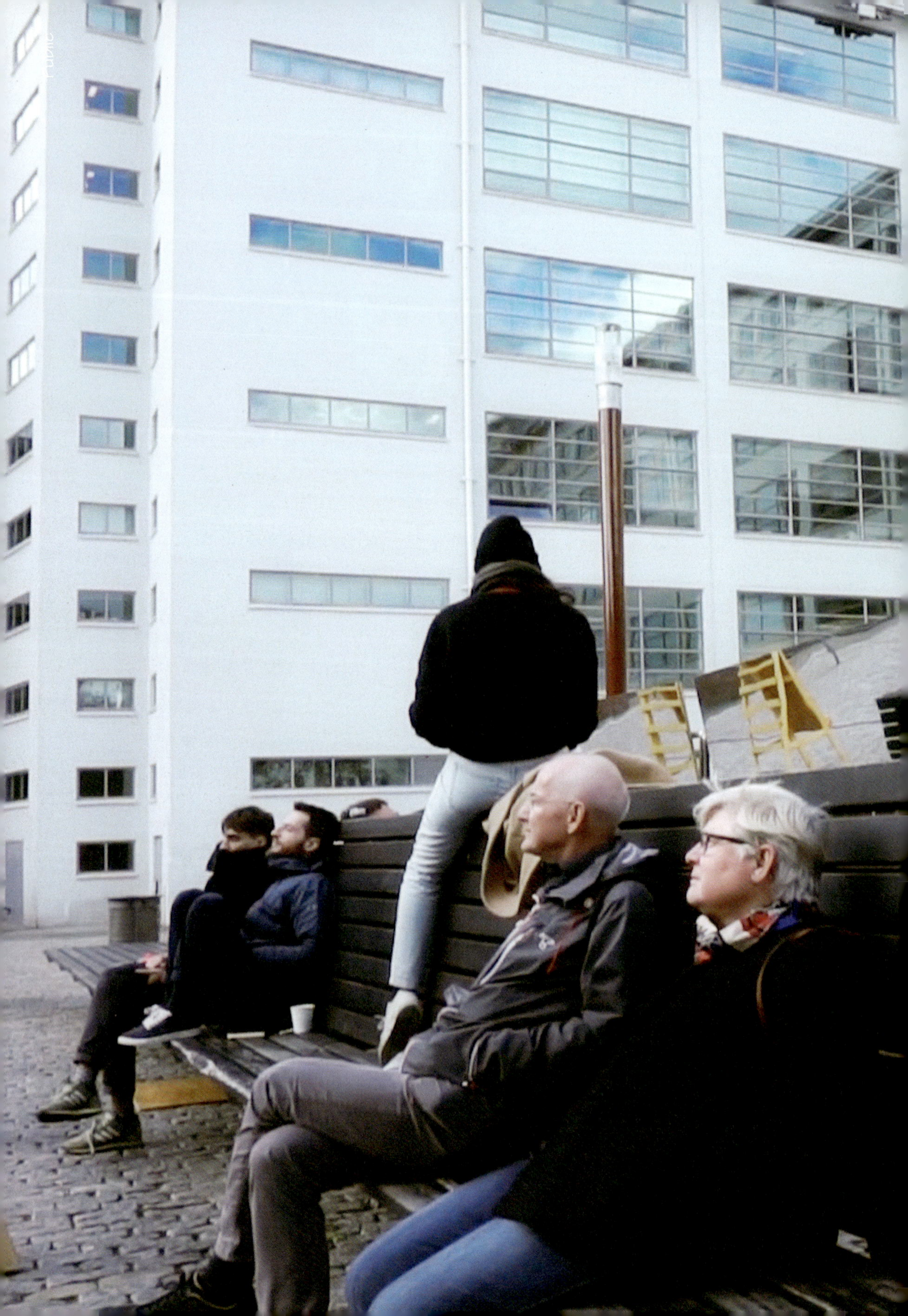

ACHIEVEMENT #11
EVERYDAY CRITICALITY, COLLECTIVELY RADICAL CRITICALITY

is a multinational collective consisting of seven creative practitioners*, who contextualise Design as the production of Everyday politics. The collective embodies a critical and analytical attitude to question themes and engage with the public through a debate. Dialogue, discussion and critique are their modes of discourse, while examining how collectivity can evolve in multi-facetted structures of trans-disciplinary and socio-cultural diversity.

With *We Are The Market!* the collective offered an open conversation through concentration, focus and circumstances that nurtured conversations such as shared meals and a public seating platform. They intervened in the public sphere, by offering performative collectivity.

* Pablo Calderon Salazar, Amelie Lisa Develoy, Silvia Dini Modigliani, Zeno Franchini, Christine van Meegen, Giovanni Pezzato and Jeannette Petrik.

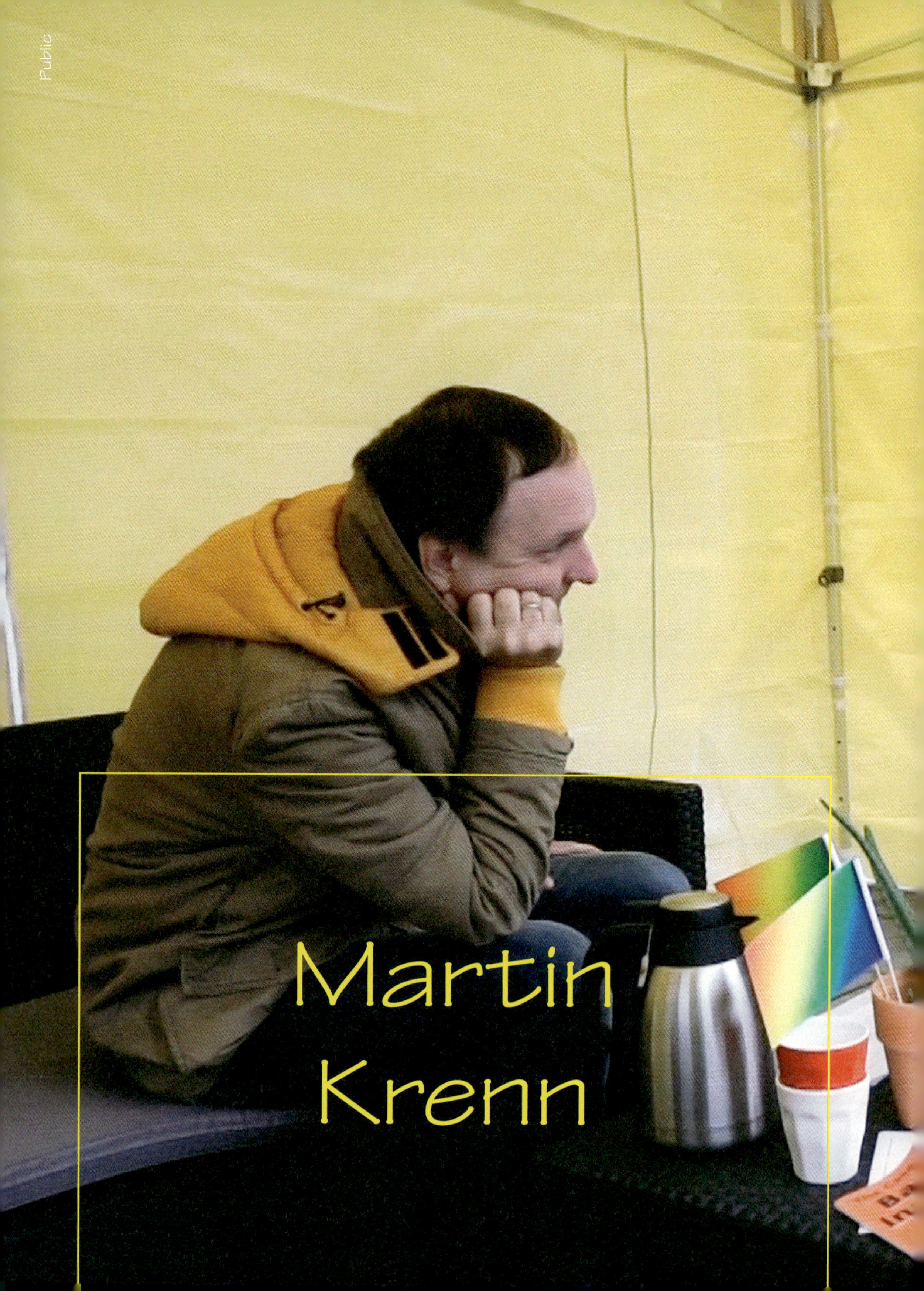

Martin Krenn

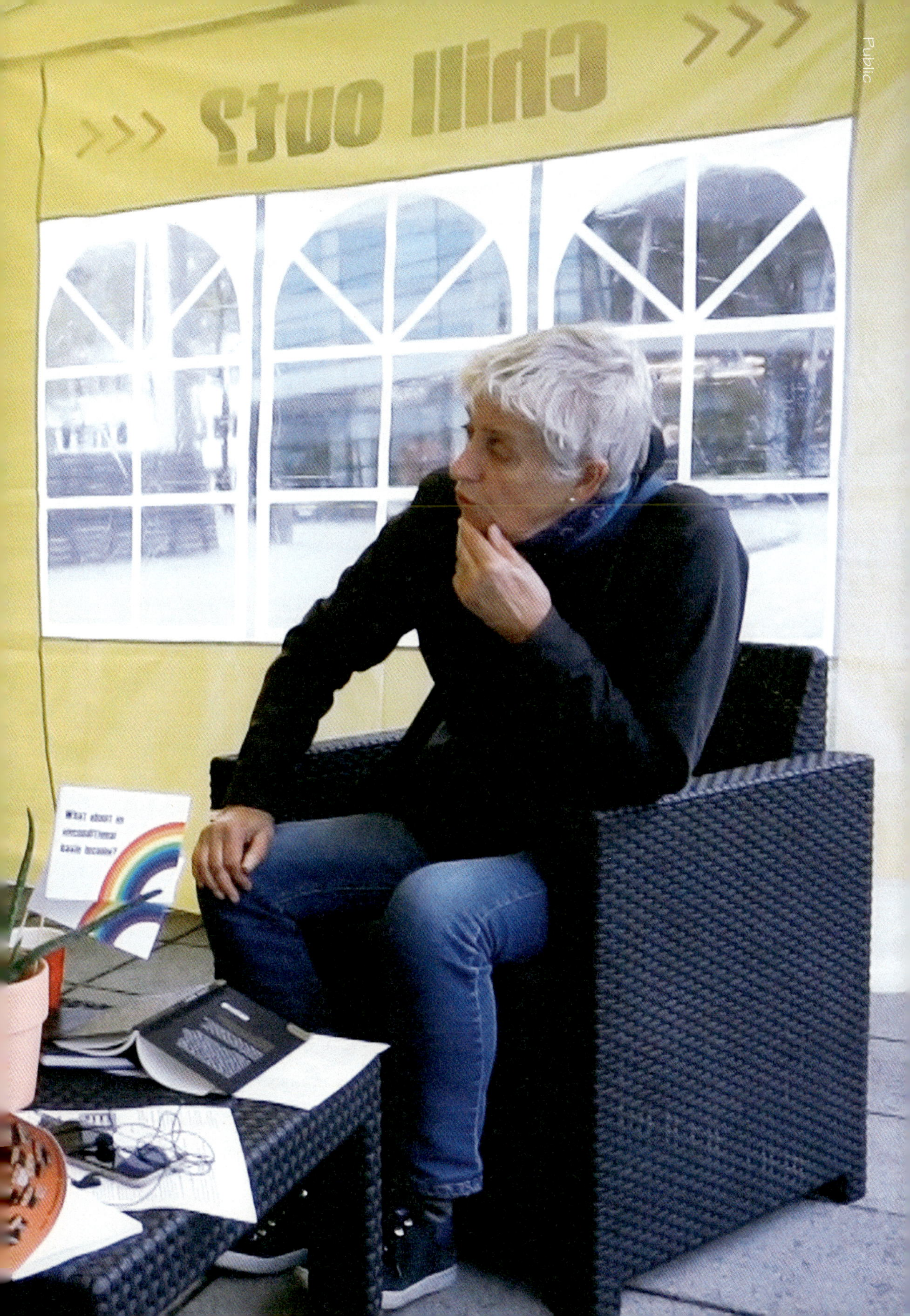
Chill out?

ACHIEVEMENT #12
POINT OF LEISURE
MARTIN KRENN

Triggered by the strained relationships between art and society, Martin Krenn's social-practice as an artist opens up to symbolic exchange in an increasingly immaterial manner, turning from visual identification to social engagement. By consistently expanding the field of art, he tries to initiate discussions about socio-political topics and to challenge thinking, exchange and engagement.

For *Point of Leisure* Martin Krenn set up a party tent with phrases such as "Slow down?", "Wait a second?" and "Leisure as work?" on its sides, creating a place to discuss the unconditional basic income with the public. People joined Krenn to contemplate about its urgency, necessity and opportunities while reading relevant literature and drinking coffee or tea. Krenn uses the opportunities of unbiased yet progressive artistic exchange to challenge and question political concepts, he exercises democratic mobilisation in response to a political agenda and uses the visual and architectural means of conventional campaigning to serve debate on urgency over agenda.

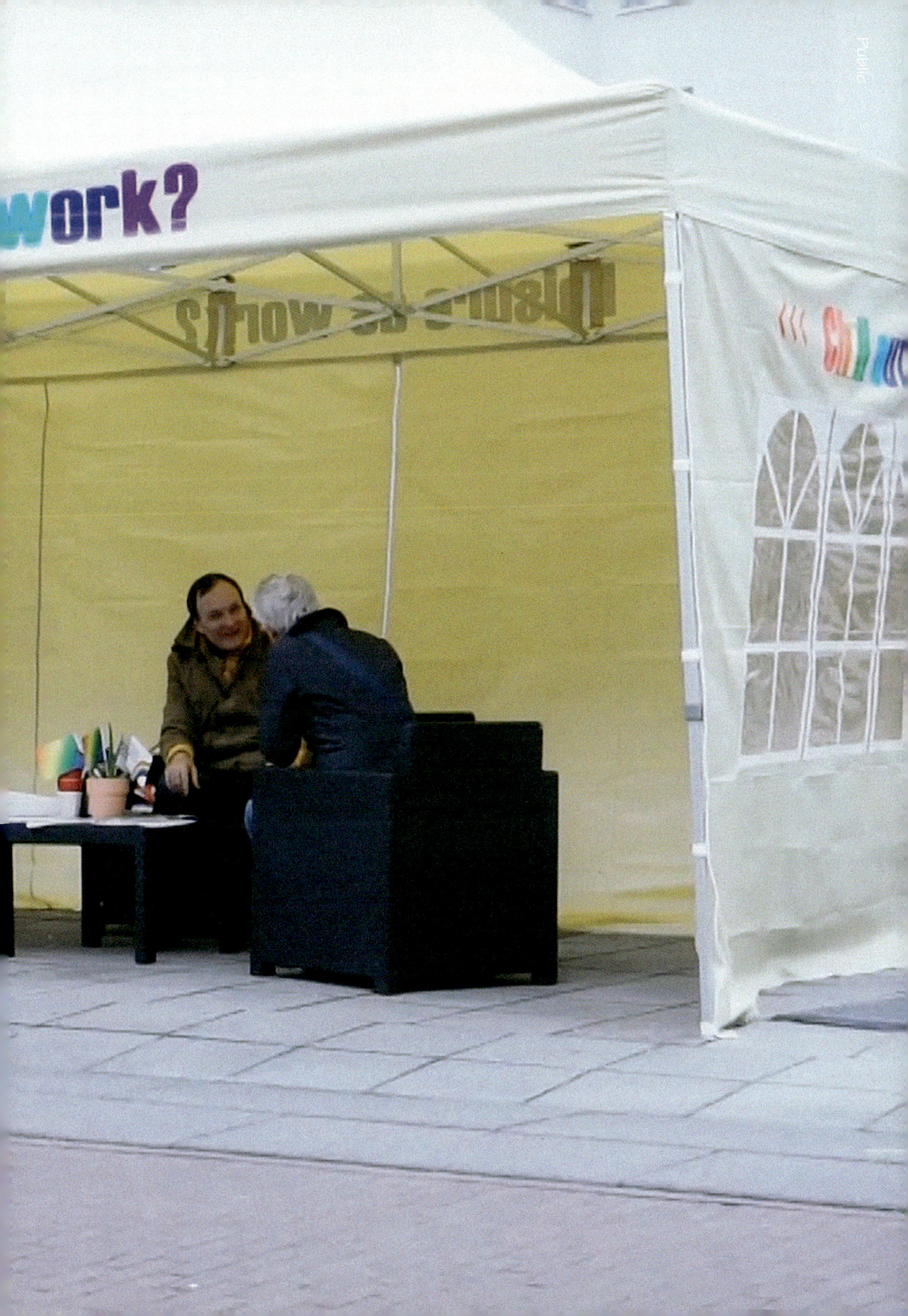
work?

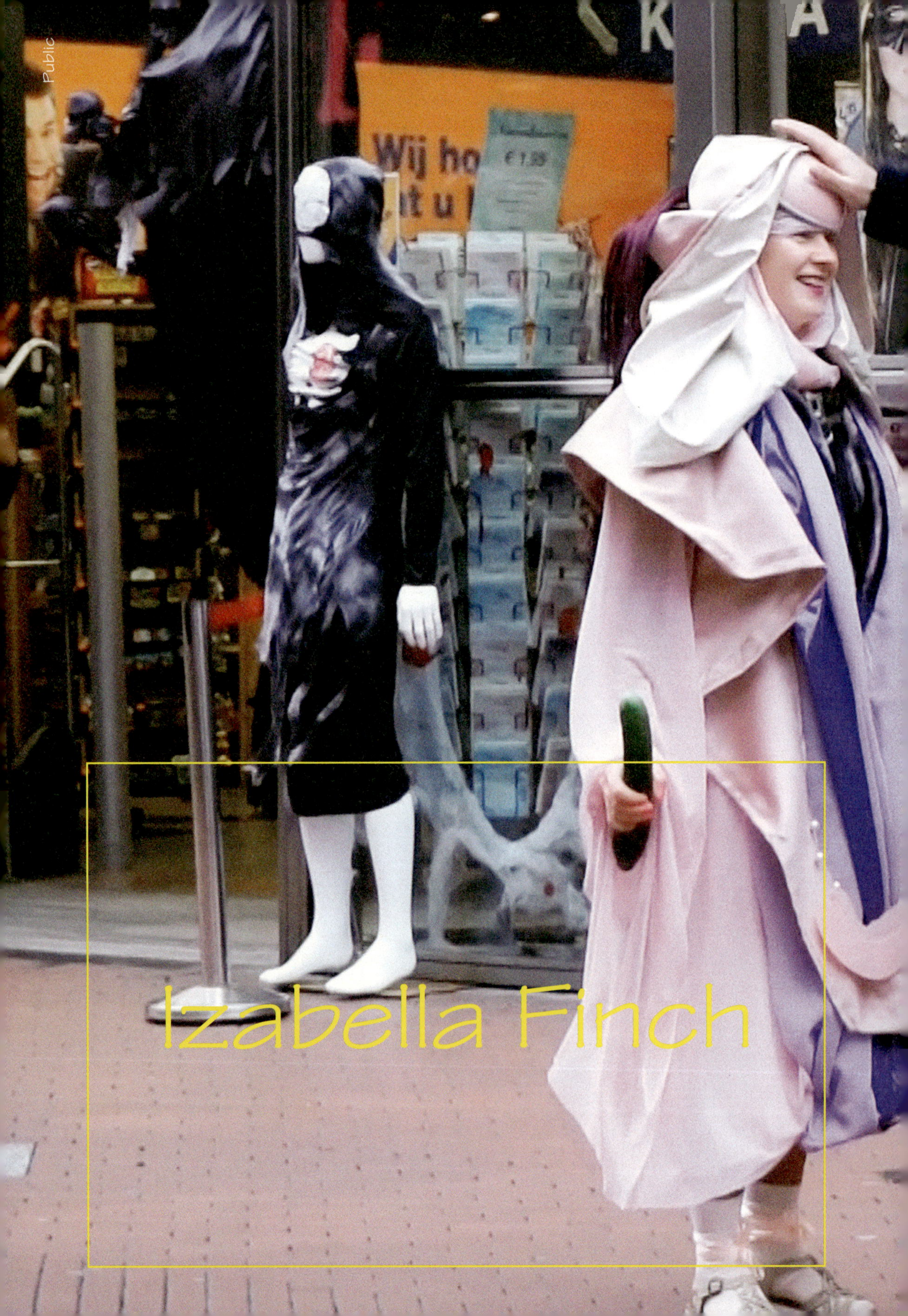

Izabella Finch

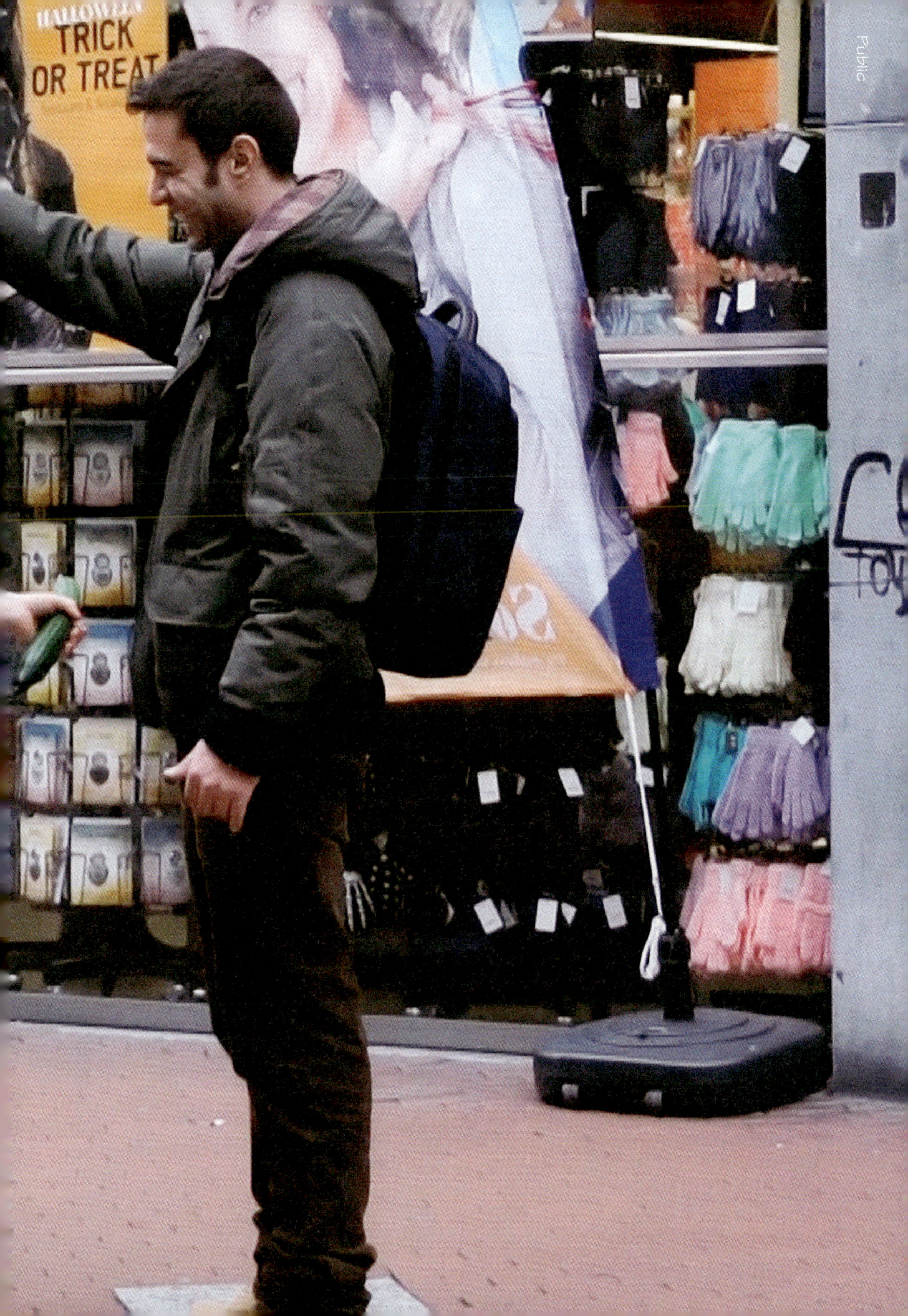
TRICK
OR TREAT

ACHIEVEMENT #13
TEMPLE OF TEASE ON TOUR - WITH PRIESTESS PUSSYLICIOUS
IZABELLA FINCH

Privacy might be safe, might be ethically harmless as it is a closed-off perimeter, but what occurs in privacy should not be repressed and is still in need of being challenged. Izabella Finch is a British artist and trained choreographer, based in Amsterdam, who aims to generate open conversations around topics such as sexuality, feminism, sex education, masturbation and sexual anatomy through performances that include singing, expressive dance and conversations with or in front of the public.

One of the personalities which she embodies to transfer her message, and who she refers to as an 'alter-ego' is *Priestess Pussylicious*, who wears a costume representing a vulva. She manages to draw the public's attention on to herself, through her outrageous and provocative display of behaviour and encourages people to be confident in their sexuality and sexual actions, while offering advice to the public as part of her interaction; an alternative service to the people of Eindhoven.

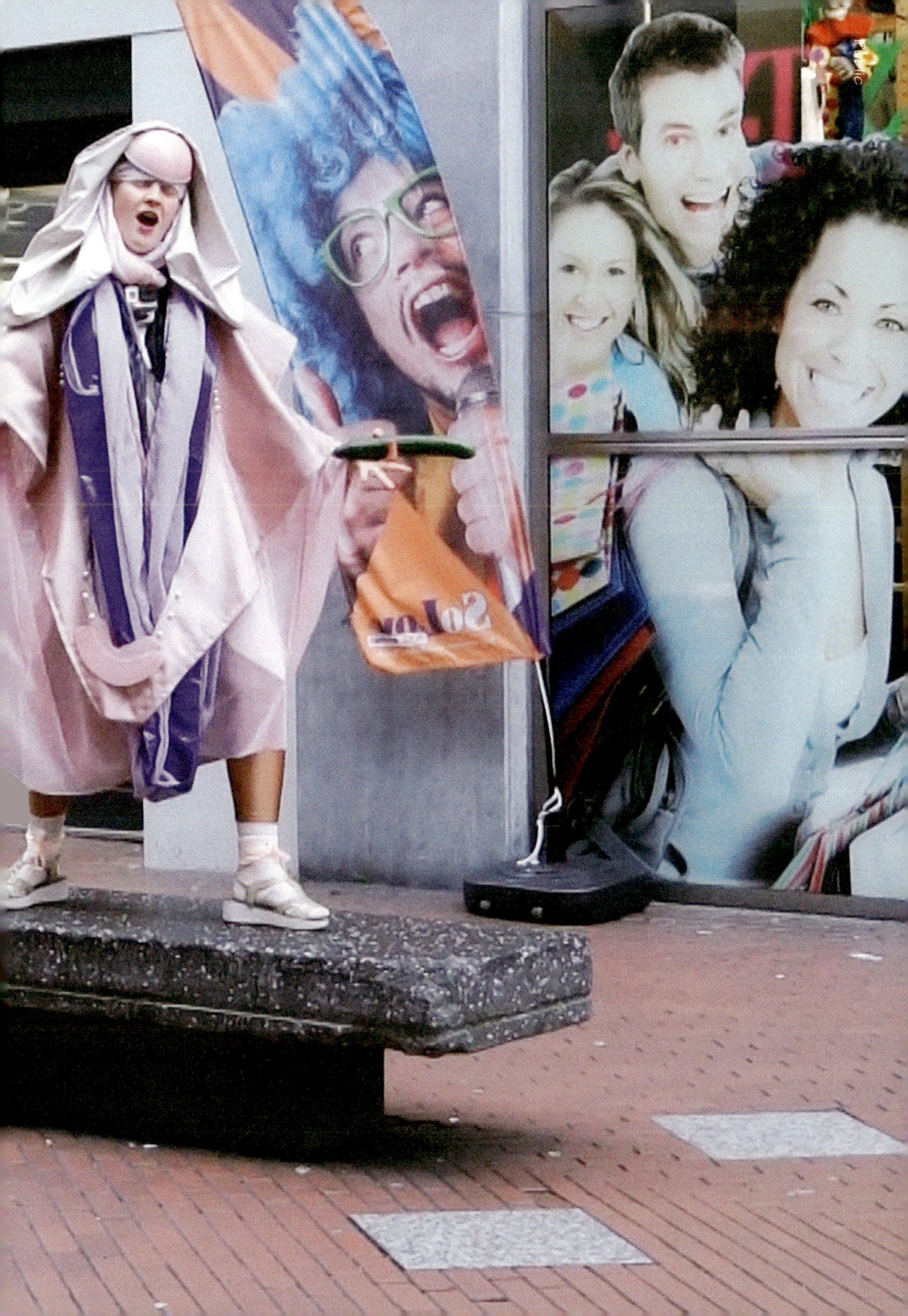

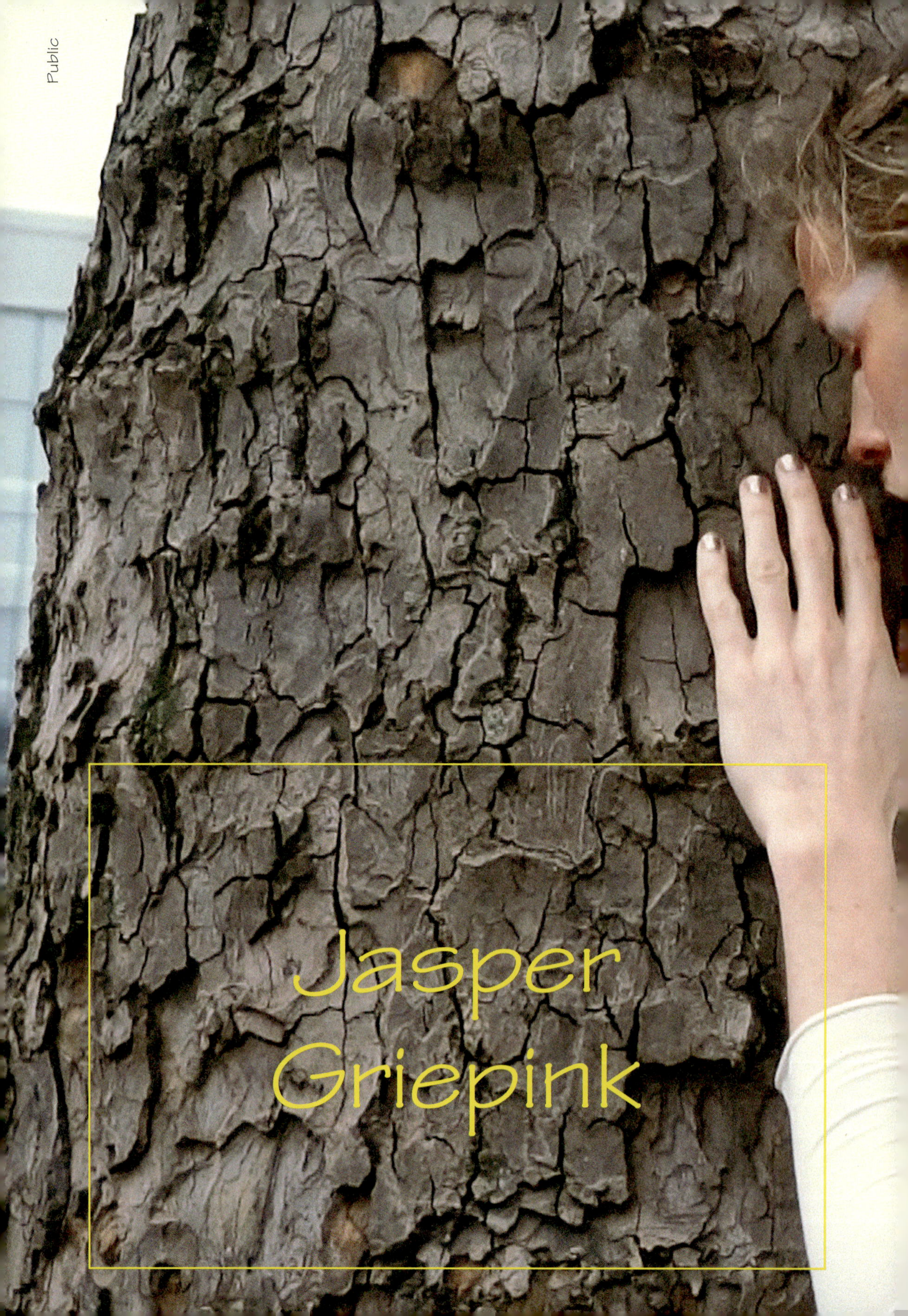
Public
Jasper
Griepink

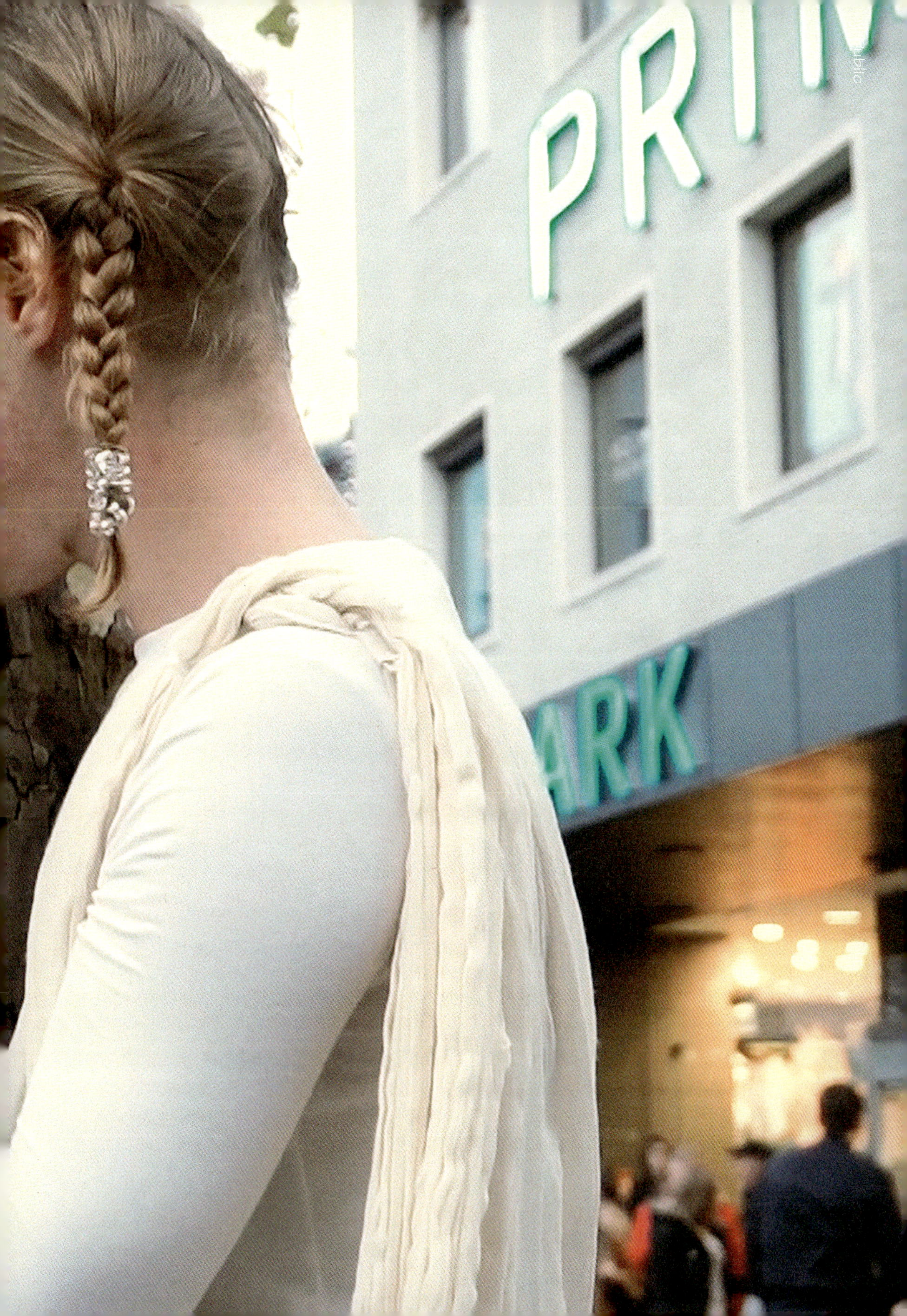
PRIM
ARK

ACHIEVEMENT #13
ULTRA ECOSEXUAL POLYAMORY
JASPER GRIEPINK

Jasper Griepink is a performance artist who aims to connect humans with each other and nature, through performance pieces, engagements, happenings and New Wave Druidry. His aim is to build a counter movement and momentum against a capitalist mentality, through personal and deeply emotional interactions, lead by feelings and intuition. In many cases Jasper uses the body as a tool within his practice, whether it's his own or that of others, through interaction in relation to others or nature.

His intervention in Eindhoven stood up to the wasteful, and commercial nature of the shopping centre by focussing entirely on the expression and affection for plants and nature, creating a stark contrast to the backdrop of his actions.

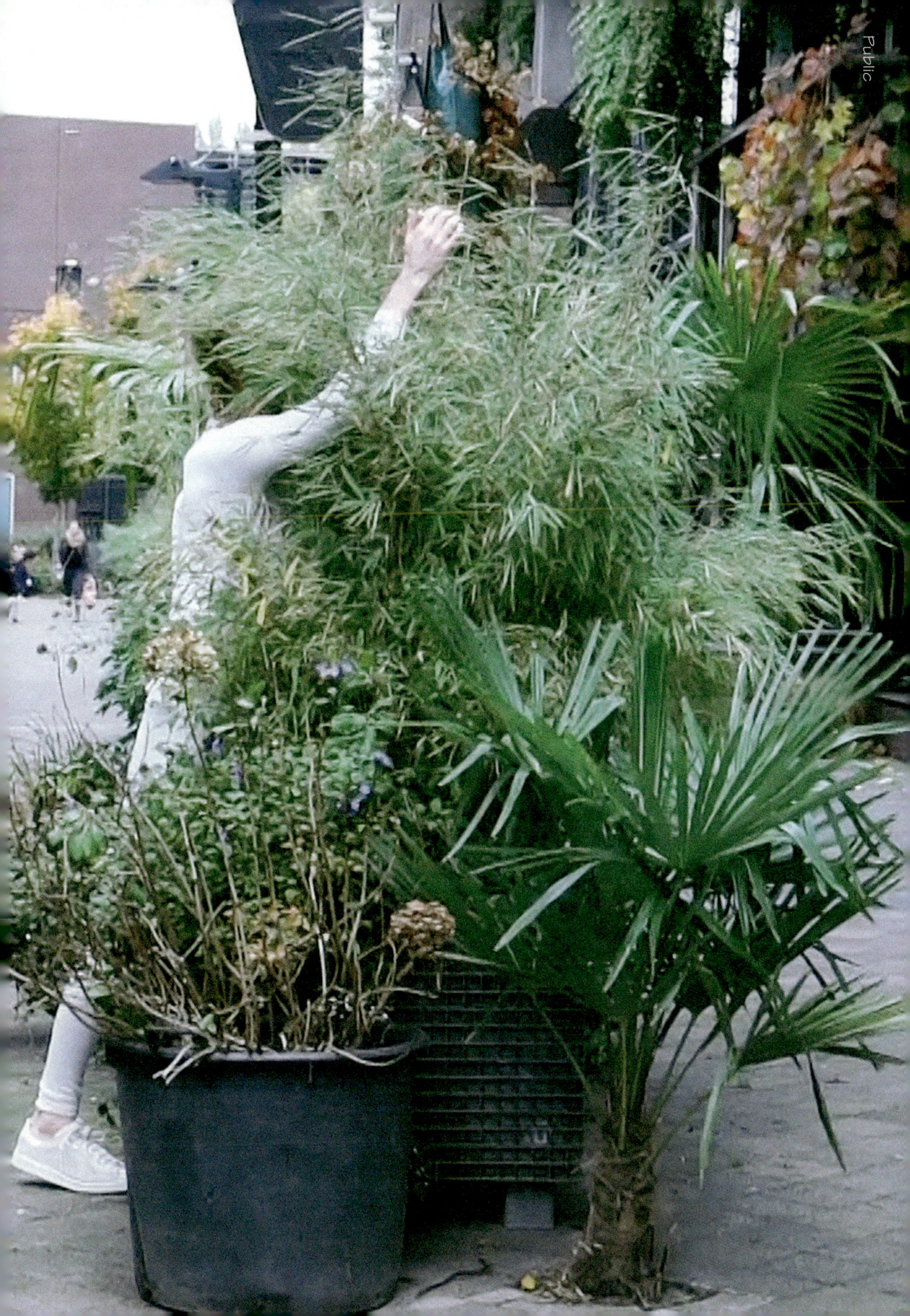

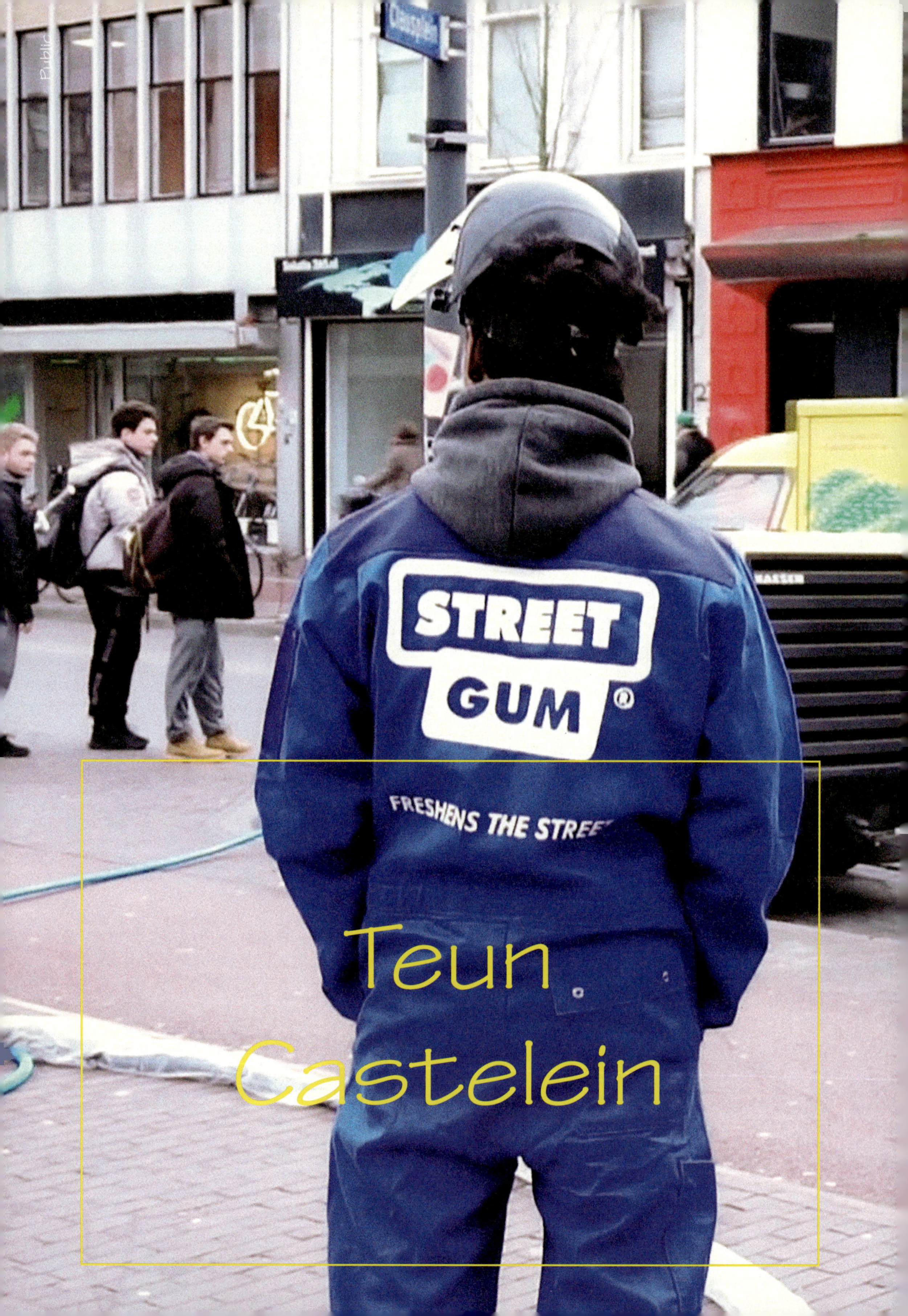

Teun Castelein

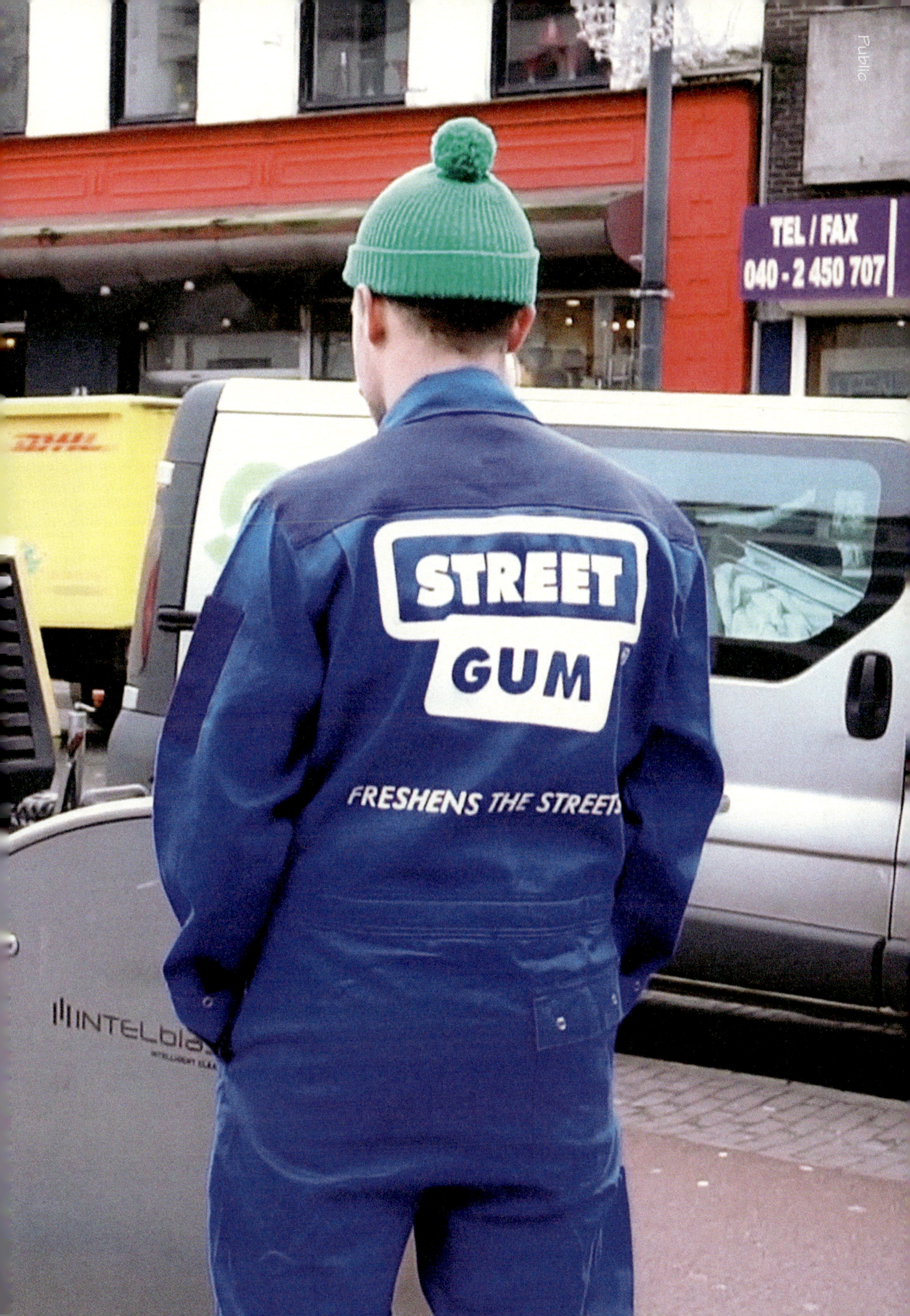
TEL / FAX
040 - 2 450 707
DHL
STREET
GUM
FRESHENS THE STREETS

ACHIEVEMENT 15
STREET-GUM
TEUN CASTELEIN

Innovating, inventing and engineering make the world a better place, as this entrepreneurship is needed. These qualities are characteristic of the wide-spanning-practice of the cultural entrepreneur that is Teun Castelein. Fundamental to his innovations are controversial ideas, that explore opportunities in the market and express the gaps in the market's culture.

Street Gum is a closed cradle-to-cradle system as it reconnects waste and product with each other. Gum is taken from the pavements, cooked, flavoured and ready to be re-sold. Easy, good and tasty.

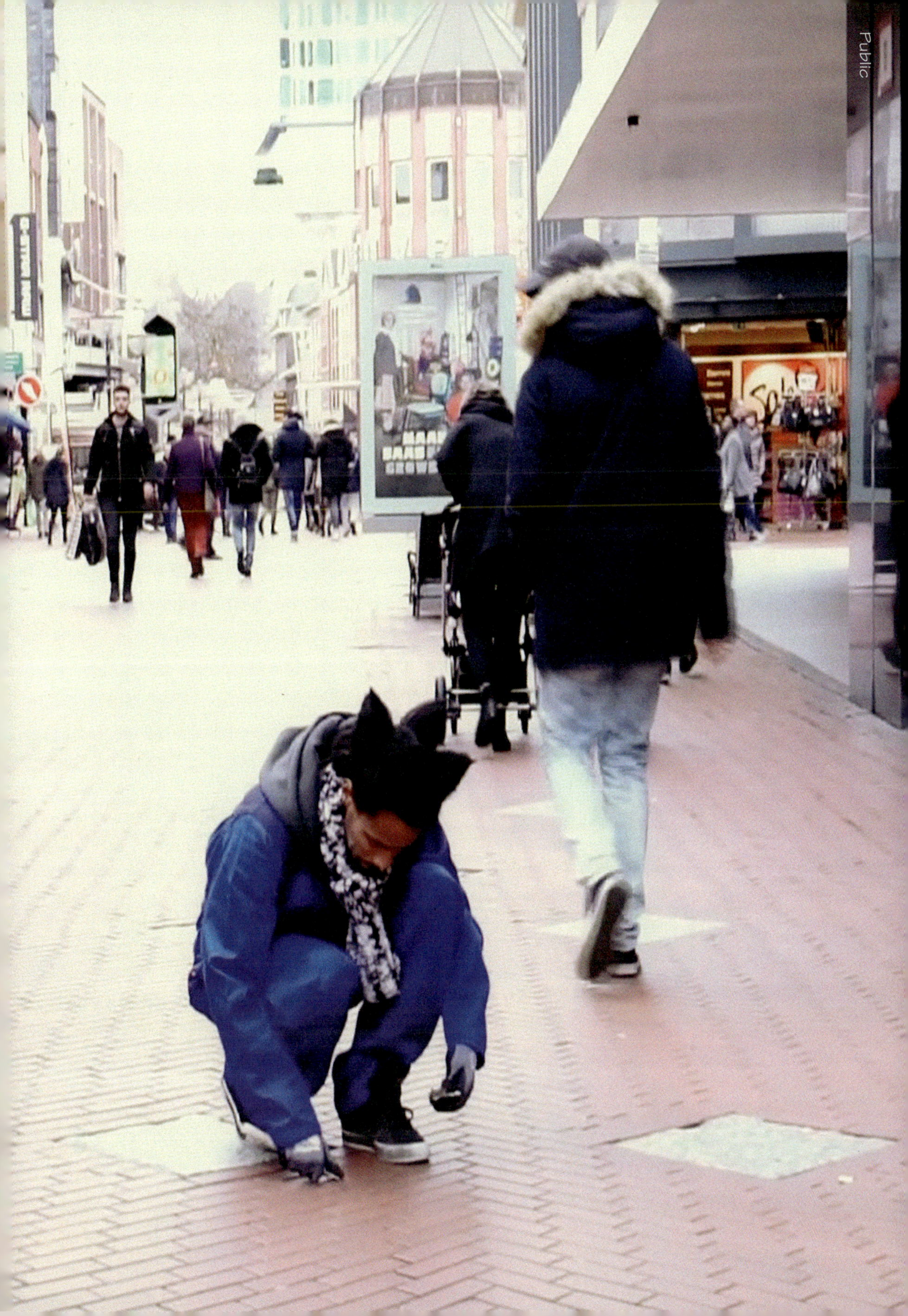

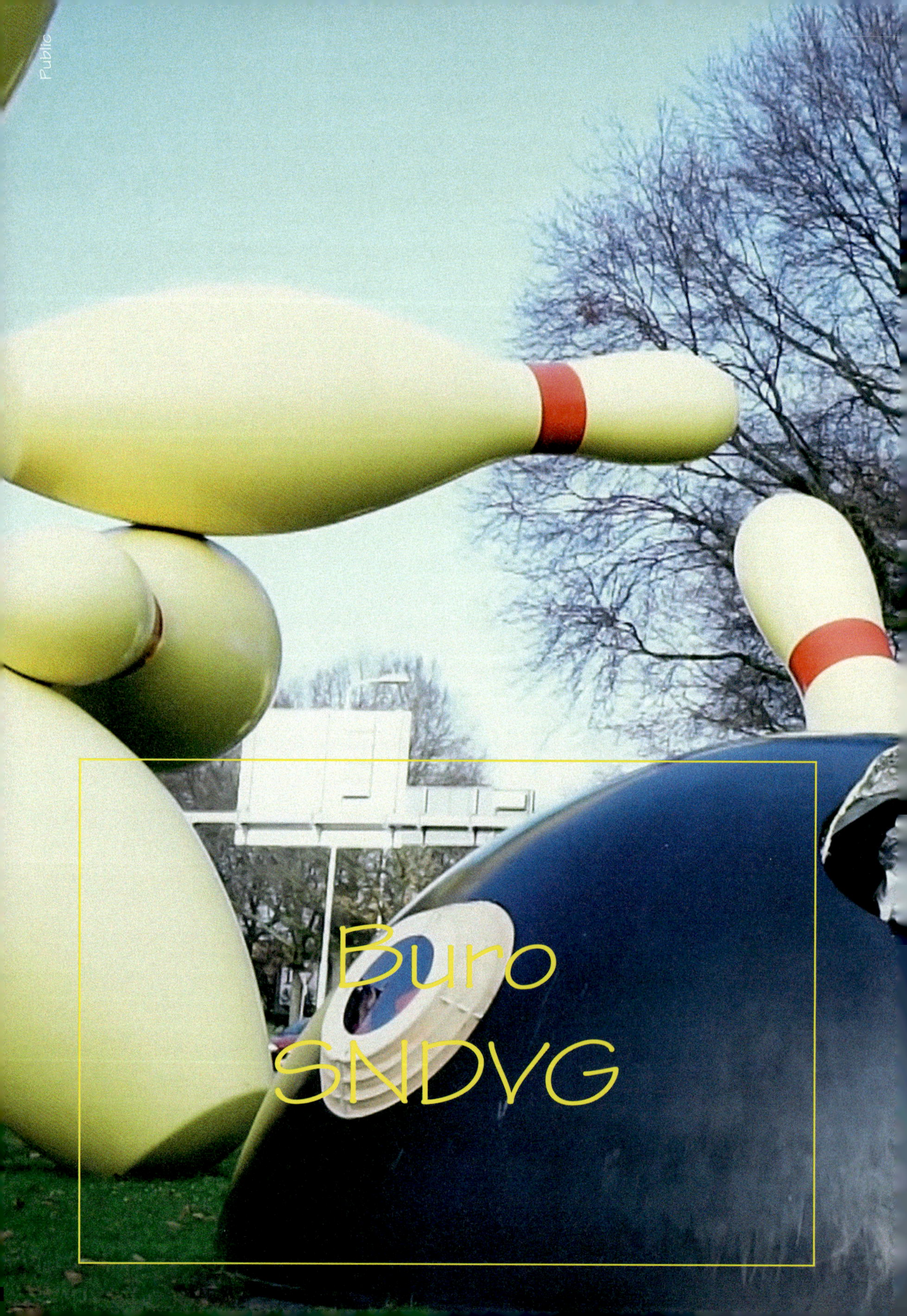

Buro SNDVG

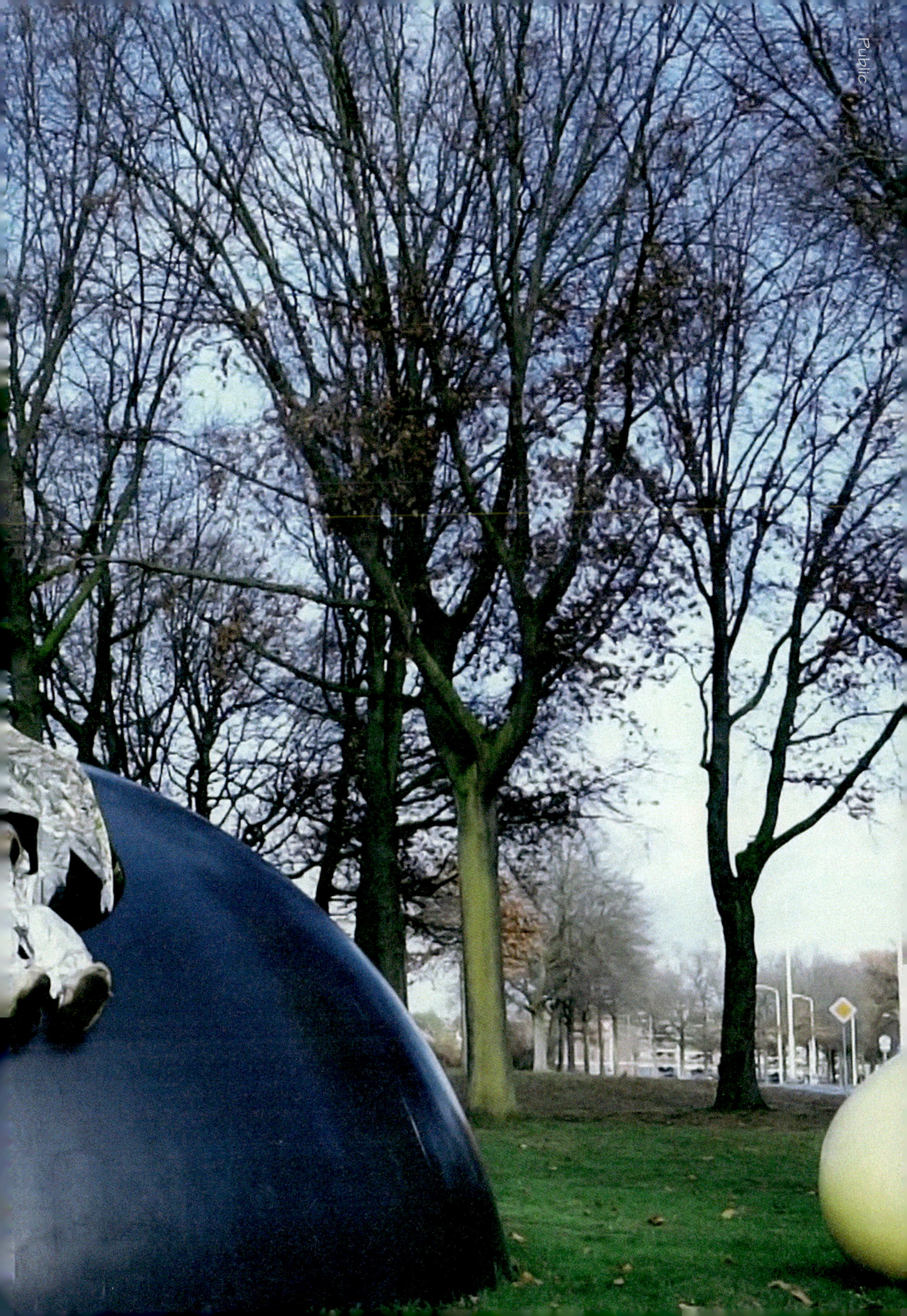

ACHIEVEMENT #16
CONTEMPORARY ARTCHITECTS
BURO SNDVG

Sly designers might design like artists; a bit into the unknown. The Eindhoven based Snodevormgevers, offer alternative placements for the cultural products of modern industry: objects, architecture and spaces. These convincing props claim respect, by offering a sense of sly humour. They also engage one in a desire to escape, as their mechanical or sculptural excess of imposing modernity often establish capturing installations.

A similar theme is visible in their *'We Are The Market!'* proposal as Buro SNDVG, in which they decided to invade a public sculpture in the centre of Eindhoven and inhabit it as a tiny-house, a Bed and Breakfast or an Art-Hotel-like place, questioning ownership and right of use over public property and art, challenging the line between art and common ownership.

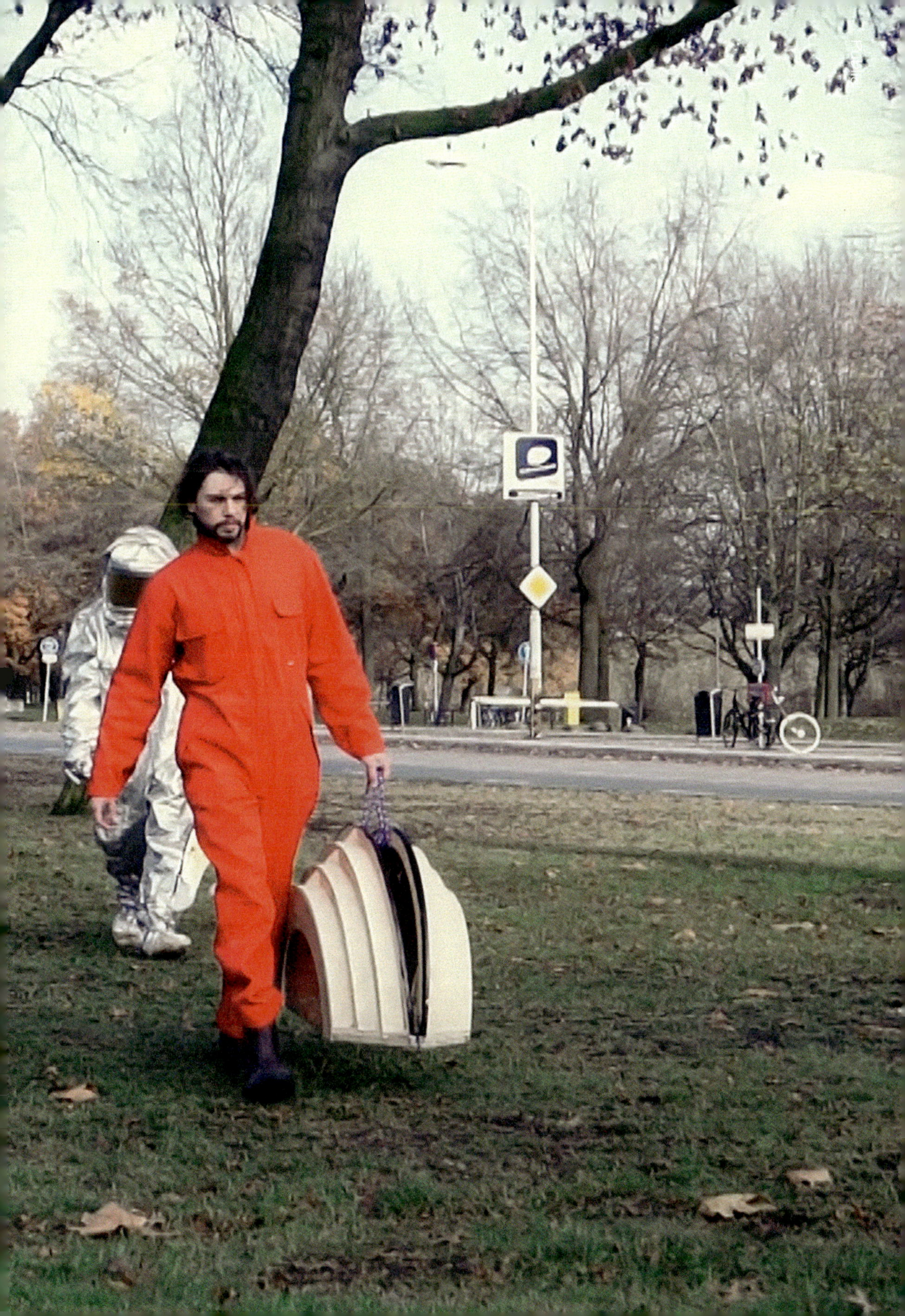

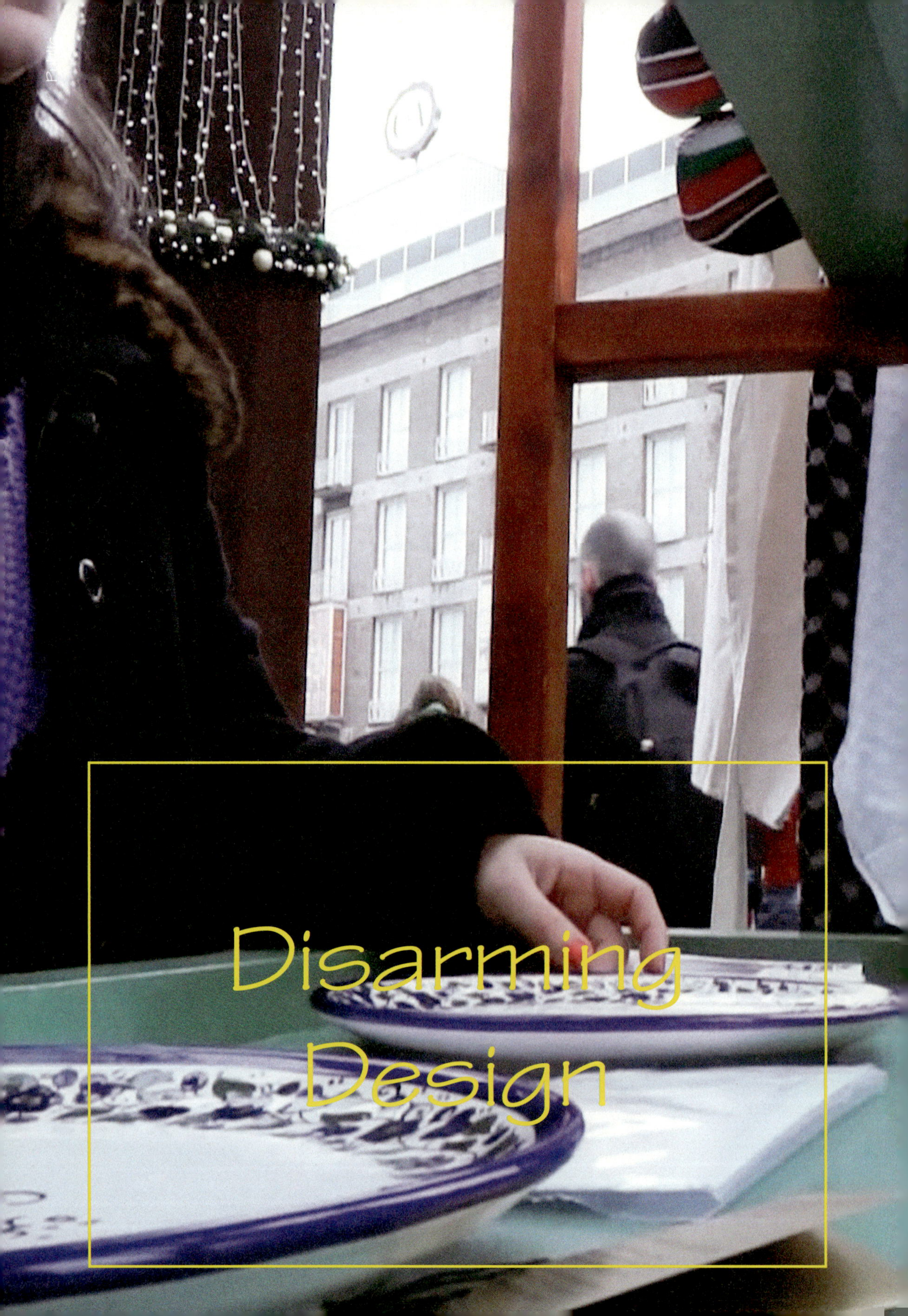

Disarming Design

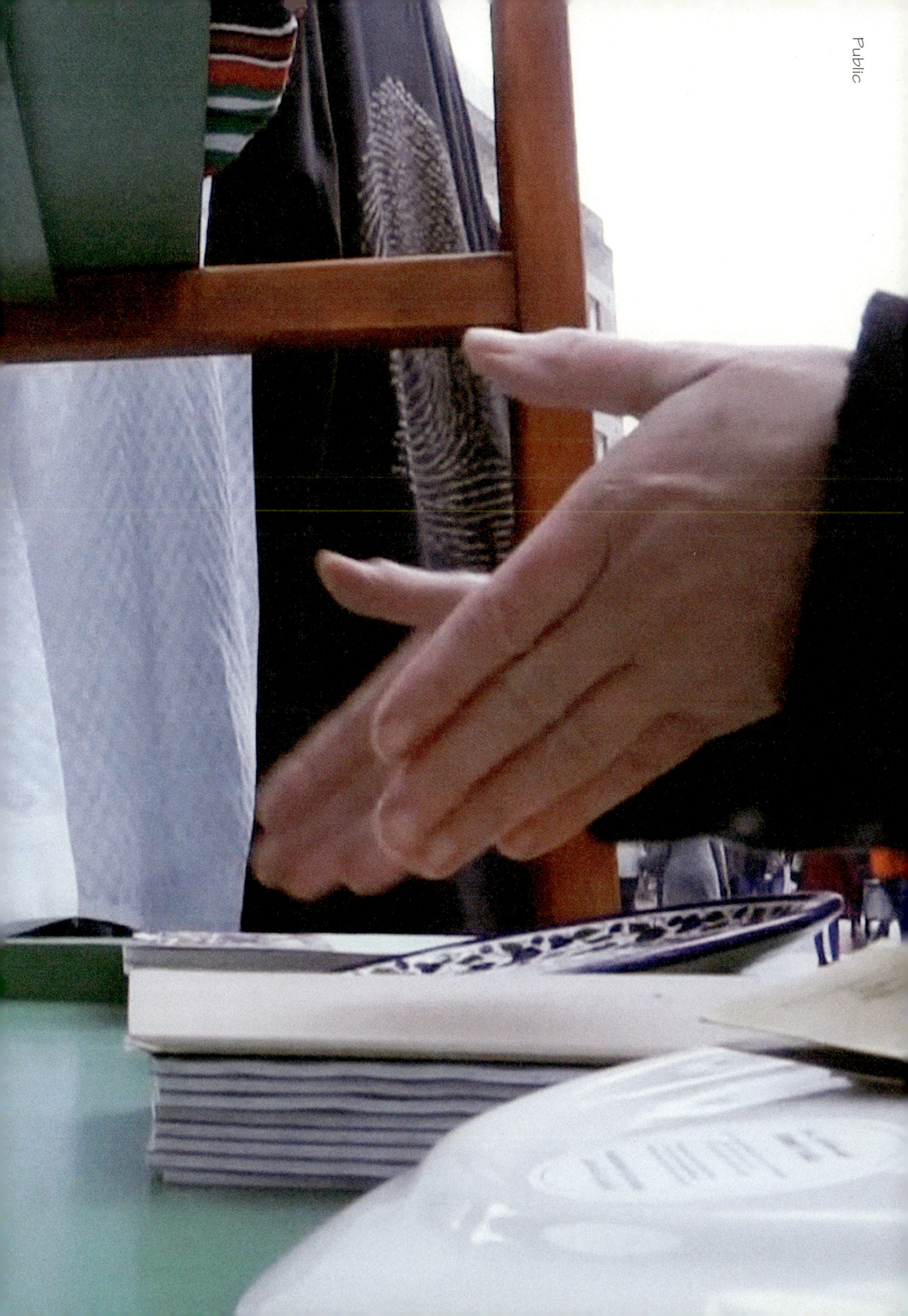

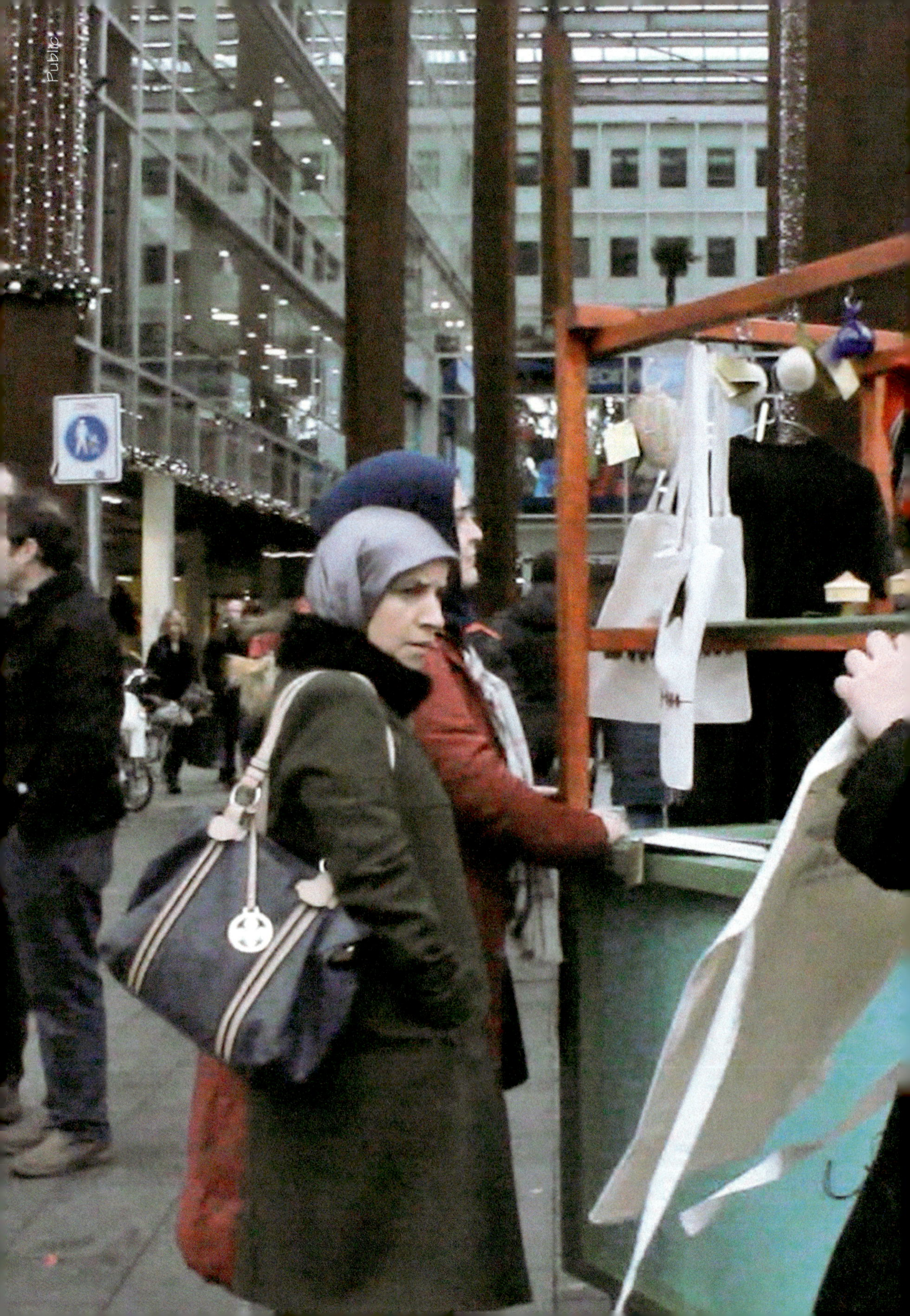

ACHIEVEMENT #17
DISARMING DESIGN FROM PALISTINE
DISARMING DESIGN

The design label presents and sells useful goods from Palestine, designed by contemporary designers and artists in collaboration with local producers and artisans. The project focuses on the development of local design and production capacity, through creative processes. By stimulating interdisciplinary working relationships, new artistic models are empowered. Art and design are deployed as powerful tools that allow serious discussions within a community about the political, social and cultural realities. It approaches design as a platform for discourse. How can creative practices contribute to a more sustainable society and human-centred economy?

The collection of products is presented and sold locally and internationally, through pop-up shops, exhibitions and a web shop. For *We Are The Market!* a special vending carriage was designed and built, inspired by Palestinian street-vendors. Items were promoted and sold on the streets by a Dutch female of Palestinian decent and a Syrian man, familiar with the conventional applications of the fabrics, the habitual usage of the items and the process of the labels' manufacturing.

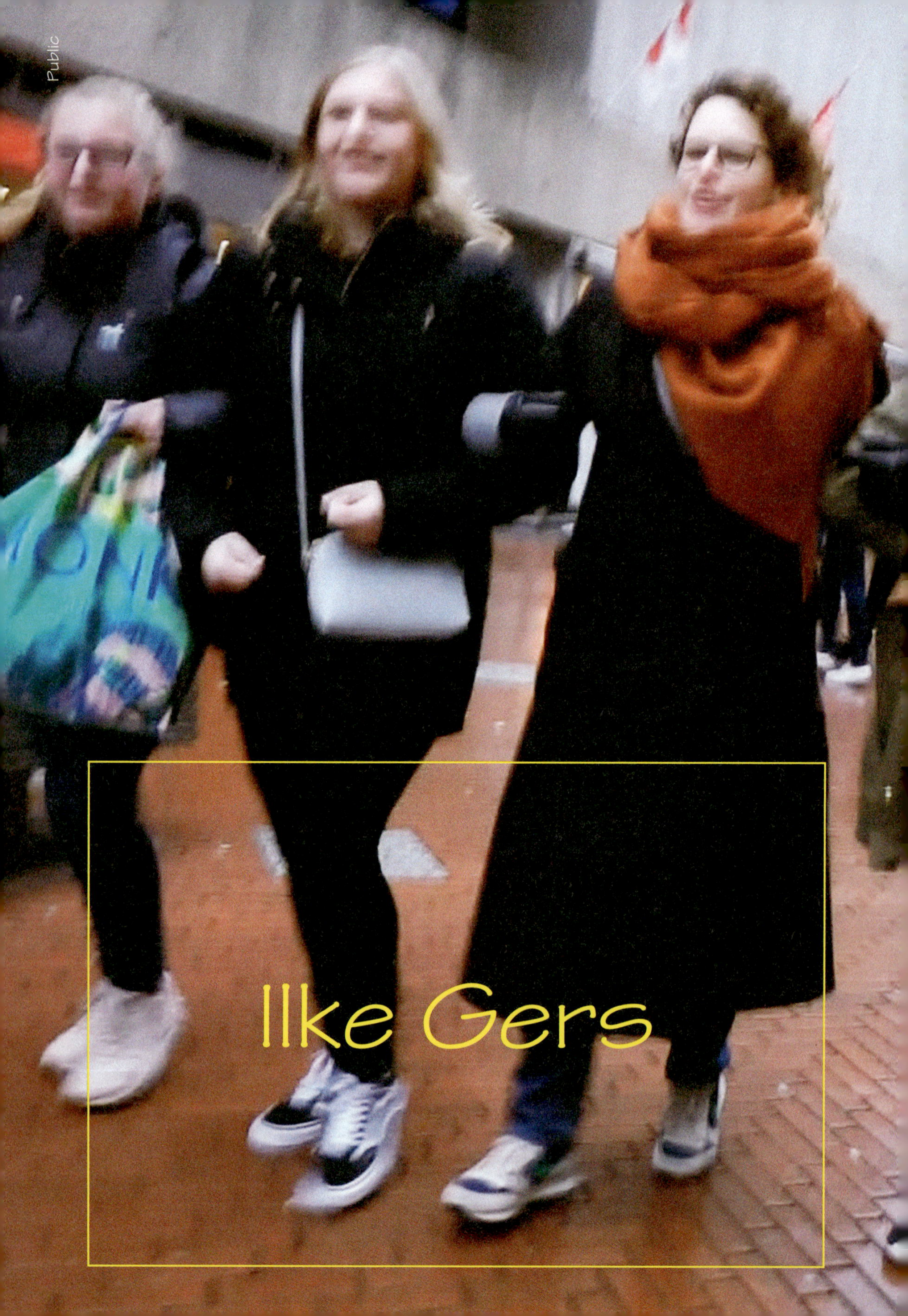

Ilke Gers

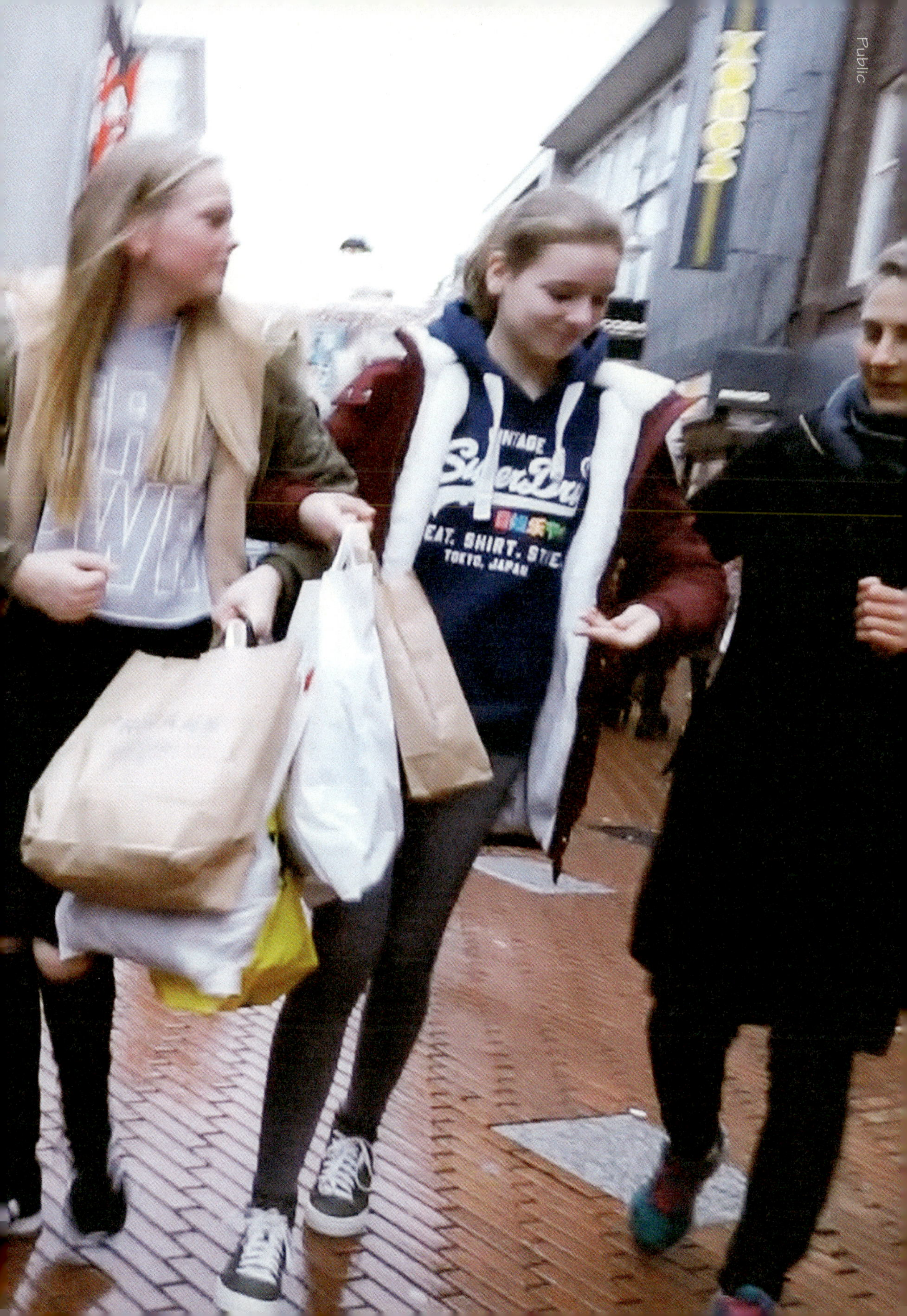
SuperDry
TOKYO, JAPAN

ACHIEVEMENT #18
ELBOW TO ELBOW
ILKE GERS

Literally and figuratively speaking, Ilke Gers brings movement, behaviour, social and spatial conditions into play. On a Saturday afternoon she walked down Eindhoven's Demer, the busiest shopping street in the centre, while inviting people to join her arm in arm. In effect by doing so, she manages to block the street, making others join her or crawl underneath the arms to get to the other side. Generously, Ilke claims the street for everyone to be in solidarity and united.

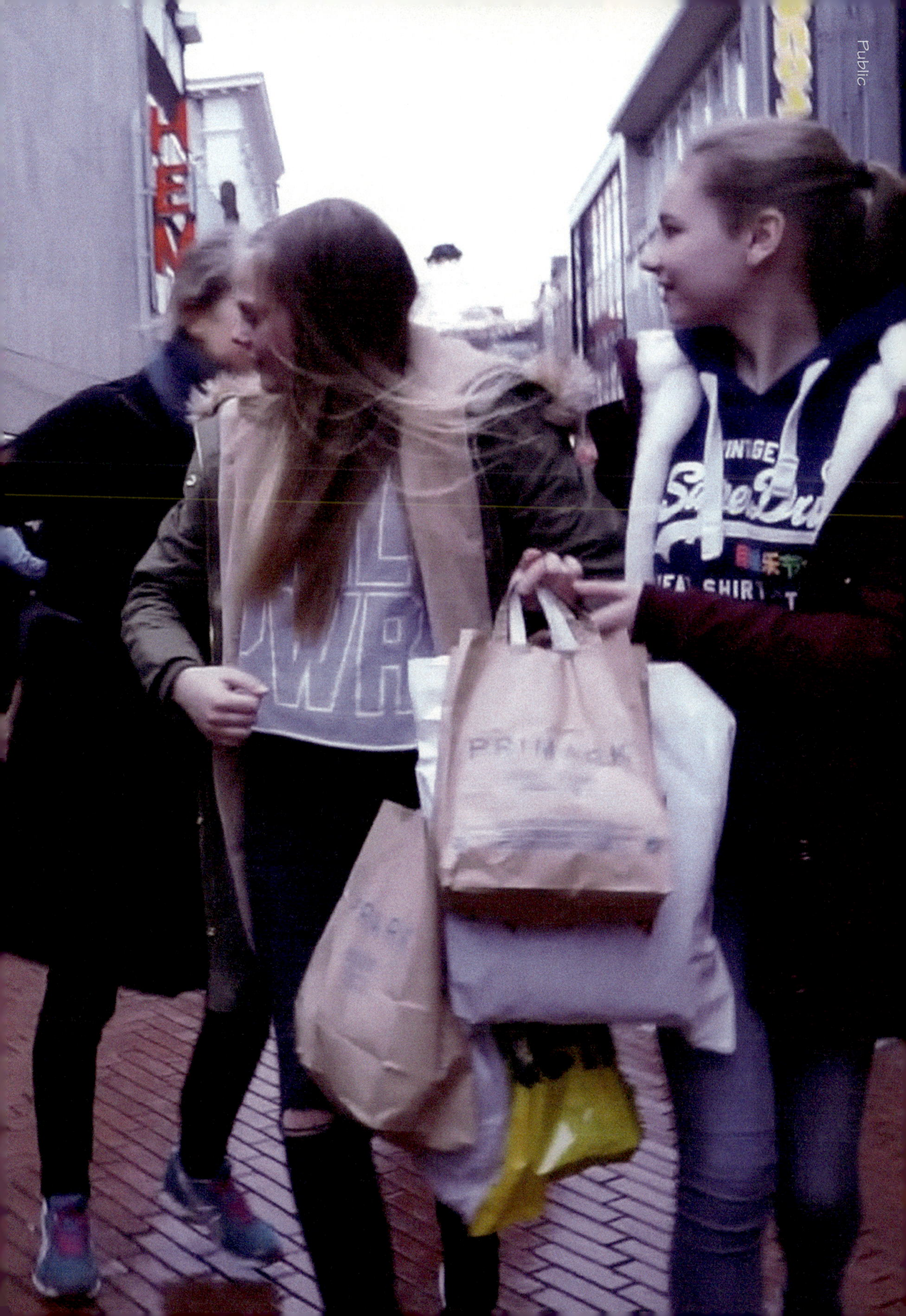

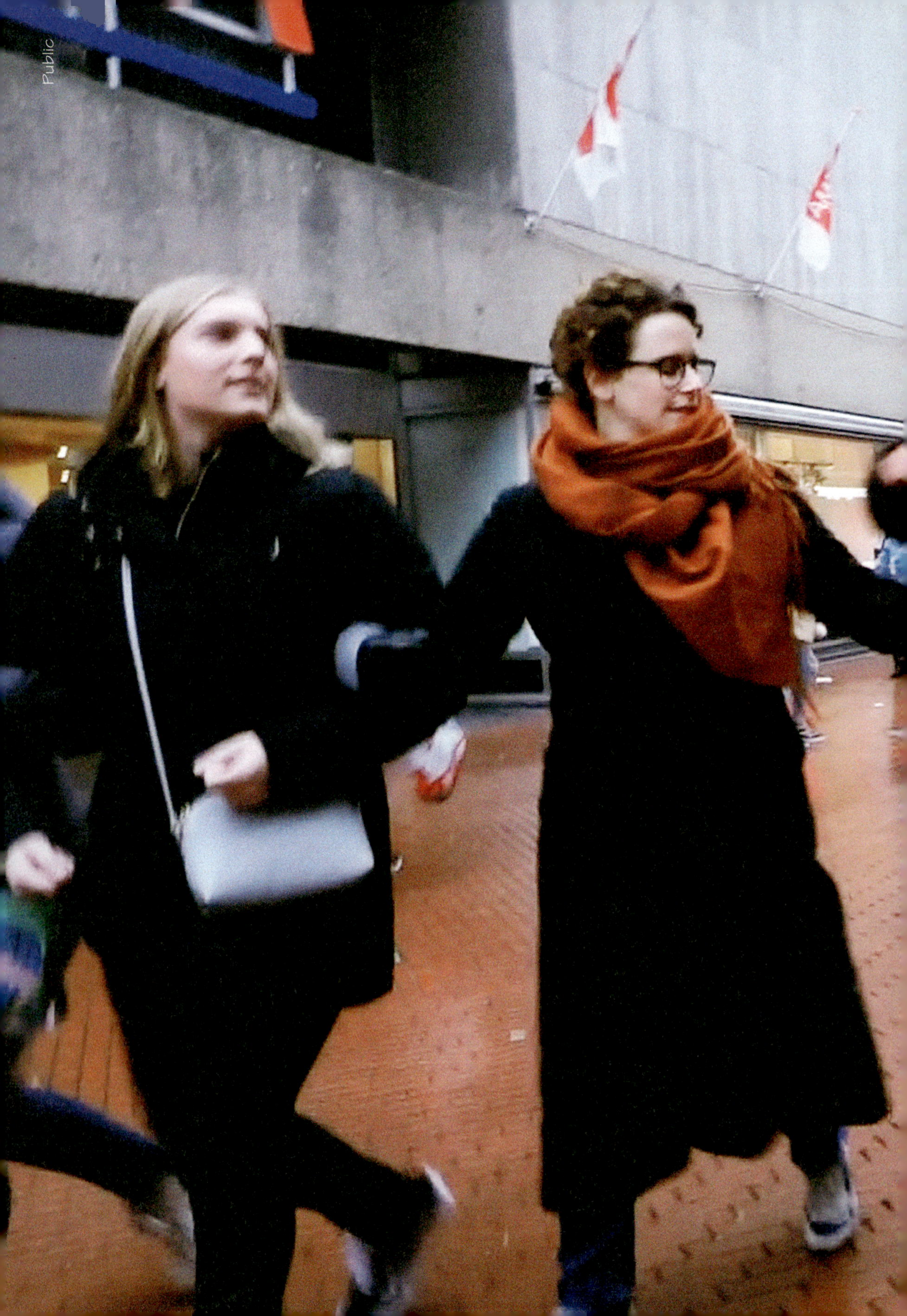

By Michel van Dartel

JP: Can we consider the public gallery as a situated being? I ask because you describe galleries as 'designated spaces for aesthetic experience' that are 'outside our natural habitat'. How then does a situated art or design piece function in a space like Onomatopee?

MvD: To answer your question, I need to first introduce the notion of 'situatedness', which I first became familiar with through my previous work as a cognitive scientist. Although the term 'situated' first appeared in late 1980s feminist theory, the notion of situatedness became hugely influential in the cognitive sciences in the decades following. There, it facilitated a shift from the dominant idea that the mind works on the basis of representations in our brains, to the realisation that the mind emerges from interaction with the world around us.

As the psychologist Edwin Hutchins points out in his groundbreaking book *Cognition in the Wild*, this interactive view of the mind makes studying cognitive phenomena in laboratory environments highly problematic. If cognition is emergent from interaction between a human and his/her environment, then that entails that the mind is entangled with the social, cultural and environmental factors that surround us. It can therefore not be understood without taking that context into account. This is what cognitive scientists emphasise when they call cognition 'situated'.

A laboratory is however set up with the purpose of stripping away contextual factors, as these may interfere with the variables under study. As a result, one could argue that cognitive phenomena studied in the laboratory are not quite the same thing as these phenomena 'in the wild'. This decontextualisation, ensued from moving the cognitive phenomenon from an everyday context into a laboratory environment, does not only change the phenomenon that the psychologist is interested in knowing more about, it also might place (part of) the potential explanation for the phenomenon out of view. Seen from this perspective it is no wonder that laboratory studies in the domain of cognitive psychology translate notoriously poorly to real-world situations. Imagine studying the cognitive aspects of drug addiction without taking the context of drug-use into account, for instance. This is something scientists have done for decades, until they realised that cognitive processes in the addicted mind are triggered by, and interact with, all kinds of environmental factors, such as social contacts, objects or places. In other words, they realised that cognition is situated and, consequently, cognitive phenomena such as addiction cannot be fully understood without taking into account the context in which these phenomena occur 'in the wild'.

Now, let's apply the notion of situatedness to the domains of art and design. Galleries are great places to focus on works of art and design without all the distractions of everyday life. And when the artworks or designs on display refer to other things that happened in such spaces, as autonomous art often does, then it of course makes perfect sense to look at these artistic or design reflections in a gallery setting. However, much work in these fields reflects on matters that exist outside of the gallery space, and this is where things get more complicated. Suddenly the audience is asked to take in something that is not actually there in front of them, and never was, but is represented by the work. Now the artist or designer is facing the same problem as the psychologist researching cognitive phenomena in a laboratory: How well does the work need to represent the subject that it refers to in order to make a reflection that remains meaningful outside of the gallery? Here, art and design professionals often make the same fundamental mistake as many psychologists did before the realisation that the mind is situated; they isolate their subject from the context in which it exists.

Instead of implying that there is a wrong and a right way of engaging with real-world issues through art and design, which is what the public debate on artistic engagement often seems to boil down to, the notion of situatedness brings more constructive views on these matters. It simply poses that representations of the real world are by definition limited and biased. From there, one can only either be very cautious with declarations of (critical) engagement with a real-world issue, or find a non-representational way of engaging with it. Such non-representational engagement always begins with the artist or designer becoming familiar with the situation that he or she intends to engage with. This generally entails embedding oneself in the context of the subject to experience it first hand, as it is impossible to fully understand a real-world situation from text and images. Such an 'embedded position' goes beyond merely observing a situation closely; to truly understand a subject and engage with it is to become an actor in its context.

However, even with a full understanding of a subject, based on such an embedded position within its context, a work that represents that subject in a gallery space is never complete and always biased. To overcome this, also a more situated mode of presentation should be sought after. A curator could for instance bring the context in which the subject is situated into the gallery, or bring the audience into the context. Although this may sound like an impossible undertaking, sometimes it is surprisingly simple. I am thinking, for instance, of some of the work that I have been involved in that addressed food ethics. People do not make ethical judgements related to food looking at representations of it on a plinth; they make them when they stick their fork into it. Therefore, instead of organising an exhibition with creative reflections on food, we produced a live event that presented artistic and design statements as an actual dinner. While artists, designers, philosophers and chefs introduced their ethical perspectives on the ingredients used to prepare the meal, the audience was subsequently left with the choice to eat a dish or not. Obviously, a dinner-event in an art space is still very different from the meals we have at home, yet situating art and design perspectives on food-ethics in the act of eating does bring such reflections closer to the real-world context of having a meal. So, looking at these matters through the lens of situatedness does not only inform artistic processes, curators may benefit from it in their processes as well.

Sometimes, however, it can also be extremely difficult to bring the context in which the subject is situated into the gallery, or to bring the audience into that context. To make an audience travel to a certain place can prove incredibly difficult to realise for instance. Besides the logistics of moving people around, one often also has to deal with limited accessibility, special permits or liability issues. Such endeavours may even exclude part of a work's potential audience from experiencing the work, or worse, the work or its subject may be negatively influenced by incoming audiences. Making art and design more situated may therefore not always align well with other stakes surrounding the gallery and its audiences.

Nevertheless, I believe that the best questions to start from as a curator are: Where does the issue addressed 'live' and what does the project intend to do there? Only then can the question of how the art space and its audience fit in be addressed. Following this basic principle, a gallery can create incredibly meaningful relations to the world outside of it. In the current cultural climate, however, curators are often forced to prioritise the stakes of an art space over the ambitions behind exhibited projects. This makes projects such as *We Are The Market* incredibly brave. Although it may seem obvious to go out onto the streets if you want to address 'how the capitalism of the high street is producing exclusive public spaces', for a publicly funded gallery, such actions are often not in the interest of its own sustainable future. It requires a relatively large amount of resources to organise such actions in public space, while they moreover result in neither of the things that most (public and private) funds like to see in return for their investment—high visitor numbers and significant revenue from ticket sales. Why then would Onomatopee even care to send performance artists out into the streets? Because they want their aesthetics to be productive 'in the wild'.

By engaging with the subject directly, rather than representing it in the gallery, the risk of misrepresenting it is annihilated and its potential impact is immediate.

JP: Michel, thank you for such a detailed reply! There are a few things I would like to draw out from your response. The main one being Eindhoven, and the city as an entity in which the public gallery inhabits. But firstly, to call We Are The Market brave, is for me surprising. This is mainly because when I reflect and write about the individual projects I am guilty of focusing on the micro aspects—the relationship to environment, the public, etc—which do bleed into the bigger picture. But, are sometimes lost to me when immersed in the details, so thanks for shaking me and refocusing my gaze.

As for the situatedness of the projects, one specific achievement jumps to mind, Toine Klaassen's *Exercises in City Hybridisation*. You mentioned earlier that the mistake artists and designers make is that they isolate their subject from the context in which it exits. Toine, originally from Eindhoven, embedded himself in the city. So much so that he developed a whole new persona, through whom he interacted with the city and its population. The way I read this intervention was through its transformative abilities, it dragged people away from the concrete of Eindhoven and in to its dirt—something that I want to see more often. It situated Loves Stones (his character) and the public in a different, 'alternative' city. One that wasn't forcing the mantra of being 'smart' on to its citizens.

This is where the situated public gallery gets its strength! We have also brought some 'artefacts' from the achievements, and the city, and placed them in the space. Yet each piece on 'display'—I hesitate to use that word—is a node that links the spectator to a specific time and place in Eindhoven.

With all this in mind it allows me to finish with a question for you, Michel. Where do you think the agency lies for a situated entity—artist/designers/gallery—in a 'smart city? You wrote about the shift from the dominant idea that the mind works on the basis of representations, to the realisation that it emerges from interaction with the world around us. Reading this statement I start to think that the locus of critique changes in relation to Eindhoven. I say so because the city is described as a 'dense network of sensors and actuators': implying that it too, as an entity, is situated. So it develops a direct relationship with its citizens and therefore the cultural production that goes on inside of it. So, I wonder how the relationship changes between the situated art produced when it's placed in a city like Eindhoven?

MvD: From conversations with historian Orit Halpern I learned that "smartness" predominantly promotes a perpetual dissatisfaction with the present, rather than offering real solutions to pressing challenges. A dissatisfaction, to which the answer always includes more technology to make things even more "smart" in the near future. A performance like Klaassen's may help shift our gaze from this technologically optimised future that is always just out of our reach, to the people, bricks and dirt that actually make up our city in the present. I consider it one of the most important contributions that art can make in these times to 'reconnect' us with the world around us. What greatly worries me is that as more and more of our private and public behaviour is mediated, shaped and steered by technology, we end up knowing less and less about the consequences of that behaviour in the world. Again, based on the premise that humans are situated beings, I believe that it is in observing the relationships between our behaviour and its consequences that we make sense of the world around us, as well as understand our own position in that world.

Take the simple example of 'online trolling', for instance. Imagine what would happen if we would unsolicitedly tell people off in a public space. Likely, we would instantly be socially corrected by others. Telling people off online however, such consequences are easily ignored, if they become visible at all. Obviously, trolling can be extremely harmful for a victim, but I think that there is a bigger issue at stake here: When technologies keep the consequences of our behaviour out of view, we lose the ability to explore the world around us and our position in it by probing it with behaviours and observing what they set in motion. Trolling is just a simple illustrative example of where insight into this feedback loop between human and world is lost, but it can be observed anywhere where technology is claimed to make things 'smarter'. It is no secret for instance that many of the products that we consume are produced under dreadful working conditions, yet we hardly ever need to face these consequences of our consumer behaviour. The 'smarter' the logistics that mediate between producer and consumer are, the more removed we will feel from the effects of our consumer behaviour towards these working conditions.

JP: What the smart city highlights for me is this lack of adequate language, something that James Bridle writes about when he describes the cloud as being 'both an inherently distancing metaphor and a potentially harmful one'. As Onomatopee is both a public gallery and a publisher there is, at least for me, a huge potential for becoming this locus—or maybe even the locust, an entity that gnaws away at the technocracy.

The novelist Jonathan Franzen wrote in his novel Purity: 'the terrors of the technocracy, which sought to liberate humanity from its humanness through the efficiency of markets and the rationality of machines...this impatience with irrationality, this wish to be clean of it once and for all'. I feel this quote works well applied to both the 'smart' city and the gallery. What's more inhumane than the both of them? The steadfast belief in big data and the rationality of ones and zeros doesn't really allow for humans dressing up as giant vulvas, for people falling in love with trees, or for others expressing their heartbreak through song in a public square on a Saturday afternoon.

Are the public and the social body becoming less engaged because of technology? Franco Beradi writes about how it's bringing about a radical reframing of the relation between media and self-perception, and how we don't deal with the other's presence anymore, something you mentioned earlier. Maybe the public institution will become even more important than ever in mediating a new kind of relationship... or is that wishful thinking?

MvD: The anthropomorphic metaphors that are used to describe such technologies are probably not taken literally by anyone, yet I increasingly feel the need to emphasise their nature to remind people that they are anthropomorphic for a reason: to win over our faith in technology for the benefit of economic and political agendas.

Your comparison of the 'smart city' with the 'white cube' as arenas that both 'liberate humanity from its humanness' is incredibly intriguing. Although I find it hard to imagine a 'smart city' that embraces humanness, and the irrationality that entails, I have less trouble envisioning an art space that does so. While the 'smart city' is a disembodied entity entirely organised around the efficiency of markets and the rationality of machines, a gallery does not have to be. As we touched upon before, a gallery is physically situated in the world. If we want to use that space to critique the efficiency and rationality of markets and machines, I believe that we should engage with them more directly than is currently done within those spaces. Public art and design institutions should facilitate and promote practices that embrace the irrationality of the world that they are situated in, instead of attempting to represent it in the work displayed. There is a lot more risk involved in the first than there is in the latter. Such is a risk that should be encouraged by funders and institutions, and shared rather than avoided or delegated down to the artists and designers.

Such endeavours indeed always require some 'patience with irrationality', because working 'in the wild' entails that a curator, artist or designer cede some of their control or authorship over their critique. At least in part, in the wild, aesthetic is co-produced by other, human and non-human, actors in the world. Actors that might behave completely irrational in response to the artistic or design intervention.

Coming to think of it, perhaps a truly 'smart city' may be possible after all. All we need to conceive however are technologies that are not informed by efficiency and rationality, but by inefficiency and irrationality instead. I suggest that we do not call such a city a 'smart city', however, let's just call it 'our city'.

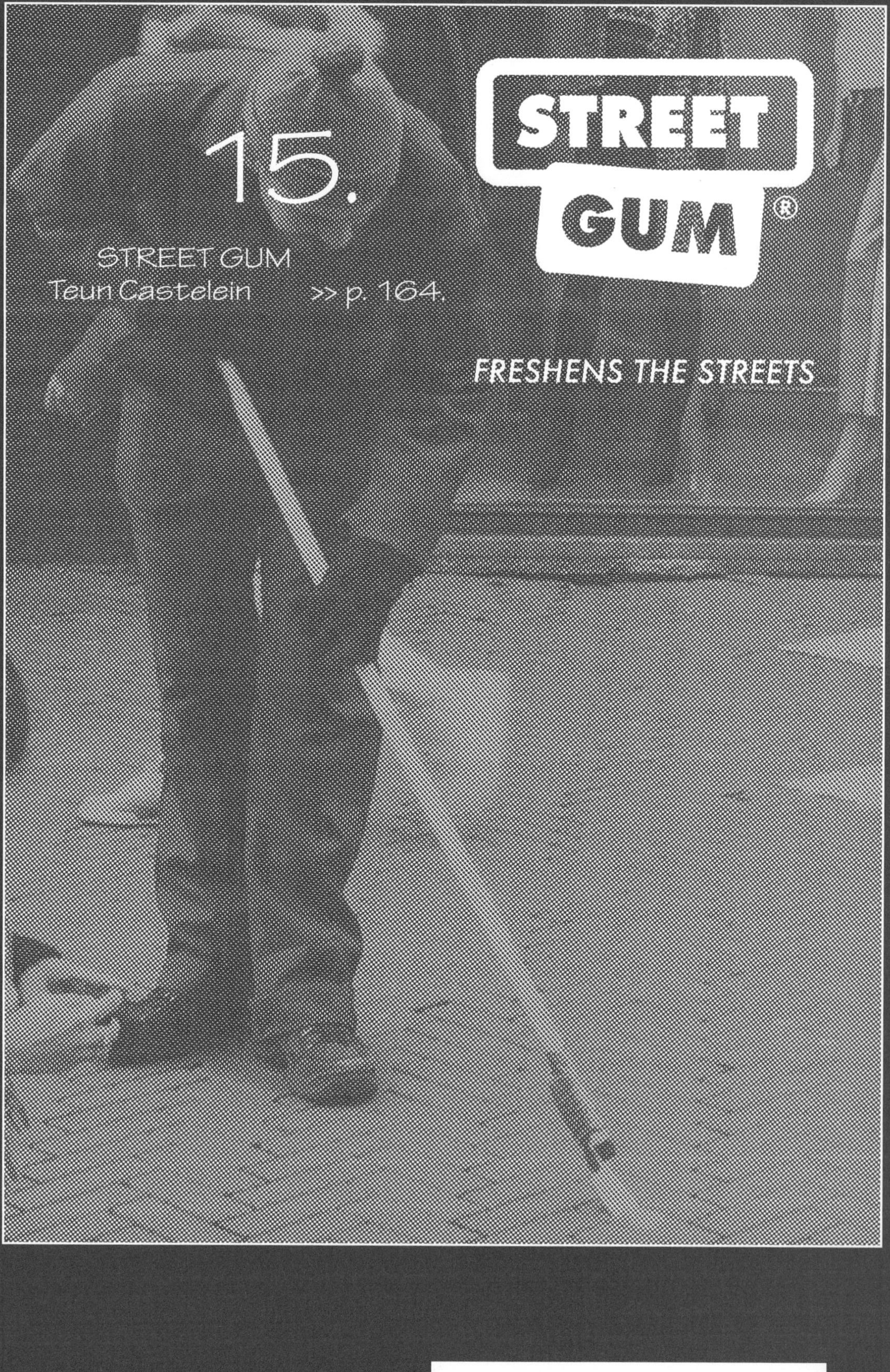

15.

STREET GUM
Teun Castelein >> p. 164.

16.

CONTEMPORARY ARTCHITECTS

Eindhoven 365 >> p. 168.

Achievement #16

Two Alternative living spaces in the design capital of The Netherlands. Artfully repurposed by a local studio to investigate the re-purposing of public art. Doing what they do best, Contemporary ArTchitects have twisted the notion of purpose and turned this 'iconic' art piece into a useful object. The local train station, supermarkets and other useful amenities are just 5 mins away. With no neighbours to speak of, this location is one the most exclusive in the city.

Hosted by Onomatopee, We Are The Market and local studio Contemporary ArTchitects.

The Neighbourhood
Eindhoven is bursting with energy. And we are glad to share it with you. When you google innovation, it is no coincidence that the first images you find are light bulbs. Over 125 years ago, Philips brought light to Eindhoven. The company transformed the city into a vibrant industrial success story. Nowadays, Eindhoven is a bustling city in transition, with a constant flow of new developments in the fields of creativity, innovation, technology, design and knowledge.

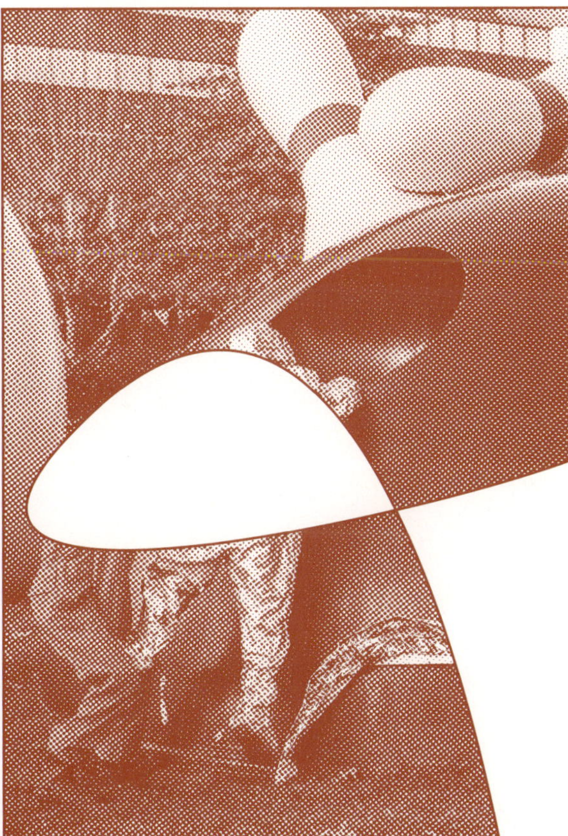

photo: Robin Heemstra

Overview
2 Habitable spaces in the bustling centre of the city

Private rooms in public art—Eindhoven
2 Guests
Spaces
0 beds
1 Bath Room; The Great Outdoors.

€ Free: Just get the door to the space through BURO SNDVG

17.

DISARMING DESIGN: FROM PALESTINE

Your reporter >> p. 172

On the 6th of December, a chilly Saturday in mid-winter, warm breezes from heartfelt charity interlaced the pattern of by-passing consumers near the Piazza shopping mall in Eindhoven. The Piazza area is an impressive landmark in the city of Eindhoven, with its big rusty pillars, the big brightly lit high street-fashion windows, the adjacent iconic '60's building of the Bijenkorf, and the open rooftop structure; its tastefulness being debatable. In front of the entrance to the mall lies the 18th September square. The 18th September, 1945 marks the date of Eindhoven's liberation from the occupation and the fascist terror of the German national socialists, brought to an end by the Canadians, the British and the Americans. How pleasantly ironic that this square, which is dedicated to peace, is now used to pass from McDonalds to H&M, two multinationals that spread global pain and suffering amongst animals and human beings alike. And how more pleasantly suitable that this location was being used by Disarming Design to display, sell and promote their original Palestinian products.

Since the settlement of Jewish colonizers earlier in the 20th century, and the declaration of the Israeli state in 1948, Palestine has been a place of political war, social injustice and religious- and colonialist-inspired violence. It's a place of constant conflict and debate, heavily fuelled by international affairs, and what we know from our news feeds. Our view from Palestine can almost feel like what Baudrillard would call a simulacrum, a copy without an original. Because Palestine is more than war and conflict, and more than what the media wants us to believe. Having never left the stage of political news, the country is now in a specific spotlight again, both positive and negative to me. Negative, because the American president Donald Trump has declared the city of Jerusalem the capital of Israel (problematic because Jerusalem has both Palestinian and Israeli parts, and thereby denying the Palestinian right to the city and disavowing the Palestinian state) and positive because of the brave young girl Ahed Tamimi, who physically confronted an Israeli soldier and is now being honoured all around the world as the Palestinian protest-princess. Despite the support from various left-wing groups and activists and due to her bravado, she is still locked up.

Within this view that we have of Palestine, fuelled by the media and international politics, it's difficult to grasp the real Palestine. What are the people doing there, how do they express their craft, their creativity, their culture? These questions are inherently and partly answered within the products that Disarming Design sells and promotes. On the flyer, that was distributed in the city of Eindhoven, the initiative is described as follows: 'Disarming Design from Palestine is an inclusive design label that develops, presents and sells useful goods from Palestine, designed by contemporary designers and artists in collaboration with local producers. The label aims to spread alternative narratives about contemporary Palestine and reflect upon the function of creative practices in situations of conflict." The label is registered as a non-profit company in Ramallah, Palestine and as a foundation in the Netherlands with a studio and warehouse in Belgium. The products are not only sold on the Palestinian market, but are offered for international distribution as well. And today, in the framework of *We Are The Market!*, every consumer in Eindhoven can get a piece of Palestine.

The products are displayed on a beautiful handmade wooden cart, built especially for *We Are The Market!*, based on an original Palestinian design. Two people, a Palestinian- born woman and a Syrian man, are there to enthusiastically speak about the project and sell the products. My eye falls on a book about specifically Palestinian culture: its wildly growing flowers, its original street art, its lovely traditional recipes. The objects such as the notebooks, Christmas ornaments, tableware, clothing and accessories, all bare typically Palestinian elements that are interwoven in a design that wouldn't feel misplaced in a Western living room. One of my personal favourites is a sheer white blouse, that bares the design of a traditional Palestinian scarf. My mother used to call those an 'Arafat shawl', or less politically correct, a "Turkentot".* I like how the interchanging, all-white, houndstooth-like pattern is subtle at first, but clearly visible when you know its origins. The shirt also seems light to wear and could belong to anyone's everyday wardrobe. Another set of objects that are both conceptually and aesthetically pleasing are the plates with the decoration of arabesque imagery on the front, and the distance to Gaza written on the front. That is, the distance from a specific Western city, like Brussels or Rotterdam, imprinted on the bottom of the plate. When you're finishing your plate of food, you can always see how far or how close your Palestinian friends are. Plus, it makes you painfully aware that, when filling up your plate, others might not be so fortunate and might have to survive in times of war without any food, or might have to eat without their families who have been killed. Food brings people together, and by using this plate, it becomes apparent how your togetherness, both national, as on a family level, is organised.

Artefacts (man-made objects) have layers of meaning. Through daily usage of a notebook that a Palestinian person has made, for example, you can really feel a closeness to this person, whose hands have touched that same paper. Objects can also make you travel through time, marking the journey from the glass blower to your Christmas tree for instance. By being in touch with the objects that Disarming Design produces and promotes, you can experience a piece of the real Palestine. Palestinian artists and designers also receive royalties for the sales of their products, and producers are paid according to fair trade standards, as stated on the flyer. Those agreements are undoubtedly positive, and I think many Westerners feel attracted to buying something, of which the profit is equally divided and of which a part goes straight to the designers and the producers. From our wealthy, rich and safe positions we want to do something about the crisis over there, but we don't know how or what. So to fill this longing for goodwill and charity we can buy from Disarming Design, and fill our warm safe houses with beautiful Palestinian products. However this is also where the project pinches a little. Disarming Design is originally a Dutch and Belgian initiative by Annelys de Vet. Despite all its best intentions, opportunistic Orientalism can be lying in wait. The products that are sold here today, are mostly bought by wealthy shoppers of Eindhoven who are already interested in contributing to the good cause and/or fair trade businesses. Palestine is presented here by Western mediation, and they're bought by Western people who feel attracted to "doing something" about the perpetual conflict in the East. I'm curious how the people on the Palestinian market respond to the products. How much can Disarming Design really do for the people in Palestine, for both the producers as the consumers? I don't know, but while I'm investigating I'd love to write my thoughts in the notebook, whilst playing with the stress ball made of wool and stone, wearing the white blouse and being surrounded by little pieces of Palestinian craft and creativity, in the comfort of my safe city.

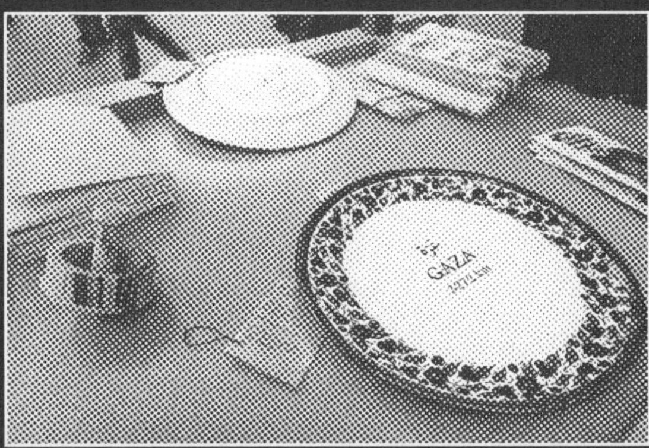

*The Dutch problematic saying "Turkentot" in English means "Turkish rag".

18.

ELBOW TO ELBOW

Your reporter >> p. 176

...Visualise a group of 15 people, entirely engrossing the breadth of a main shopping street, giving bystanders the choice of joining the chain or having to crawl in-between arms and legs. *If you can't beat them join them.*

Ilke Gers, a New Zealand born artist who is now based in Amsterdam, frequently uses performative games and group dynamics within her own practice to explore and strengthen interpersonal relationships between strangers and in groups. As part of this she staged a march with strangers, which started at Eindhoven's historical landmark, the St. Catharina Church and arrived on the 18 Septemberplein, a symbol of capital commerce, over which the large Piazza shopping mall looms, with an ever watchful eye.

The process went as follows: Ilke would ask people to join her walking down the street, some would link arms, others refused, then Ilke moved to the edge of the chain to try and convince more people to partake. Many were persistent in not wishing to participate, others hesitantly agreed once being reassured of the possibility of leaving or 'getting off' of the symbolic train at any point, to continue their shopping spree.

Although not wanting to support the hugely widespread gamification of everything, which is becoming an increasingly used marketing strategy to nurture interest for brands, programs, processes and apps, making the action playful worked positively. The aim of the game here was not to create an environment of gain but that of pure, simple and innocent human interaction and engagement. But challenges and games seem to touch upon a deeply rooted instinct. Despite there being no parameter to compare or measure the action against, no level of success or failure even existing, people of the public suddenly became competitive, likely inspired and animated by the high energy levels and motivation which Ilke was able to display throughout, encouraging the participants to also ask strangers to join. Approaching the finish line and trying to increase the amount of people holding on to each other, people's dedication also increased, one man repeatedly exclaiming, *"There's not enough people, it's just not enough!"*, displaying a feeling of despair at the apparent lack of engagement by some.

It was a process of trial and error. Touching people before having caught their attention lead to abrasive reactions as people were overcome by the fear of being robbed. Other people ran away, without listening to the warm invite. Too deeply engrained is the self-enforced training of walking through town with blinkers on, in fear of being engaged into a conversation one would rather not have, about a charity which one is too selfish to give to or would rather not hear about. And for fear of one's own ignorant perfect first world bubble being pierced and therefore popped, bringing one back down to earth with a bank. It became apparent that the choice of words with which people were invited to join in the activity was vital, some attempts working better than others. Unsurprisingly people questioned the purpose of the action. What was met with a lack of understanding was the explanation of it being part of an art project. Has art and the white cube acquired such a bad reputation, that it stops people from wanting to participate?

Other people's eagerness to partake exceeded all expectations. Two young teenage girls walked the entire stretch and having celebrated the achievement at the end through applause, laughter and cheers, had to walk back most of the way to continue their trip, but they did so, in no way begrudgingly, which was a refreshing sight. Having staged the group activity, we felt a huge feeling of gratitude towards the people that had joined. A sense of achievement connected the group, the pointlessness of the exercise losing its relevance, because as a team we had reached a common something. Highlights also included a line of children who didn't speak English but with smiles and hand gestures were convinced to join and happily did so, while their parents and grandparents trustingly let two women take the children ahead while they caught up at their own pace. Other times parents were wanting to turn off in a different direction, but the children were apprehensive to let go of the chain. When Ilke persuaded one person of a group of teenagers, the rest was easily motivated too, not being able to refuse being part of this movement that suddenly took over and attracted looks and attention by many. One man was willing to take Ilke's arm but refused to link up with his other male friend, which left Ilke speechless and baffled. Needless to say they weren't part of the chain for long.

The achievement was successful in the physical establishing of bonds, making people literally connect and in some cases reconnect. Possibly even more significant was the fact that this human chain was able to symbolically disrupt the entire street and atmosphere. Humans having to pay attention to one another again. *"You change the whole space by doing something opposite to the expectation of the space"*, says Ilke.

NO MORE INVISIBLE HANDS!

By Fred Dewey

(Los Angeles & Berlin) 1.31.18

I It is hard enough for ordinary people to get leverage over and govern their daily conditions - in all the places where they live, work, breathe, meet, exchange, and think. Why do things happen the way they do, and what can we do about that? This is clearly an important question, yet somehow it is the hardest in the world to ask. Indeed, it has become nearly impossible to ask, and even *less* possible answer.

It is impossible because the biggest force blocking our way, preventing a healthy model of exchange, community, and self-government from being enacted and secured is something *invisible* - the invisible hand of the so-called "market." A spectre is haunting the West, *the spectre of the invisible hand*. It is precisely this that hides countless important matters, modes of relationship, and not only blocks but robs us of our power. It seeks to conquer and rule all exchange. This invisible hand, rather than making exchange and conditions clearer and more just, more open, free, and equitable, makes them more opaque and unjust, more closed and slave-like, and renders all our conditions less and less friendly. There is a paradox here. Much of this "magic" is because this thing we call "the market" has become a fiction. It has been called *free*. An ordinary market is one thing. A free market is different. A "free" market has never existed in human history. It is a myth, a fiction, because it is at best a term of art, at worse a ravenous, global ideology. Any *working* market larger than the town square must be guaranteed by government, laws, and good will. When saturated by deception, by thieves, by ill-will, by parties—in short by *invisibility*—it offers no freedom.

A global market is invisibility expanded to a global level. This myth and fiction of the free market has been used again and again to hide moves of politicians and economic figures wishing to protect their power and rule in society. The rest of us, beyond the top 5%, must live in a world defined not by the people who must suffer it but by power *taken* from the people by an invisible hand.

II In September 1997, protesting a government budget in Mexico, buttressed by the Zapatista movement, protesters produced a poster whose slogan spoke volumes: "Neoliberalism: a crime of the state." Neo-liberalism is the great defender of so-called free markets. Its espousal of so-called freedom enforces a fantastic, well-crafted, totalizing fiction to disguise robbing people of things, power, rights, lives, options, and finally appearance itself. Early on in this program, on May 3rd, 1980, Margaret Thatcher spoke plainly to the London *Times*: "Economics are the method: the object is to change the soul." We have experience of such soulcraft in the United States by now. Wrecking the social and political contract has been under way for decades, all in the name of the market. Gambling, extortion, speculation, de-solidarization, and precaritization are very far advanced. But something more serious is at work even than this. Europeans are less experienced in this cynical array, and the trick that underlies it. Most people did not expect that the "social market" was a Trojan horse for the economic market. The bitter trials of Greece, Spain, Ireland, Portugal, Italy, and northern countries like Holland, Sweden, and Denmark, and increasingly Germany and France are a sign of what is really at work: the untrammeled rule of parties, center systems, and an invisible political and economic caste bent on political and economic *slavery*.

Sadly, our critical apparatus comes not from the democratic-republican tradition, and from reflecting on its core principles—where markets, wealth, parties, and power concentration are forcefully restrained, and public space, public power, and accurate representation of the people are demanded, built, and protected by law. Instead, again and again we rely on a body of writings that put economics, labor, markets, and capital above all. Part of this comes from the Marxist school, a school that has clarified much but also obscured much. One does not need to go to the Chicago School of Economics, the "fresh water school" as it is called, the "free-market school," to find rule by fiction. To focus on and rely upon economics, labor, classes, and capital is to refuse the fact the machinery governing this, and governing our lives and conditions, is political and existential at its core. Markets and *political* accumulation go hand in hand, and this accumulation is relentless. Capital is an instrument of the social. We speak in terms of social capital, human capital, cultural capital, and so on. But this machinery is human and political, and as long as it is subjugated by an invisible hand, we are at grave risk.

Isn't it past time to find a new critique? We hear often how we are puppets of technology, or history, or nature, or some mysterious group. By far the most common argument is the most far-fetched of all: that we are nothing but functions of capital and markets. Of course "markets" act upon us, and classes form to answer markets. But they also dissolve. They are made and unmade. But by whom? Classes are like the invisible hand. Can we not probe deeper? Where does power lie? How do we gain traction in the world if we turn from human, political decisions and exchanges made by plural, concrete, and organized people and instead rely on mysterious, invisible forces?

When The Market is turned to as a description, a solution, as a prime mover, as a so-called "reform" tool, when it is our only choice or opponent, things always seem to inextricably become more corrupt, more unequal, more deceptive, and crucially, more disempowering. The Market is a recipe for invisibility. Why is it not clear, and an outrage, that The Market again and again, as our description and our agency, results in elimination of people, history, full democracy, and finally, the right to rights and the space of appearance itself?

III The global movement based on this invisible force elevated to supremacy is neoliberalism. Neoliberalism is designed to undo public life, to make it inconceivable, to rule with unquestionable tyranny and coercion, to reduce everything to "markets." It is economics, the quintessential manufactured reality, triumphant. Everything becomes confused and opaque. The point is not that "market" signals challenge and balance public signals and signs; the point is "market" signals *supplant* public signals and signs. Exchange is subordinate to accumulation and invisible power. This *obscures* a world where people are unique, are responsible, organize for and against power, and have the full right to govern conditions, not as classes, but as unions of differing and distinct people, organized for power. Generous exchange, free exchange is continually subjugated. Is it any wonder market signals teach us to give in? That is the point. We are supposed to give up before this great and global dynamism that supposedly leads to the best of all possible worlds. We no longer can lay claim to power, to *our* politics, but stumble inside a vast, global, and invisible system created by experts, for experts, for every ruling political and economic caste aimed at robbing the people of their power and their capacity for and right to *political* freedom.

Today, market logics saturate every facet of life. They are used to speak of reform. They are called a way to open things up, to make life *more* free. In the United States, such fiction has preceded dissolution of public financing, public programs, and public governance. This is now fully underway in Europe. Community control and grounding in place are rendered an ancient memory, and forgotten. The local no longer is the place of our assertions and protections. The people are pushed, through soul-changing schemes, onto their back foot, rendered unable to answer and challenge. Gary Olson, a critic of neoliberal culture, described the results of this recently, echoing his book Empathy Imperiled: neoliberal "culture" "deadens feelings of social solidarity, pathologizes how we view ourselves and stunts our natural feelings of empathy and moral responsibility." The results of this are fatal. What precisely is the difference between letting The Market dictate and a dictatorship of one or more parties? Or of states? Or some conspiratorial group that has no name and can't be located?

All of these form what Solzhenitsyn labeled a great Red Wheel. Hannah Arendt, in a barely explored section of her best-known book *The Human Condition*, confirmed Solzhenitsyn's intuition, concretely. She cites the sociologist Gunnar Myrdal, who called the invisible hand, this hidden hand of markets, a "communistic fiction." This is ingenious and clarifies things instantly. The Market is a hallucination of the social sciences and a tactical tool of political elites. It does not exist. It is useful to technocrats, managers, and politicians because it collectivizes and depersonalizes a plural world of differing and resisting human beings, dissolving their rights to govern, forcing everyone to speak in terms of a statistical fairytale, defining politics away. While it is true in a small-town market that people trade openly and can see what they get for their money or for another object in barter, this is not what rules in mass society. It is no model for our lives. The Market is a vast, faceless, totalizing machinery whose workings remain invisible and unaccountable. It allows expert and secret rule, and more still, fiction to be gussied up as a science. In reality, the Market allows those with power and wealth to rig things and to never to be seen or caught doing so.

This is why ruling political castes the world over *adore* the Market model. They have "the Market" as a scientific explanation for all they do, as the thing they need to "unleash." Because when people get screwed, when inequality soars, when public support programs end, when precious places and spaces close, one by one, the political and economic caste can deny any responsibility. It's magic! They are only following, and respecting the laws of The Market. So and so must be cut back or shut down because The Market has shown it is inefficient and unworkable. Indeed, if something vanishes, it was meant to vanish, it was never legitimate. So and so must starve, or change their stripes, or say up is down, because the Market ordained it. This is a final solution to how to disenfranchise people without fingerprints, without anyone accountable, and without a way to fight back, except by focusing on the problem on its terms: capital and markets. How can one possibly envision a market that does not fall to this logic? The only way answer and response is through The Market, whose rules are wielded by the invisible hand.

IV Thinking in terms of a market is, in the end, a block to thinking politically. While the idea things work out by each person being self-interested and commercially oriented might appeal to those who lack poetry, history, and a capacity for thinking, while people might love a bottom-line calculus to make decisions and exchanges more easily, this is a utopian hope akin to dreams the working class is going to heaven, the revolution is coming automatically, or, in the end, that the moon is made of Swiss cheese. What exchange is possible when the Market defines it? How can the "we" in politics break free of this? What ordinary human being would want to have their life, their world, and their future determined by buying and selling, by cost and profit? This is nothing but a slave ideology.

The Market triumphant is not only the enemy of the people having power and the right and ability to exercise it, it is the enemy of culture itself. Rule by the market is a way to destroy any chance for grass-roots politics, communal spirit, an atmosphere of generosity, and the idea decisions, exchanges, choices, and certain made things need to be public, accountable, non-economic, and grounded in place and time, in neighborhoods, in communities, in spaces, in a body politic. It is a way to destroy the principle that people, politicians, and parties must be held to account, that what we create and assemble in a culture matters and must last, and most of all that the people as a body and individually have the right to govern, experience reality, exchange freely, and *hold reality and conditions to account*. What do the people demand? What enriches their lives and hopes? What truly protects them? What undergirds their full imagination and power? Do they even know how to ask, rather than have others tell them? Is there a space for the people to learn how to conduct lives as full and rich, differing people, as equals, to know what's up, to strengthen rights together rather than group by group, identity by identity, leaving everyone fighting each other?

Over and over, market arguments overrun public things,

reality, and every public good and commonality, every sense of our shared and non-conforming world. They render our common world, the world we share, impossible to grasp and govern by those that live in it. Free exchange, free offering, open sharing again and again fall under the sway of economics. The people are left to spin in a fictional, fairytale world that serves the ruling castes very well indeed.

If one examines things historically, the rise of the Market as a model is concurrent with the growth of political tyranny by political parties, technocrats, and managers. The original theoreticians of the hidden hand served the ruling political caste of Britain very well. This has expanded out now across the world, wielded in its purest form from the halls of power in the United States and Europe. More and more the media, having killed off free presses everywhere, play along, encouraging us to believe the notion the people have the right to govern and that markets screw things up is sheer reckless populism. But what was socialism concerned with? With granting power to workers, to those who create significance, and most of all, to protecting societies and people precisely from the dangers of any and all "invisible hands." Why are markets and capital dangerous? Because they are fictions, they always favor the ruling castes, and protect freedom only for them. They render our conditions invisible, blinding people and robbing them of a full and rich language and culture, art and literature able to describe what the people need to know and see to govern and exercise their rights.

In reality, what people offer each other must be non-economic. We are not the market. If trade is the ruling model, I offer you this in exchange for that. Exchange is one form of public life. But when it becomes economic, exchange ceases to be full and richly human and political. Exchange is reduced to calculations, to machinery, to technocracy, to spurious, anti-public, and unaccountable laws. I trade a piece of something for money or another thing mediated by money. When I exchange freely, I still must turn to matters of survival, labor, and leverage. I evaluate myself in terms of money, and how much I have or do not have. I am ever more bound in wrenching and false equivalences. No one, supposedly, is in charge. Can one imagine a market that does not use money to decide and define meaning? Can one imagine a system where exchange is governed by the people? Can one imagine an offer where there is no calculation, where calculation is defied and rejected, and where more power for all, not just the few, is the result? To imagine such a world of exchange seems utopian, except this is what people do when engaged in neighborhood politics, in friendship, in governing together face to face. They exchange freely for governing to be shared. People must face each other to negotiate demands and needs, discuss their world, and figure out what is real and how to find the best solutions to problems. Invisible hands have NO place. Under neoliberalism, The Market replaces government and governing. But this of course is only fiction. In reality, governing has been rendered invisible and unaccountable. It has been taken from those who must suffer it.

That we are not and can never be mere economic units is vital. Yet calculation has invaded everything. The market and neoliberalism were carefully designed precisely to make sure such understanding would become impossible, to force people to forget their political power, their uniqueness, their plurality, to reduce themselves to units and calculations, to shut out the non-calculable —in other words, to push to the side all that really matters in living. The imagination is destroyed when rule by fiction conquers it. The extraordinary profusion, for example, in the arts and culture, of small scale and diverse publishing, small independent spaces, works, and a sophisticated level of discourse, imagining, and critical thinking depends on non-calculating, non-economic reasoning. It depends on a space in which such exchange is free, supported, and can flourish.

V The people cannot govern their neighborhoods and their world through The Market. Only technocrats, managers, and politicians can. Non-economic reasoning is vital to public life, to meaning, to imagination, to thinking, and finally, to the most important things of all, exchange empowering understanding and action. The neoliberal market order would replace these with boorish reductionism, with competitions for limited funding, with uncertainty and precarity, with the destruction of the people's capacity for governing action. Under Market rule, mentally, we are stripped of our humanity and rights. Indeed, to participate in this fiction of The Market, we must *strip ourselves* of our humanity to fit in. Pressure from every direction grows, and what took decades and enormous effort to build up can be erased in a few short years or months. This is what every society that gives in to the invisible hand, the neoliberal world movement, faces.

One cannot develop inside a market except as a market thing. This is a shining, social logic built on ruin. If the market is total, there can be no politics, no people, no human difference, no capacity even to think. All local specifics and differences are neutralized. That this could be efficient and free is the greatest and most ridiculous fiction of all. It is efficient and free for the rulers, certainly, because there is no longer a fractious body politic to contest and answer every decision. Market fiction aims to destroy thinking, public life, the feeling in every realm that we are safe, that we must have each other to rely on, that things like poetry, history, thinking, rights, and free exchange matter. Every non-functional aspect is exterminated. The question of freedom is reduced to the lowest possible form, a form so degraded human beings are forced to see themselves as units, statistics, aggregates, and slaves, spinning in the nothingness of an absurd and ruinous measure.

Economics was labeled the dismal science for a reason. Sadly, our histories countering this have been methodically undone and forgotten. Endless and brutal battles for human dignity, political freedom, and rights have been silenced, replaced with technocracy, thoughtlessness, superficialization, and finally the thing the model leaves no room to grasp at all: implacable party rule, whether by one party, two parties, or many, and most of all, by their instrument, bureaucracy. The free market is no enemy of bureaucracy. It is its architect.

The big question now is, how did the ever shifting and growing Market fiction gain a foothold, and why do we permit it? How much ruin must be exacted before the people say, enough? It is as if we must begin from scratch. That is the consequence of a totalism more thorough than those that preceded it.

One way the people are saying enough is to organize locally for power, through municipalism, through federated people's councils, through efforts to create open, democratic, grassroots structures to govern conditions. The call for these, and for as yet unknown forms, to exercise transparent and honest governance, is growing. We are becoming alert to what neoliberal and market notions have long hidden: center-system parties rotten to the core, controlling and destroying political space, destroying what Hannah Arendt so beautifully called "the space of appearance." This is so because the hidden hand is merely a veiled fist.

In the realm of culture, the effort to see clearly is difficult, and double: how to expose and break through fictions that serve to remove our power, on the one hand, and on the other, to have structures we build to protect and nurture our political, cultural, and artistic freedom, what we make and do, what we say and sense, what we exchange freely, our free public life, our plural body seeking to govern and contribute to all our conditions. Who are we? How would we begin to ask such a fundamental question, living in a vast rubble field created by ever-changing and ruinous fictions? In the end, it is up to us to challenge this global tyranny, in every neighborhood, place, and space where we come together, with our neighbors, with strangers as well as friends, no matter how different we are, indeed, precisely *because* we are different, because we have so much to offer each other, because we *need* each other.

We need each other because we seek meaning, we seek to secure it and experience it, to create it and enjoy it. It is in our plurality that reality and what is *not* fictional reside. We are not slaves, we are not in a fictional world, we are not units, we never consented to the ludicrous invisible hand. It is this world, *our* world that now totters over an abyss, and the only choice left is to say no, sorry, we are human, we are people, we are the people, no means no, and we have the right to govern our conditions and not be ruled by spectres, ghosts, and little dictators. If the people wish to reclaim exchange for themselves, they must first shed every invisible hand, and see at last all hands must be on the table, and visible. Then, perhaps, and only then, if we were to say "We are the market!" everything would again be possible.

THE UTOPIA OF THE SHOPPING STREET

By Koen Haegens

More: In that case, my dear Raphael, for goodness' sake tell us some more about the island in question. Don't try to be too concise—give us a detailed account of it from every point of view, geographical, sociological, political, legal—in fact, tell us everything you think we'd like to know, which means everything we don't know already.

Raphael: There's nothing I'd enjoy more, for it's all quite fresh in my memory. But it'll take some time, you understand.

With those words from the beginning of the seminal text on utopianism, *Utopia*, Thomas More sets up the narrative in his classic work from 1516, in which he outlines the characteristics of an apparently ideal state—or more precisely, has the Portuguese world traveler Raphael Nonsenso recount them. In the course of his many wanderings, the latter has happened upon a curious island where everything is different than in Europe—and infinitely better. There in Utopia, as the island is called, the workday has been reduced to six hours, yet no man dies of hunger, and the impulsive capriciousness so prevalent in the European rulers of the day is entirely absent. If we are to believe the mysterious Raphael, then, Utopia offers a supremely intelligent political alternative for those willing to think logically and rationally.

It is 500 years later, and Utopia is no longer an island, nor if we are to believe the proponents of the free market, is it still even a "utopia" (from the Greek "*ou-topos*") in the literal sense of being "nowhere". Far from requiring years of wandering to reach, it can be accessed by a brisk stroll down to the city center, where amidst the shopping streets, neon signs, and vandal-proof street furniture, a *real* utopia awaits.

The greatest thing is perhaps that you need not be a world traveler on the order of, say, Raphael to see these wonders with your own eyes. Everyone can immerse themselves in this earthly paradise every day. The cultural pessimists, of course, view it all as nothing but blind mass consumption, greed whipped up by commercial deception. But why is it so busy there then? And why is it that this is where all those diverse population groups that artists, museums, and political activists are trying so desperately to reach—mostly without success—can be found?

Economists have pointed to various qualities that help make this place so attractive. For one thing, in the market utopia, every single person—correction, "consumer"—counts, whether they are black or white, man or woman, straight, L, G, B, T, or any other orientation. Even people without a passport can take part, as long as they possess the means to do so. This is not the case in government-controlled economies; dissidents and other undesirables can be excluded from the system, as the economist Milton Friedman pointed out in his book *Capitalism and Freedom* from the early sixties. But not in the market economy. "No one who buys bread knows whether the wheat from which it is made was grown by a Communist or a Republican, by a constitutionalist or a Fascist, or, for that matter, by a Negro or a white," he wrote.

Those limits to government intervention create space for pluralism and freedom. That means anyone who wants to can buy themselves a completely new identity. Friedman and his predecessor, Friedrich Hayek, took it a step further, however. In their view, even democracy itself was in better hands with the market than with traditional political institutions. If health care were to be fully privatized tomorrow, voters would have little more to say about it. According to liberal economic thinking, however, that loss in democratic participation is compensated by an incredible increase in influence through other avenues. Unlike the electorate who dutifully check off boxes on a ballot once every four years, critical consumers bring out their vote every single day—with their feet. They exercise their power by signing up for a particular health insurance policy (or purchasing any other product or service)—or not. That direct form of participation represents a gratifying contrast to the developments undergone by traditional democracies. It is increasingly the case that all real decisions—about cutbacks, the future of the social welfare state, incomes policy, etc.—are made by grey-haired technocrats working for institutions that prefer to keep citizens at a distance. An example of this is the immense increase in power acquired by the unelected European Central Bank in Frankfurt. This is exactly what the term "post-democracy" was coined to describe, and it is something other than a dictatorship. A post-democracy still scrupulously holds elections, including discussions about such topics as whether students should be required to sing the national anthem at school, because that generates a lot of votes.

As opposed to that, the market utopia would appear to embody a superior form of democracy. "When you enter the voting booth once a year, you almost always vote for a package rather than for specific items... When you vote daily in the supermarket, you get precisely what you voted for and so does everyone else," Friedman wrote in his bestseller *Free to Choose*. The economist Paul Samuelson, who would hardly be considered a market fundamentalist like Friedman and Hayek, appropriately calls these "dollar votes". We, as consumers, use them to dictate what needs to be produced and "not every 2 or 4 years at the polls, but in [our] daily purchase decisions."

In a variation on the deeply cherished political desire for a so-called participation society in which proactive citizens voluntarily take over duties from a cost-cutting government, this might be called the "participation economy." And its beating heart will be found not in the halls of power of the nation's capital but in the shopping streets of cities and larger towns around the world. In other words, a utopia, but one that really exists. Right?

"The Utopian way of life provides not only the happiest basis for a civilized community, but also one which, in all human probability, will last for ever. They've eliminated the root-causes of ambition, political conflict, and everything like that. There's therefore no danger of internal dissension, the one thing that has destroyed so many impregnable towns."

Thus Raphael concludes his report of his stay in Utopia, with an enthusiasm bordering on propaganda. But upon closer inspection, something in his ebullient final words rings false. Is there truly no longer any internal strife in Utopia? No political conflict? That sounds too easy, too seamless – as if the "end of history" envisaged by Francis Fukuyama had already come to pass in the sixteenth century.

It would seem Utopia is not always as wonderful as Raphael would lead us to believe. The government (i.e., a collection of old men) intrudes profoundly into the populace's daily life, frighteningly so. If it gets too crowded, for example, then a group of subjects will simply be told to leave the island; they must establish a colony somewhere else. Moreover, it turns out that the estimable six-hour workday is made possible, in part, by slavery. Their enlightened attitude toward crime—by late-medieval standards—also has its bounds. Criminals who refuse to better their lives, according to the travelogue, are "just slaughtered like wild beasts."

Small wonder that the philosopher Hans Achterhuis once renounced the text as dangerous, even totalitarian. Yet it is equally possible, as the sociologist Merijn Oudenampsen has noted, that More was deliberately sowing seeds of doubt. Toward the end of the book, reflecting on the interesting views just propounded by Raphael, the author concedes, "I cannot agree with everything that he said, for all his undoubted learning and experience". And in his epistolary introductory letter to the book, More ridicules the lack of humor amongst the majority of readers in his time: "Some are so literal-minded that the slightest hint of irony affects them as water affects a sufferer from hydrophobia."

The utopia of the shopping street chafes in a similar manner. You might call it the iron law of the ideal society. As soon as a social system appears too good to be true, with no signs of conflict nor someone exercising power, you know some form of hidden manipulation is at work. In More's Utopia, that manipulation is exercised by the state. In the shopping street, it is the so-called market that is infinitely more controlling than all the lovely theories on laissez-faire might imply. Is it the ultimate democracy? At best, it could be called a failed democracy. In terms of acting as a permanent ballot box, through which consumers express their every preference and desire, the market certainly conveys the appearance of a "pure", direct democracy. Anyone can participate, as long as they pay. But therein lies the critical catch: the rich possess exponentially more influence than your average Joe. The ruling principle, after all, is "one dollar, one vote." It is a modern spin on selective suffrage.

And there are other concerns worth noting. Anyone who looks closely will notice that just about everything that transpires in our city centers is less spontaneous, neutral, and apolitical than we might be inclined to think. A set of very specific rules apply. Not only do these create an unfair distribution of influence, in terms of exercising Samuelson's dollar votes, but they circumscribe the topics up for decision.

What passes for "the market" saddles us with thousands of decisions, from which health insurer to choose to the color of your toothbrush. These small decisions of the shopping street consume vast amounts of our time. Yet when it comes to the most important decisions in life—how do I want to live, where is the country headed, how can we save the world – silence reigns. Political protests on city streets have been on the decline in recent decades. In terms of commerce, the emphasis continues to be on such things as what colour shoes you want. And that makes for a very sorry vision of humanity.

Despite all the promises of freedom, pluralism, and authenticity, the city center of the 21st century curtails the possibilities for the public. The logic of the shopping street forces us to assume one role and one

role only: that of a calculating consumer. But that is only half a life—actually, a fraction of one.
Try the following thought experiment. Take an average day in your life. What roles do you fulfill in the course of it? At breakfast in the morning, we do not lay out the table for our partner, children, or other roommates because we expect something in return, nor because we hope to thus favorably influence their work or school performance and potential future earnings, as some economists might suggest. At home, we behave in some sense as communists, as the American anthropologist David Graeber has provocatively suggested: each giving according to their abilities and receiving according to their needs.

Then, perhaps we go to work. There, too, the market thinking is much less predominant than you might think. Companies are sometimes called "mini planned economies" for good reason. Some run on cooperation, teams, and creativity; others by virtue of bureaucratic processes and hierarchy. But in no instance are they peopled with automated individuals who view everything as a transaction to be negotiated; any such company would quickly go bankrupt.

In the evening, at home or in the city, we cease to be an employee or co-worker and adopt other roles. At the bar, maybe you are a friend; in the theatre, an enraptured spectator; or back at home, that garden-variety communist. Personally, on many such days, my direct interaction with the market is limited to maybe fifteen minutes in the supermarket and a couple of episodes at work. In any event, those are not the times that stick with me.

What does all this have to do with the city center? A true utopia might look like this: a place where people go to engage in all those various roles - not only as a shopping consumer, but also as a social animal, a person seeking beauty and knowledge, or a politically engaged citizen. We are a long way from that, of course, but there is hope. The manipulation in our city centers is so embedded, with so many millions spent on TV and radio advertising, not to mention billboards and shop windows, all to imprint us, that we have become calculating, utility-maximizing individuals. Is it not a wonder, then, that we obstinate, many-headed beings still choose on occasion to sit and chat for hours on a bench? Or that we might decide on a whim to go look at beautiful things, go against the flow, or just stroll around—without consuming a thing?

MISCELLANEOUS

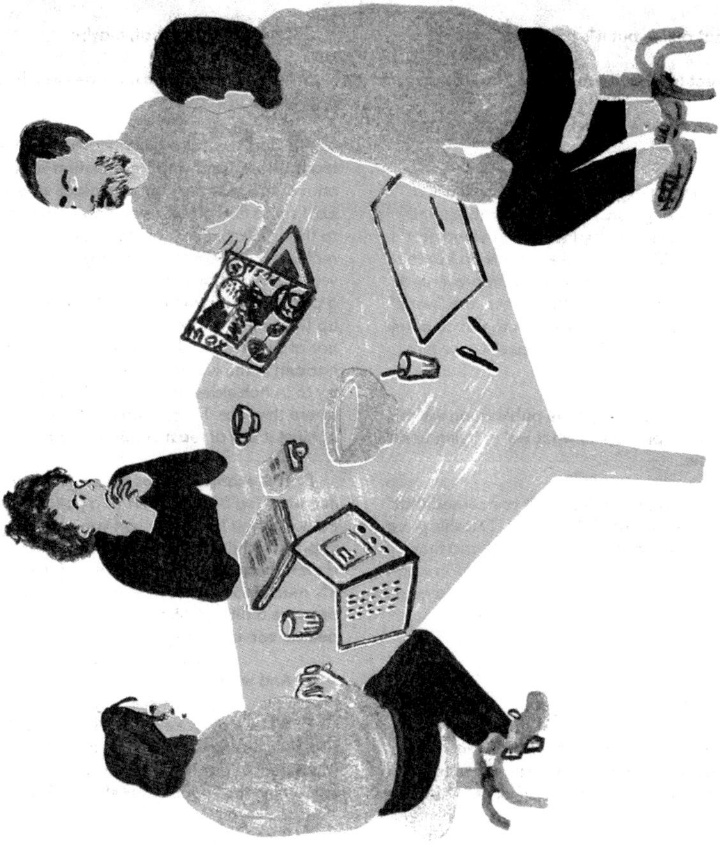

A: I'm not sure if this is what we want but if we would reach a consensus that we want a "weak" criticality, something that is very difficult or weak opposed to a strong, in the face, aggressive critique – if we say.

B: What is criticality within your collective? To me, it seems like if you have a meeting place and an honest conversation, all cards on the table, it's one-on-one, it's face-to-face, you know. If you go face-to-face it becomes more urgent for you because you also put your cards on the table. It's a bit like social therapy, in a sense, right?

C: To me, this project was all an online thing. What you said about the table that we're having now, this idea is not present there.

B: You can also add that offline but it's not face-to-face.

C: The idea of the project has been evolving, it's been changing.

D: It's quite a long time that we've been speaking about this project, one year almost.

A: Right now, we're switch from digital to physical, which is a necessary thing for us in order to go on. Maybe this is the point where it creates a doubling. We don't need to decide whether it's one thing or another. It's very difficult to make a decision like this. Maybe we should rather decide which elements are represented digitally and which take place physically. In that sense, the "weak" idea – yesterday I wrote something which I keep in the back of my mind - we all agree that this idea of a "weak critique" is our aim. Then we maybe keep things a bit more open.

C: Isn't this interesting for issue no. 2 of the publication we're making tomorrow? To show the process of what we're trying to do? Instead of just having a topic.

A: This is what we're trying to do. I'm just a bit concerned that it would become a totally self-referential thing. Like "Ok, this group of people met and they're talking about being critical and they were critical about being critical." Then it becomes this loop where you're reading this thing and you think "these people should go out a bit more."

B: If criticality doesn't have the capacity to reach out further, you know, if we can't find a proper platform, it has to become this viral thing that goes via all of us, that we carry out ourselves, that we take responsibility about ourselves and share that in the conversations we have, you know. Cultural change in that sense will come through one-on-one contact. I think that's an interesting idea, too, that the communal would make a change, right? It would work bottom-up and without any instrumentalisation. That would be true empowerment of people. It's emancipated. It's totally individual. We're sitting here all the time as individuals. The only thing we share is that we're interested in expanding our horizons and see what we can do within the social environment we are part of. Then collaborative practice works with a lot of different nodes. That's much more viable, I think. So, the only thing we can count on is that we have a bunch of nice people together, willing to do something. Then the tone will also become less pretentious and much more open. It becomes an economy of trust, you know. So if we all follow up to people who suck up to other people part of the Design or Art community and their capitalist logics then things are not going to change. That's something that you need to turn your backs towards. You need to create this other environment where you want to create a different truthfulness. That's really important. It's also about how behaviour is conditioned by logics that you want to oppose and about how to make that real.

D: It's also nice besides involving people at this stage that we're testing out how these dynamics work. We can be critical with very simple language, as well. We've been spending all day looking at misused words. It's about reconstructing critique in very simple terms. That already is democratising.

A: From this conversation we could have a political line to follow. We already know we want to be quick, open, simple, down-to-earth.

D: And independent.

A: Right now I really feel the need to find a certain hook to reality and try and connect a certain text from the publication to reality, applying it to a certain context. It would give each of us a hook to reality, something to identify with.

B: It's parallel narratives in a similar universe.

A: Something like that, maybe.

B: Parallel narratives as nodes which might intersect, things you might have in common.

A: I don't want to be critical just for the sake of it. I want to really understand what my position is. For example, I want to be critical towards the common place of being opposed to politicians. So, I try to find a text as an entry point into this topic. Then I try to think "Okay, I'm a politician who studied political sciences. I realised that I can't just do any shitty job and I ended up being very excited about certain political views and I ended up joining a party. I got instrumentalised and went up the ladder and ended up thinking that I'm doing good for the people when actually I'm not at all." This could be a way for me to understand how things happen in the world even if that's not how things actually happen. I try to switch sides and tell myself a story about how people arrived where they are. Then, I can accept that this exists. I can still be against it but at least I understand how it came to be.

B: This example shows the structure of sucking up to hierarchy, in a way. You become part of a political party and help people out with their interests, then you get votes. But that's not about improving the choice people can vote for. Of course you could sketch that as scenarios but that's a negative scenario. I think, it's much more interesting to start speculating about how you can propose a different kind of organisation. How this can go viral. How people can become part of this.

D: And what space there is within a reality.

B: What's at stake is a kind of social ability about getting together, sitting together. You are offering people a seat next to you. Most people don't. That's already generous and interesting. This is something that people feel strong about.

D: It can also be nice to just go to people and ask for opinions. Nobody actually wants to know the opinion of anybody else. It's more like "listen to my opinion and shut up."

B: How can you create a social reality if you never sit together? What's the worth of collectivity if you're never sitting together?

D: This is also why we're here, talking about this.

A: It's like what you were proposing to sketch out alternative models of our ideas of the project. This, we need to do. For me, this goes hand-in-hand with sketching out the status-quo, the context. If I don't understand why designers do the things the way they do I can't imagine an alternative.

B: Dynamics is good. I think you should just now DO stuff. If you just have the name, Radical Criticality, everything that happens under that umbrella is valid. If you always debate on how you should do it nothing is going to work. Just DO stuff!

"There are never perfect conditions for an act— every act by definition comes too early. But one has to begin somewhere, with a particular intervention; one just has to bear in mind the further complications that such an act will lead to"
Slavoj Žižek

Trying to wrap back the past days of Radical Criticality workshops in order to understand if this collective and very fluid effort could already get to some conclusion, I asked around if anybody felt like we were retracing a much-dreaded communication model: bar talk. Quick conversations, anecdotes, broad themes and very general questions all seemed to suggest such a direction, at first sight. And bar talk with its highly charged points of view and heated discussions is usually not valued as a perfect 'critical' model. Probably we could grant it to have a 'radical' attitude but it would perhaps be more fair to call it "radicalised", which definitely guarantees a shift in meaning.

Despite the very informal attitude and 'open-end' approach the project has taken, despite the 'bar-talk danger' surely on sight, Radical Criticality did manage to maintain a very distinct position. Slowly, from steadily taking unconscious choices, a defined idea emerged. If a lot of communication - including critical and theoretical - acts from an aggressive, strong position attacking the reader with propositions and structured critique we are opting for what we called "weak critique" and "weak criticality". Here, non-structured conversation, simple language and high aims protect content and discussion from jargon issues, context-dependence and dominant influences.

Giving space to "the common" — 'Common' often stands for shared heritage or political choices — here plainly means giving space to the common man. This became a choice and a strength of Radical Criticality. If a common space is created, free from an often misused jargon, promoting face-to face interaction even if on "different sides of the fence" (see Everyday Criticality, Issue No.1), striving to be far from influences, trends or soft-power tendencies of the design community, then, a new space as pleasant as a bar is defined while discussing 'the truths' (even when they're openly bullshit). One would think that an assemblage of an exhibition such as DDW should bring such 'truths' to the table.

In the end, you are happy to be handing out a publication to an interested guy asking him what he's looking for in Eindhoven and to be confronted with the answer: "hashish".

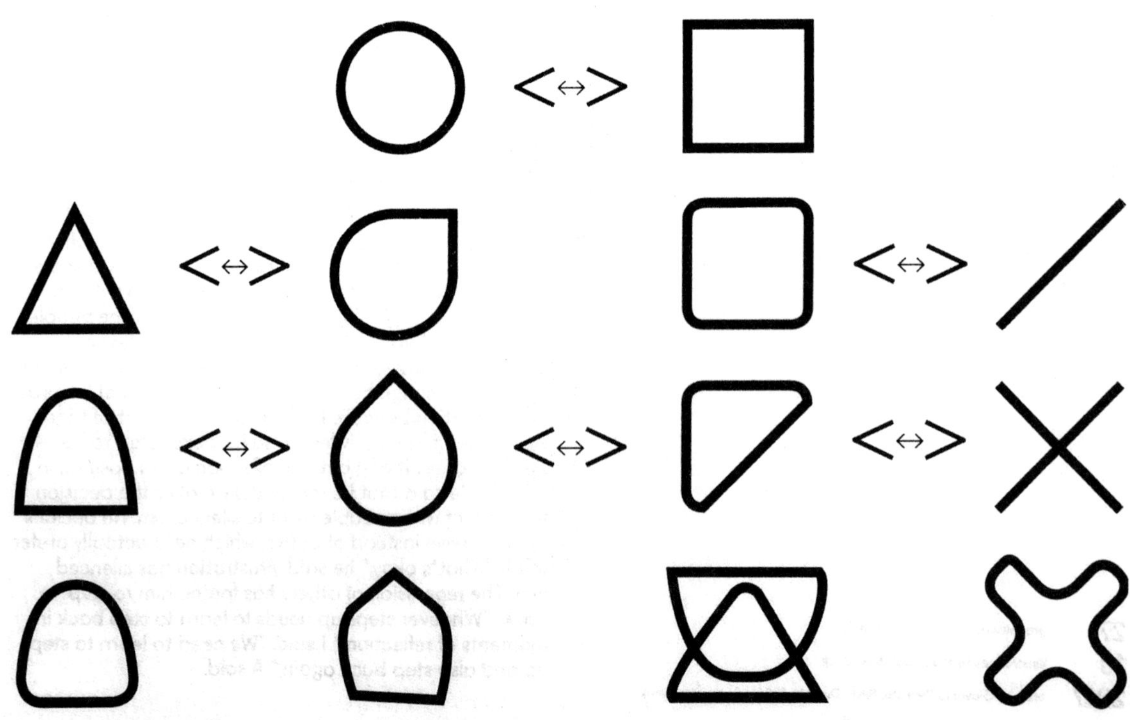

Everyday CRITICALITY

www.radicalcriticality.net

WHAT DO YOU DO WHEN IT RAINS?

Inactivity has become a taboo, something forbidden. To please others' expectations of doing, whatever they may be, as individuals we constantly need to reinterpret our own identity and desires, hiding our real nature. This leads to an irreversible distance from our feelings and to dangerous behavioural phenomena: the new 'sudden sleep' – people out of energy that suddenly collapse to the ground, getting usually hurt, and sleep – and the increase of emergency recovery from food overdoses and workaholic syndromes. Bodies are changing shape since running is a common activity when no other ideas come about. This 'normal' comfortable couch wants to foster inactivity and trigger the imagination of whoever is not able to do nothing, constantly in need of doing something.

Digital technology has been powerfully present in our lives for so long now that being active and improving everyday life away from technology has become an extremist's attitude. Eating food with the shape of digital devices is a way to transform the symbol of the future into a present need. Through eating a chocolate smartphone we can understand that usual digital devices don't provide physical energy and they don't have any taste.

← This text mirrors project descriptions distributed by designers as part of their presentations during Dutch Design Week 2017. It contains unmarked direct quotations and inconsequent reproductions of grammar and syntax.

27
10
2017

graphics by Amelie Lisa Derveloy
illustrations by Priscilla Suàrez Bock
texts by Giovanni Pezzato, Silvia Dini Modigliani, Jeannette Petrik

A fictionalised recollection of an encounter with A and B

"Action" means "acting" means "doing things". Talking to strangers is "doing things".

I met A by chance. We talked about our project, the collaboration with Onomatopee and things we've started thinking about. We sat down on the sofa upstairs. The video of "Achievement #2" (also part of Onomatopee's "We Are the Market" project) was playing. The video started, slowly and A and I waited for the titles to change and the action to be shown. When waiting, I had the urge to ask A about her opinion on the introductory paragraph to DDW's map. It reads "The world is manufacturable. The future is stretchable. Designers have revolutionary ideas and innovative solutions for the future. DDW presents mind expanders, horizon extenders and boundary pushers. Warm-ups and stretch exercises for people who want to stay agile. Move with the times and stay supple. It all starts at DDW: do the #stretch."

Me: What do you think about these lines? What's this supposed to mean? I really don't understand. "Stretchable" what a terrible word, no?

A: [Reads the paragraph. Shrugs, laughs, then puts on a thoughtful facial expression.] Well, I think this is what "Stretch" means. [Turns the map around and points at the illustration on the cover. A rendered three-dimensional blob of tactile patterns.] "Stretching" means to take something which is actually nothing too special - [points at the random looking cover graphic] - and blowing it up, making it look as if it was something big and important.

Me: Bloated.

A: Yes, bloated. This is what "Stretching" means in Design. You magnify something mundane and make it appear like something exciting and spectacular. That's exactly what Design shouldn't do, in my opinion – stretch.

Later I met A again at the entrance of the space. B was sitting at the front desk, I was sitting at the desk opposite, writing. B and A started speaking in Dutch. A switched to English. We got into a conversation. B spoke about the issue of being a white, male person with an assumed social privilege and the repulsion some people experience when he gets into expressing his desire to engage in inclusive social interactions. He said sometimes he feels as though he's not entitled to be critical towards discrimination because he's perceived as part of those who cause it. He's privileged, so he's expected to be silent as a result of a critical reflection of his position in society. He said that he respectfully makes the decision to be silent when people want to silence him. He decides to be passive instead of active, which he'd actually prefer to be. "That's okay," he said. Frustration has silenced him. The repression of others has forced him to step back. "Whoever steps up needs to learn to step back in moments of reflection," I said. "We need to learn to step up and also step back again," A said.

Issue n° 1 — COLLECTIVITY 23 Oct 2017

COLLECTIVE AUTONOMY: AN OXYMORON?

Collectivity cannot be autonomous, or can it? From a perspective of Western thought, autonomy is associated with individualism, locking yourself out from the rest of the world. But that's not how it has to be. From the Greek αὐτονομία (autonomía), autonomy literally means "self government" (autós, "self" nómos, "law"). Chilean biologists Humberto Maturana and Francisco Varela coined the word autopoiesis (autós, "self" poiesis, "creation / production") to refer to the ability of systems to create and regenerate themselves. Systems (both biological and social) need to develop a logic through which they will function, a logic based on which they will also connect with other systems. Think of a local indigenous community in the Colombian Amazon able to define the rules for the functioning of their community, the boundaries of their territory, the roles of its members, etc. Once this is defined, they can establish relations with other systems (other community, mother earth, local or national government, etc.) through what Maturana and Varela call "structural coupling". The struggle of such community is a struggle for autonomy, understood as a collective effort by and for the community. Only by understanding autonomy from a collective perspective (as opposed to an individual one) can we strengthen our communities and the relations between them. Then, we can really say, "Apply autonomy."

DAY 1 - COLLECTIVE REFLECTIONS - INDECISION-MAKING

The culture of western societies is drifting towards interactions based on visual proximity and physical distance. I use the verb "drifting" since I don't consider it to be a conscious decision: it's hard to imagine that a "general intellect" could exist in our society to be able to take the decision to stir the direction of a "ship of fools" toward a more intermediated culture.

It's easy though to think that a society with further separation within groups and communities becomes more and more manageable, this is one of the most basic principles of power, definitely nothing new to social critique; nevertheless, yesterday in Clausplein this concept became self-evident and with a concrete spatial manifestation in the moment in which sitting on two sides of a wall we realized we could look at each other in the face looking through a reflection of two mirrors. Sitting on the benches in the public square we couldn't see each other, in fact, the backrest was working as a division; through an instinctual intervention, we subverted this perception managing to create an assembly across a clear urban interruption. As a first physical encounter of the working group, we started to reflect on how this simple intervention and singular design was affecting our collectivity and language, involving passersby, that little-by-little started to gather at the extremes of the benches.

The discussion pivoted around collectivity, as a condition, as self-reflection, as an aim. Slowly everyone who was sitting on the bench became more and more comfortable with its position, learning to use the mirrors both as shelter from the square and as observation points to control the surroundings. The benches became a living room in which participants were agreeing on the difficulty of participative processes to get to a decisive moment.

These moments are necessary even though clearly dysfunctional; however assemblies don't necessarily aim for decision-making, decisions are nevertheless taken, whether consensually or not. This consideration about the time frame of collective processes and necessary pragmatism is a daily issue when working on a publication and we are the beginning of path where a lot of decisions need to be taken. Do we position ourselves within or at the borders of the design scene? do we use design to critique or we critique existing designs? do we situate ourselves in the ongoing discussion topics or we reframe the discussion toward our experience? These are open questions that allow us to unpack the issues we are discussing, but only through the topic of the next day, "action", can we will effectively understand how we move forward in our trajectory.

EVERYDAY CRITICALITY

RADICAL CRITICALITY

Exploring the themes of 'Collectivity' on 23 Oct, 'Action' on 25 Oct and 'Critique' on 27 Oct, the critical analysis and discussion of contemporary issues during the events will feed into the production of three publications to be distributed on 24, 26 and 28 Oct.

Each event will be followed up by a collective dinner offered on donation for workshop participants. 'Madame Jeannette', a vegan food truck from Enschede, will prepare a delicious meal which forms part of the workshop experience.

Participation to the workshops is open to all and free of charge.
The communal dinner is limited to 20 participants.
Please send an email to everydaycriticality@gmail.com to register your participation.
Besides, you can always drop-in!

At the root of 'Radical Criticality' stands a thoroughly analytical and critical attitude which it aims to explore together with a diverse group of participants. Dialogue, discussion and critique stand at the heart of the project while examining how collectivity can evolve in multi-facetted structures of trans-disciplinary and socio-cultural diversity.

'Radical Criticality' is the initiative of seven young creative practitioners who contextualise 'Design' as the production of Everyday Politics. With 'Everyday Criticality' the initiative introduces itself and its methodology. As the project is set to evolve as a diverse platform for dialogical critique, this intervention within the framework of the Onomatopee 142 project 'WE ARE THE MARKET!' will provide an experimental ground for the further development of the project through Onomatopee. 'Everyday Criticality' will offer concentration and focus and intervene by offering performative collectivity.

EXCERPTS OF A TRANSCRIPTION

A: I don't really care about elections because I don't feel like I'm part of the society that's voting.

B: Participation is not total. It's never fair. Some people are not participating just because they don't trust the system or they don't believe in the structure that's holding the system.

C: What do you do then? In Sicily there are regional elections and there will probably be the lowest turnout in elections ever. What do you do then?

B: You get divided. But that's also a statement.

A: But for whom?

A: How does it feel to be in the minority?

C: I don't think where I am now is better than where I grew up. I think that I can stand people better now. If I was now where I grew up there would be people that I just wouldn't talk to. It's like 'I know your kind and I don't want to talk to you.' Then I don't listen what they have to say. While, since I'm in a different environment, I allow much more people to be listened to. I also like that somehow I can also talk to somebody who, I don't know, a fucking politician, mafia guy. I'm still going to listen to what they have to say. Whereas, I might otherwise just say "Fuck it." That's fine. I don't think that they're stupid and I'm smart. It's like I need a safe distance to where I was born.

B: It's also different to grow up in a place and to arrive in a place when you've already grown up. You connect to people. You decide who you sit next to. When you grow up in a place together with a bunch of kids, along with growing up people make decisions, get possessions and then suddenly a person who you've felt fond towards you don't connect with anymore in terms of ideas of visions. When you arrive in a new place you start from the surface and get deep with some people.

C: I chose it like that, yes.

A: I've had the same experience as you decribed. Actually with performance art or conversations with strangers I've often needed more time to process what I've experienced. When you're in the moment I might not have thought that something actually did something to me but after some time I realised that actually it has influenced me.

D: That's particularly interesting if you are in charge of a process. If you want to include a dialogical process in what you do, you have to be ready to change your mind.

E: Speaking about the example of the room with ten fascists. You have several choices. One is to just speak out and say "Well, I don't agree, blablabla, blablabla" or you can just shut up. Or you can push them a bit, I mean not physically, you can challenge them by pushing them to extremes with their own conviction. If it's a racist thing, just push the topic so it explodes. At some point you must realise that what you're saying is stupid or too much.

F: This could also encourage them to go further from their fascist views.

A: Is this not just exposing them? I wonder if exposure helps them to reflect on themselves.

E: I don't know. I don't think that they're changing their minds, especially if they're ten, because…

C: I think especially if they're ten you're going to see a gradient in positions.

F: You could do this strategically. Find out who the most extreme are and who is the most likely to change positions. You can look for alliances. It becomes a strategic action.

E: You start by thinking you're the only one in the minority but you end up being the only one in control. You end up monopolising the conversation.

F: I think it's about understanding other positions and also standing in-between positions. It's not black-and-white.

D: I sometimes say something in a discussion which I don't believe only to move the point in a direction. In a moment it might be necessary to be extreme.

C: To see how people will react.

F: It's an interesting discussion to speak about convincing. We take it as very dualist. Sometimes, I don't try to convince people that my position is right but to rather convince someone that my position is as right as theirs. It's about the existence of a multitude of valid positions. This comes more from Non-European thinking which is non-dualist and accepts different truths. This dynamic is going more towards opening up possibilities instead of closing them. It's about accepting that there are different truths.

A: What if you have a group of people that need to make certain decisions, not acting is also a decision. I generally agree that there can be lots of different opinions in parallel and they can do well existing simultaneously. But when it comes to immigration policies, taxes or other questions which are answered for a large group of people by a few. What do you do? And what do you accept that others do?

graphics by Giovanni Pezzato; illustrations by Priscilla Suárez Bock;
texts by Zeno Franchini, Pablo Calderón Salazar, Jeannette Petrik.

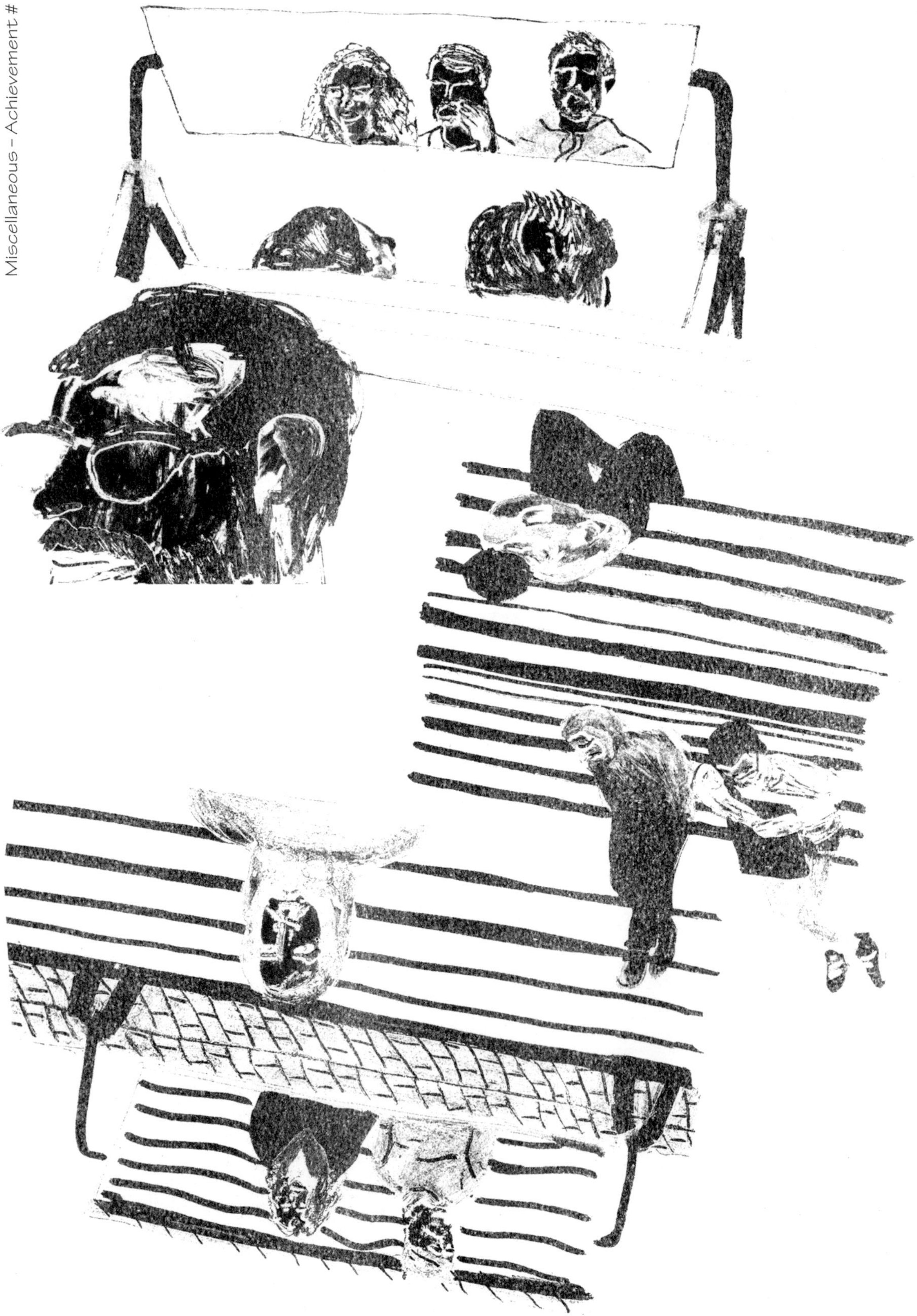

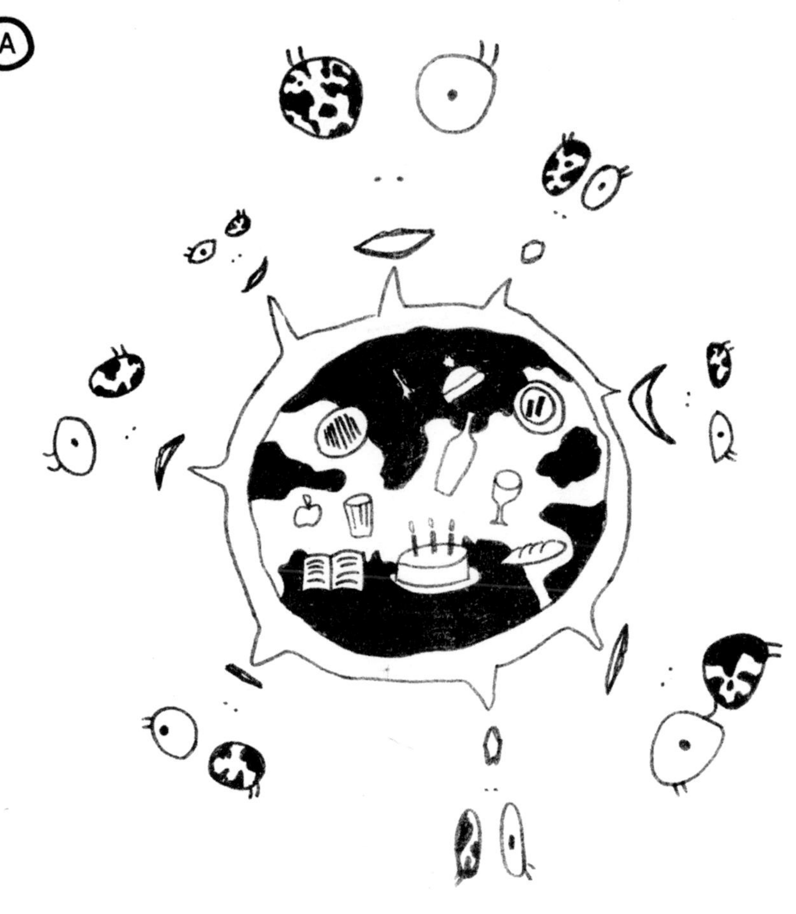

G came to join us. We had a good talk and she explained that in her perception the word "criticality" is connected to judgemental, opinionated attitudes. We elaborated that the process of developing a critical attitude is connected to self-confidence. G made a drawing for us. She took her time to think about how she was going to shape it and took about fifteen minutes to produce two sketches. We asked her to elaborate a bit on her choices. She took her first drawing and explained that criticality works as a tree. One's roots are embedded in a context and feed the organism with beliefs and meaning. The fruits are experiences and encounters which shape an individual. The leafs are opinions and thoughts one reflects and shares while the branches producing the leaves continuously form anew and add to the size and strength of the tree. Her second drawing shows an abstraction of the first. She added the element of rain as a source of nurturing randomness.

It started to rain so we dispersed.

A and I entered the space of Onomatopee and sat down at the big table upstairs. We've started talking about our thoughts on where our own criticality comes from but have not had time to make a drawing ourselves. A focussed and spent about twenty minutes drawing. I started working on the laptop, took a break and made a drawing, which I suddenly felt to have messed up because a stroke felt out-of-line. I overlaid my first drawing with another sheet of paper and copied it. I didn't mess up the same line again and continued sketching. Within a minute or two, I was done.

I sent an e-mail to the others of Radical Criticality and asked for their contribution. H sent us a diagram.

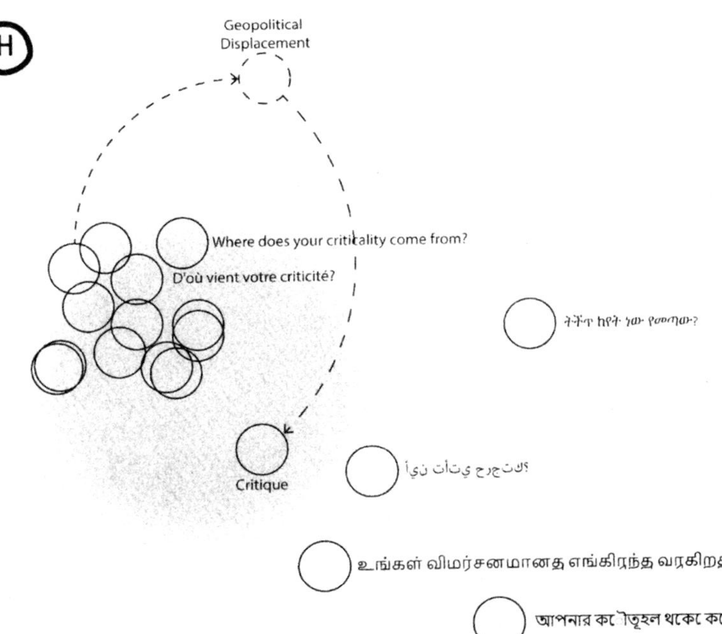

A and I went to pick up dinner which J had lovingly prepared for us. We returned to Onomatopee and had a sociable evening, continuing conversations we had had during the day and entering new conversations with curiosity.

Everyday CRITICALITY Issue N°3

28 Oct 2017

www.radicalcriticality.net

graphics by Silvia Dini Modigliani; texts by Jeannette Petrik; thoughts and drawings by Zeno Franchini and gathered in interaction with passers-by.

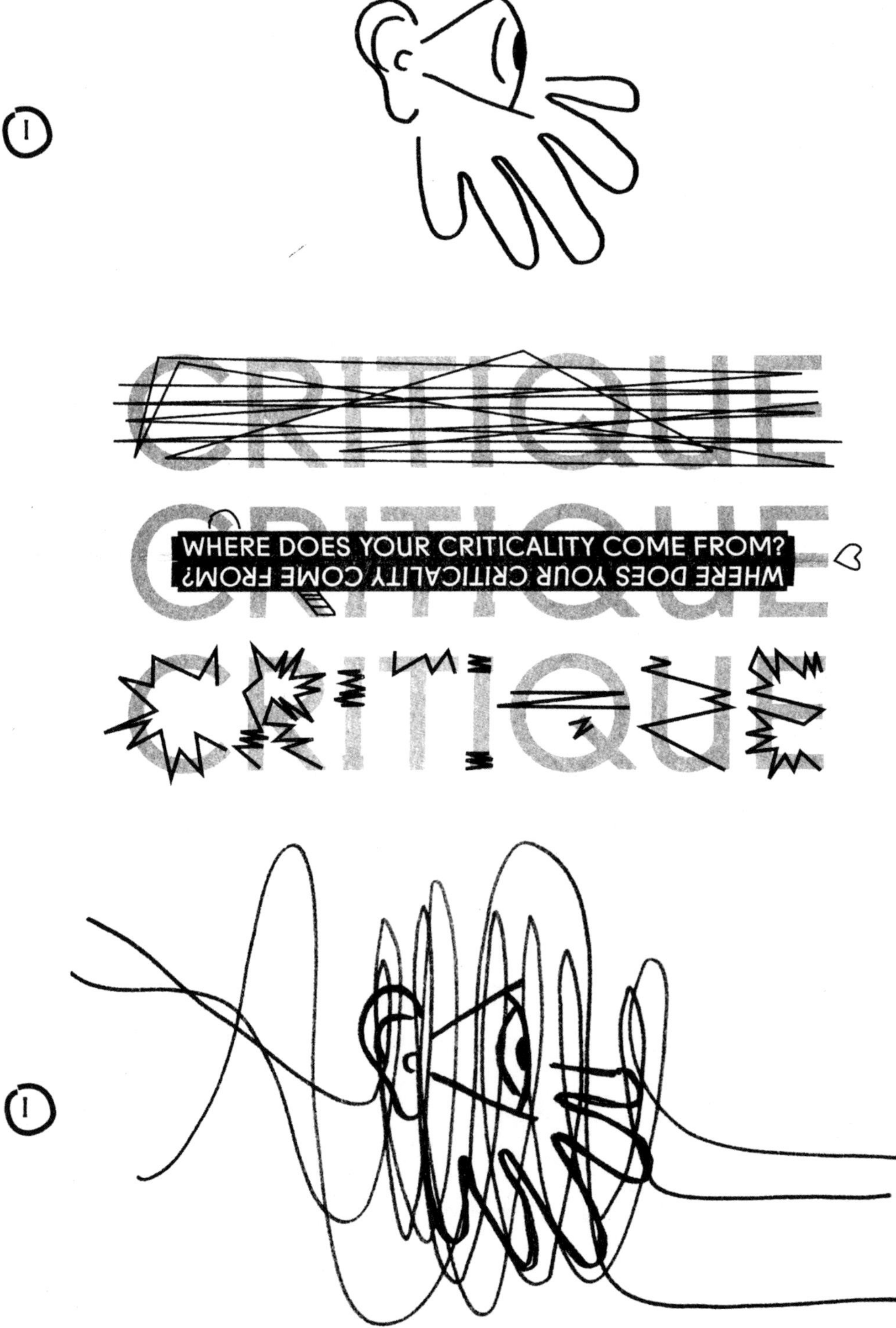

(B)

No inter-net first

MOM: worker – DAD: worker
-Drugs -Drugs
-School -Politics
-School

ME: Learner + thinker

Internet + friends

- Experiments with drugs
- No politics
- School ✓

(C)

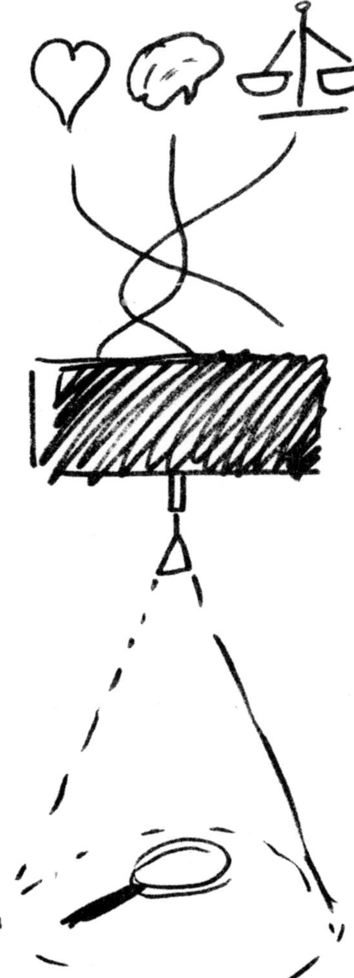

Day 5 of the intervention. After "Collectivity" came "Action" comes "Critique."

"Do you consider yourself as critical?"

"If so, where does your criticality come from?"

A and I entered Clausplein with two of our funky mirrors which allowed those who looked into one of the two opposing mirrors to see the other sitting behind with a slightly skewed vision. Having just finished to install the pieces, approached us and asked what we were exhibiting. We explained that we were not actually exhibiting anything but were rather doing something like performative research. We got into a conversation - first about his ambition to start a cab company and be his own boss and later about the perceived origin of our individual critical attitudes. Upbringing, higher education, repressive work environments, contrasting experiences in different places. We asked (B) to draw where his criticality came from. He spent about twenty minutes and produced something like a diagram.

C and D joined passed by and joined the conversation. Church, parents, friends, family, disagreement, exclusion, repression, sensitivity. (C) made a drawing for us. They left.

E passed by and explained that he liked the challenge to reflect on one's own critical attitude and where it came from. He had to leave, so we couldn't go into the topic in more detail.

B left to pick up his girlfriend and A and I sat down on the bench, back-to-back, looking at each other in the mirror. We reflected on the conversation we had just had.

B returned with F. We had a chat about the Design Academy and the master of Information Design. We shortly touched on F's critique on the lack of freedom in the working environment of an advertising agency and she expressed her desire to grow and become more independent in thought and action. B and F left to have lunch together.

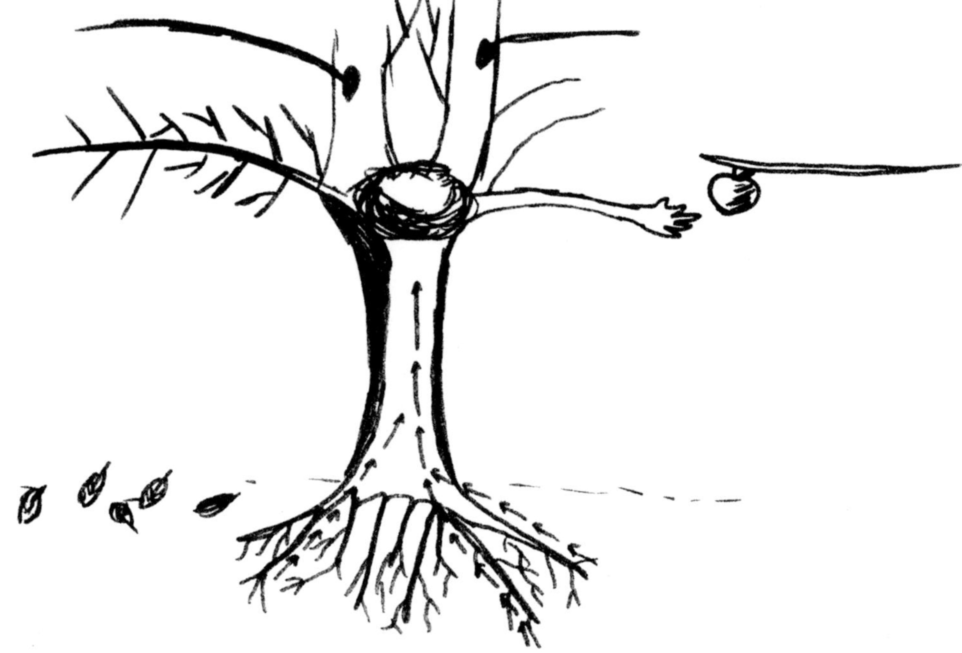

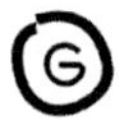

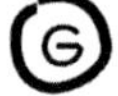

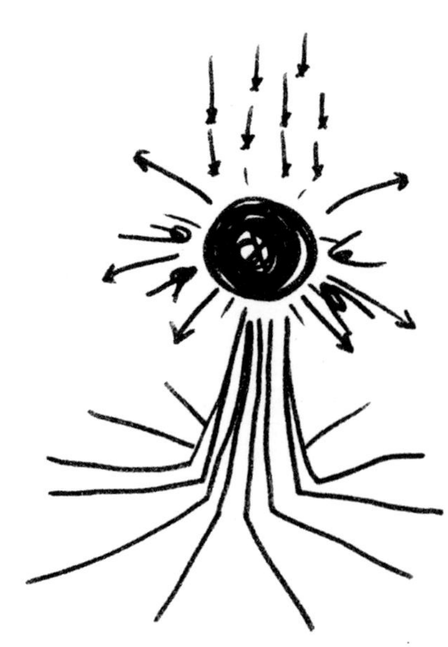

What is the 5% Universe?

To understand what the 5% universe is and how this phrase is used in revolution, we'll have to take a short journey into the cosmos—into dark matter and dark energy.

Dark matter and dark energy are unknown substances and forces that we cannot see or observe using any of the instruments we currently have. We only know it exists because of its effects on celestial bodies and the universe we can see. Together these unknowable and unobservable substances and forces make up 95% of the universe![1] That means we exist in a cosmos where we are capable of perceiving only 5% of it. Built into our consciousness, our way of processing information, is an inherent *inability* to see and interact with 95% of all that is!

Cognitive scientist Donald Hoffman claims that our brains perceive a fraction of reality to keep us alive. Evolution isn't about seeing reality as it is, it's about survival and the survival of a species is dependent on procreation. Hoffman has proven through numerous simulations that if we were to see ALL of reality, we would expend too much energy, lose sight of this Prime Directive, and die.

Hoffman likens our 5% reality to a computer desktop interface. When you click on an icon to open an application, the application itself is not that icon. The icon is a stand in for a complex application, an entire universe, hidden until we click on the icon. Similarly, the physical objects that we see in our world, including ourselves, are stand-ins, icons that obscure a much more complicated reality because it's more *useful* to conceal 95% of it. But useful for what and for whom, exactly?

If you think about human interactions, most people aren't having relationships with each other. Rather, it's our beliefs that are having relationships with one another. My belief of myself and my belief of you are having a relationship with your belief of yourself and your belief of me. Humans are essentially hosts to parasitic belief entities that have taken up residence in our minds and utilize our bodies to actualize themselves in this reality. In a similar sense as Hoffman's analogy of the desktop interface, we have become icons, belief icons. Our interface may be an elaborate configuration of constantly shifting beliefs but they are beliefs nonetheless. We have not yet learned to sift past our beliefs to really see each other, to discover who we really are, an entire cosmos contained within each of us, hidden behind beliefs.

So, our inability to access 95% of ourselves, each other, and everything that is, is useful—but not to us living and nonliving beings (whoever and whatever we may actually be)—it is useful for the survival of beliefs to maintain the systems that construct our 5% universe where we play out our 5% lives.

Remarkably, our reality may very well be like the science fiction film, *The Matrix*, where humans have become implements, tools to sustain a system whose only interest is to generate profit in the form of capital. In order to fix our position within this bizarre 5% reality, we are inhabited by beliefs that influence us to perceive everything within binaries and hierarchies.

In our 5% universe, we are continually measuring ourselves, positioning ourselves in alignment with or against everything we come in contact with. We find ourselves occupying a location either above or below another, categorizing everyone and everything within millions of hierarchies. The architecture of our language is bound within this context such that our imagining of an outside cannot escape referencing some form of division or gradation. Our system is set up so we cannot even imagine an outside, we cannot envision what could possibly exist beyond our 5% universe.

How do we begin to expand beyond the 5%? Read the pamphlet, What is Beyond the 5%?

1. Ordinary matter, baryonic matter, the stuff you and I are made of, the stuff everything on this planet is made of, and the stuff this planet is made of and the other 100's of billions of planets and stars and galaxies make up only 4.9% of the known universe. Dark matter is 26.8% of the universe. And the remaining 68.3% of the universe is dark energy.

Recap on What is the 5% Universe?

- Built into our consciousness is an inherent inability to see and interact with 95% of all that is.
- Humans are hosts to parasitic belief entities that use our bodies to actualize themselves in this reality.
- The perpetuation and creation of binaries, hierarchies, and capital keep us locked in a 5% reality.
- Even our imagination is rooted in binaries, hierarchies, and capital.

What is the 5% Universe?

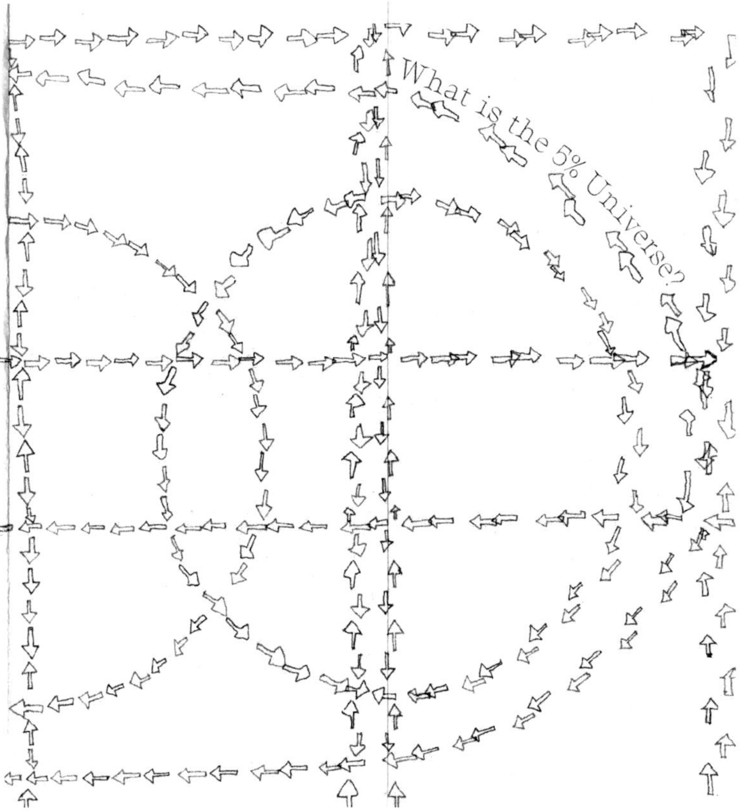

text: Jennifer Moon
illustration: laub
production: Mook Attanath + Lucy Nixon
with help from Freek Lomme / Onomatopee

Published as part of the *We Are The Market* performance
Eindhoven NL, 2017

jmoon.net
onomatopee.net

How do we embrace a death of self?

Read *Definition of Abundance* and come to the Death of Self workshop!

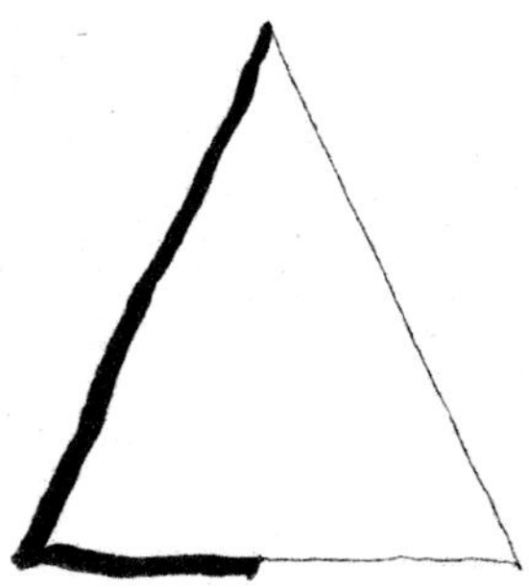

1. Refer to the pamphlet, What is the 5% Universe?, for a more detailed understanding of the 5%.

2. In many cultures, darkness is associated with fear, ignorance, immorality, and evil, lending itself to anti-blackness and racism. To then understand that 95% of the universe is "dark," so to speak (26.8% of the universe is dark matter and 68.3% of the universe is dark energy), and that that darkness will lead to enlightenment—a veritable expansion of our consciousness—is significant beyond a scientific explanation of the makeup, origins, and future development of the cosmos. How would our perceptions and interactions with each other shift and expand if they began to incorporate the 95% of "darkness" that *is* the universe? Or as Richard Panek writes in his book, *The 4% Universe*: "[Future generations] would not be seeing the same sky that [we do or once did] because they would not be thinking of it in the same way. They would see the same stars and they would marvel at the hundreds of billions of galaxies other than our own but they would sense the dark too and to them that darkness would represent a path toward knowledge, toward the kinds of discoveries that we all once called, with understandable innocence, the light."

Recap on What is beyond the 5%?

In our 5% understanding of the universe, we cannot comprehend freedom beyond the framing of binaries placed within hierarchies.

The micro realities of quantum physics exist beyond binaries, hierarchies, and capital.

Our incessant acts of measurement force us into a fixed position where we lose momentum.

We have colonized the quantum world as well as the imagination.

Embracing a death of self and a merging into many will elude all forms of measurement and allow a momentum to propel us beyond the 5%.

text: Jennifer Moon
illustration: laub
production: Mook Attanath + Lucy Nixon
with help from Freek Lomme
at Onomatopee

Published as part of the *We Are The Market* performance
Eindhoven NL, 2017

jmoon.net
onomatopee.net

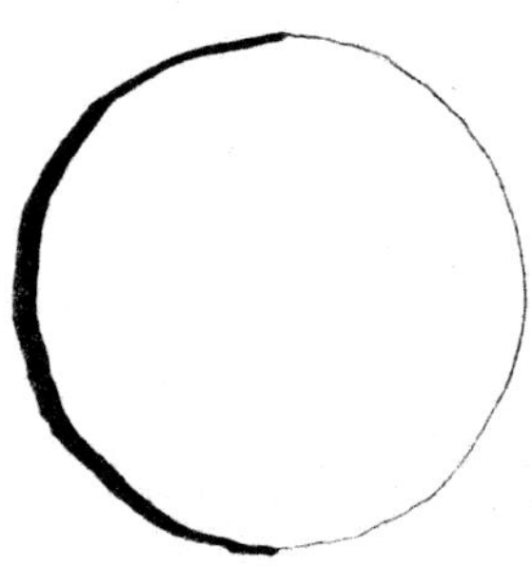

What is beyond the 5%?

What is Beyond the 5%?

In Edwin A. Abbott's novella, *Flatland: A Romance of Many Dimensions*, the narrator, A Square, who lives in a two-dimensional world, experiences a three-dimensional sphere passing through his flat 2D world as magically growing and shrinking circles. A Square believes the sphere is a circle playing tricks on him as A Square cannot comprehend depth and, therefore, cannot conceive of a three-dimensional object.

Similarly, we, in our 5% understanding of the universe[1], cannot comprehend *freedom* and, therefore, cannot conceive of concepts like justice, difference, revolution, love, and faith beyond the framing of binaries placed within hierarchies. We can only realize freedoms so much as the manifestation of our bodies allows, bodies that have been shaped to sustain a system that can co-opt any attempt to expand beyond our 5% universe into capital.

So how then can we expand beyond the 5%?

Let's start by adventuring into the quantum world of subatomic particles. In this extraordinary micro universe, commonly known as quantum mechanics, particles, such as protons, neutrons, and electrons, which bundle together into atoms—the stuff you and I and the entire visible universe are made of—behave in radically different ways than the ways we behave in the macro world. In this queer world, particles hover in a state of uncertainty, seemingly being partly here and partly there, occupying all known positions simultaneously. The orientation devices we use to ground ourselves in our 5% universe—namely binaries, hierarchies, and capital—fall away. There is no such grounding in this world where particles exist in several states and several realities at the same time, spinning in multiple angular rotations at once.

The incredible thing about all of this is that it is happening inside of us as we speak; all of this fantastic queering and disrupting of time and space is happening RIGHT NOW in the subatomic particles that make up our bodies and all the observable matter in the universe. So how does all this radical queering wash away into a system that converges into a single reality, this 5% rendering of our macro world? By our acts of measurement!

The uncertainty principle in quantum mechanics states that the more precisely the position of a particle is determined, the less precisely its momentum can be known, and vice versa. Essentially, we cannot measure the position and the momentum of a particle at the same time. In their unobserved state, particles exist as a fuzzy jumble of possibilities. However, once they are measured, the *act of measurement* forces a particle to relinquish all of the possible places it could have been and select one definite location where *we* find it. And when a particle is forced to choose a position, *we* lose its momentum.

Our singular, 5% reality is realized and sustained by our constant measuring. Our endless acts of measurement place everything and everyone, every event, every phenomenon within a binary-bound, hierarchical spectrum that washes away the possibilities of us and our world existing in multiple states and multiple realities at the same time. Our incessant measuring of ourselves with others and the world around us forces us into a position, an orientation, an identity, a behavior, a way of being. When we are forced to choose a position, we lose our momentum; and without momentum we can never expand beyond our 5% universe.

Instead of reaching to expand beyond the 5% and understanding how such acts of measurement prohibit movement, we have opted to wield this powerful act of measurement to colonize the quantum world, forcing it to conform to the rules of our 5% universe; therefore, mastering the ability to manipulate micro particles at the macro level. Yet, we have not figured out how to let go of fear, power, and control in order to exist *amongst* the micro dimensions! In our fear of letting go of control, we have similarly colonized our imagination, where even our imagination cannot escape binaries, hierarchies, and capital—imagination is nothing more than a reality sim.

How do we stop measuring? How do we let go of our insistence on grounding all that we can imagine in this 5% reality? In other words, how do we shed all our beliefs, all the ways in which we identify and position ourselves within this reality, in order to realize an undetermined formlessness, a groundlessness without orientation that will allow a momentum to propel us beyond the 5%? It is through an acceptance of death, but not death, as in the absence of life, defined by this system. Rather, it is a death of beliefs and a death of self, which will allow a merging into many, an aggregate formless body eluding all attempts of measurement.

As a collective entity that merges into many and enjoys multiple indeterminacies, we can avoid all forms of measurement that fix us in a 5% universe and venture out into the abyss, the 95% of darkness[2] where we can discover new forms of freedom, not determined by the binary, hierarchical beliefs of our 5% reality to keep us contained within it, but freedom that is beyond language and beyond anything we can yet imagine.

ONOMATOPEE OFFERS

FEE OF ... EX VAT.
This fee is for travel, residence and whatever else. No bullshit. Payment terms: half before, half after or all after.

FILMING OF THE INTERVENTION.
Filming takes no longer than 2 consecutive hours. With intro and outro by Onomatopee.

Final editing by Onomatopee. One commenting round on the edit is possible; for a second one it will cost 50-euro ex vat to pay for the editors.

TRANSCRIBING OF THE ACHIEVEMENT.
By Onomatopee, and is the responsibility of Onomatopee.

REPRODUCTION OF THE ACHIEVEMENT.
In book, publicity and more, and the artist agrees, unless they are not mentioned in a normal way: name, title, date, location, project title.

SCREENING OF THE FILM.
At Onomatopee, under conditions set by Onomatopee.

BOOKS.
5 free copies, more are available at cost price.

SERVICE.
Production, residence and support: we try and be as hospitable as possible.

ONOMATOPEE REQUESTS

AN INTERVENTION/ACTION/ PERFORMANCE.
Located in the city centre: contributing to the widening of the demand and/or offer. We will call these "achievements".

That all 'achievers' are well prepared, so we're in time and on budget.

MENTIONING OF THE PROJECT.
Like we do, or pretty much similar (basically as one would consider normal) + as much as possible because we all need more to keep our businesses going.

RIGHTS

EVERYONE IS PRIVATELY RESPONSIBLE FOR HIS OWN ACTIONS OUTSIDE OF THE ONOMATOPEE EXHIBITION SPACE.
The artists are responsible for their own achievements / including whatever they do to themselves and/or others.

Onomatopee is responsible for whatever we do, and will take personal care of our actions; like being more engaged than the government is and so forth.

IMAGE RIGHTS + REPRODUCTION.
Onomatopee will never go to court, so everything is creative commons in our case. Still, this means no one should be an asshole. Onomatopee does not engage in collaborations with assholes, so you're probably not one anyway, but by signing this you declare to trust us.

We give you the films after the project ended latest; maybe earlier.

Yes! We love this!

Freek Lomme/Onomatopee, "the" artist

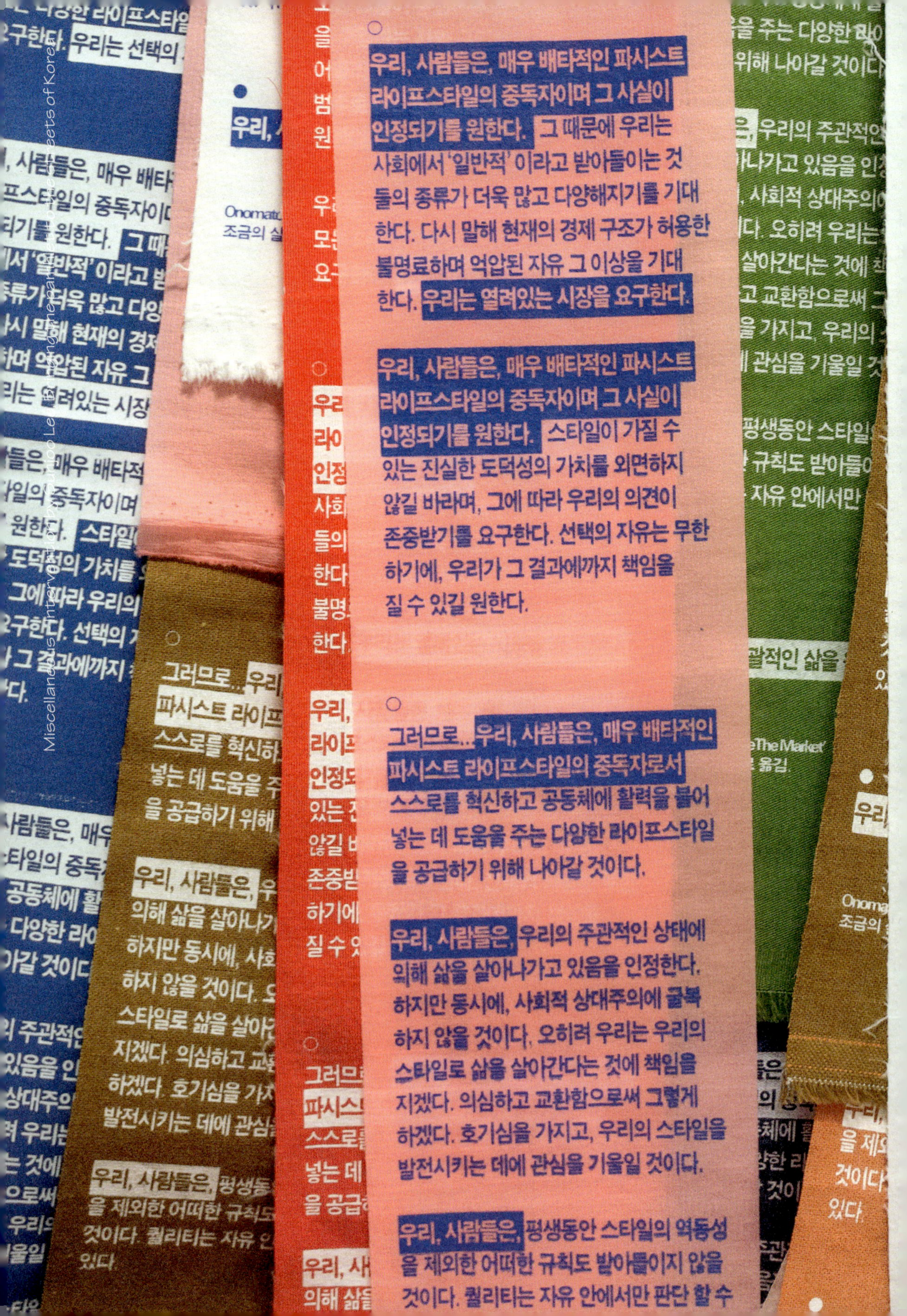

우리, 사람들은, 매우 배타적인 파시스트 라이프스타일의 중독자이며 그 사실이 인정되기를 원한다. 그 때문에 우리는 사회에서 '일반적' 이라고 받아들이는 것들의 종류가 더욱 많고 다양해지기를 기대한다. 다시 말해 현재의 경제 구조가 허용한 불명료하며 억압된 자유 그 이상을 기대한다. 우리는 열려있는 시장을 요구한다.

우리, 사람들은, 매우 배타적인 파시스트 라이프스타일의 중독자이며 그 사실이 인정되기를 원한다. 스타일이 가질 수 있는 진실한 도덕성의 가치를 외면하지 않길 바라며, 그에 따라 우리의 의견이 존중받기를 요구한다. 선택의 자유는 무한하기에, 우리가 그 결과에까지 책임을 질 수 있길 원한다.

그러므로... 우리, 사람들은, 매우 배타적인 파시스트 라이프스타일의 중독자로서 스스로를 혁신하고 공동체에 활력을 불어넣는 데 도움을 주는 다양한 라이프스타일을 공급하기 위해 나아갈 것이다.

우리, 사람들은, 우리의 주관적인 상태에 의해 삶을 살아나가고 있음을 인정한다. 하지만 동시에, 사회적 상대주의에 굴복하지 않을 것이다. 오히려 우리는 우리의 스타일로 삶을 살아간다는 것에 책임을 지겠다. 의심하고 교환함으로써 그렇게 하겠다. 호기심을 가지고, 우리의 스타일을 발전시키는 데에 관심을 기울일 것이다.

우리, 사람들은, 평생동안 스타일의 역동성을 제외한 어떠한 규칙도 받아들이지 않을 것이다. 퀄리티는 자유 안에서만 판단 할 수

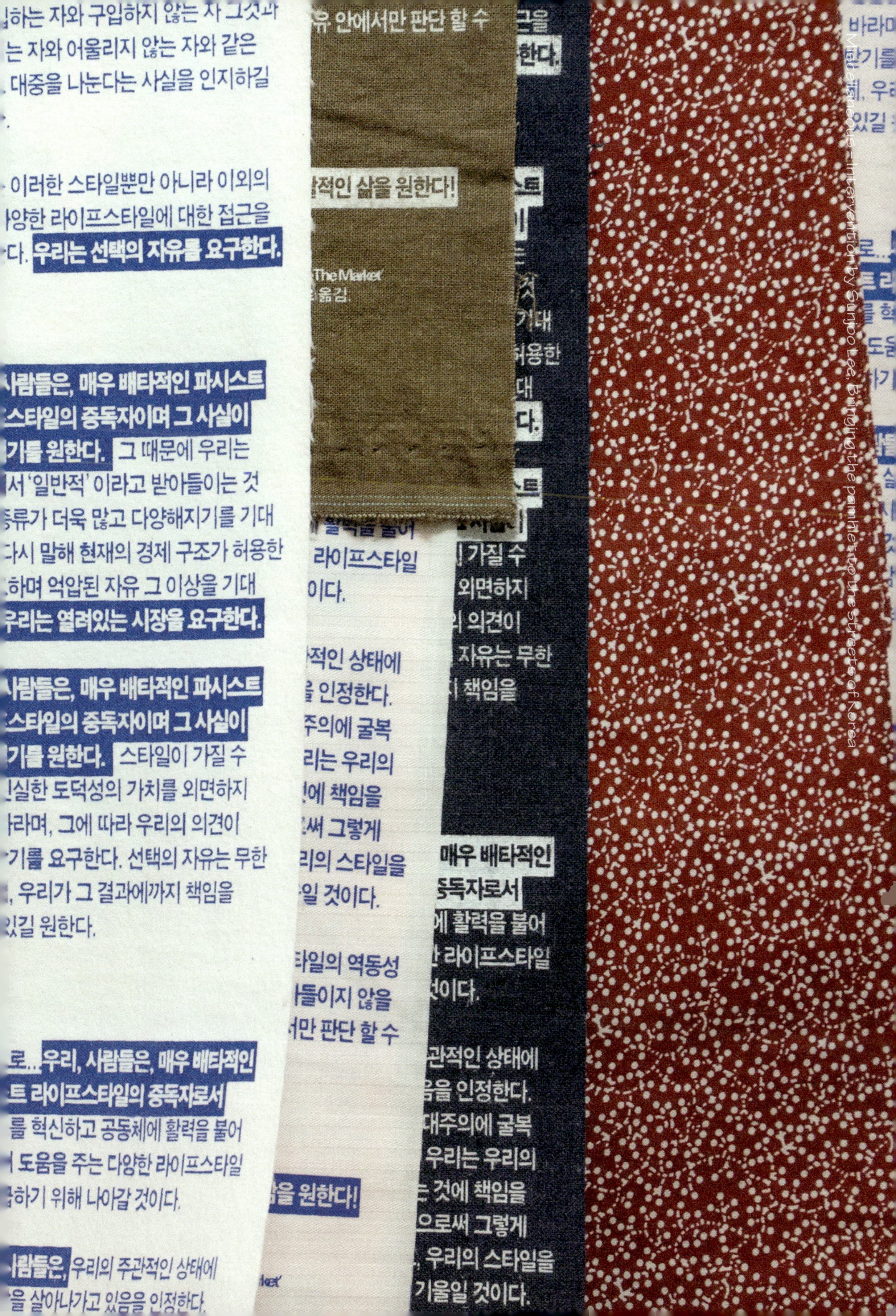

Miscellaneous - Intervention by Sunjoo Lee, Bringing the pamphlet to the streets of Korea

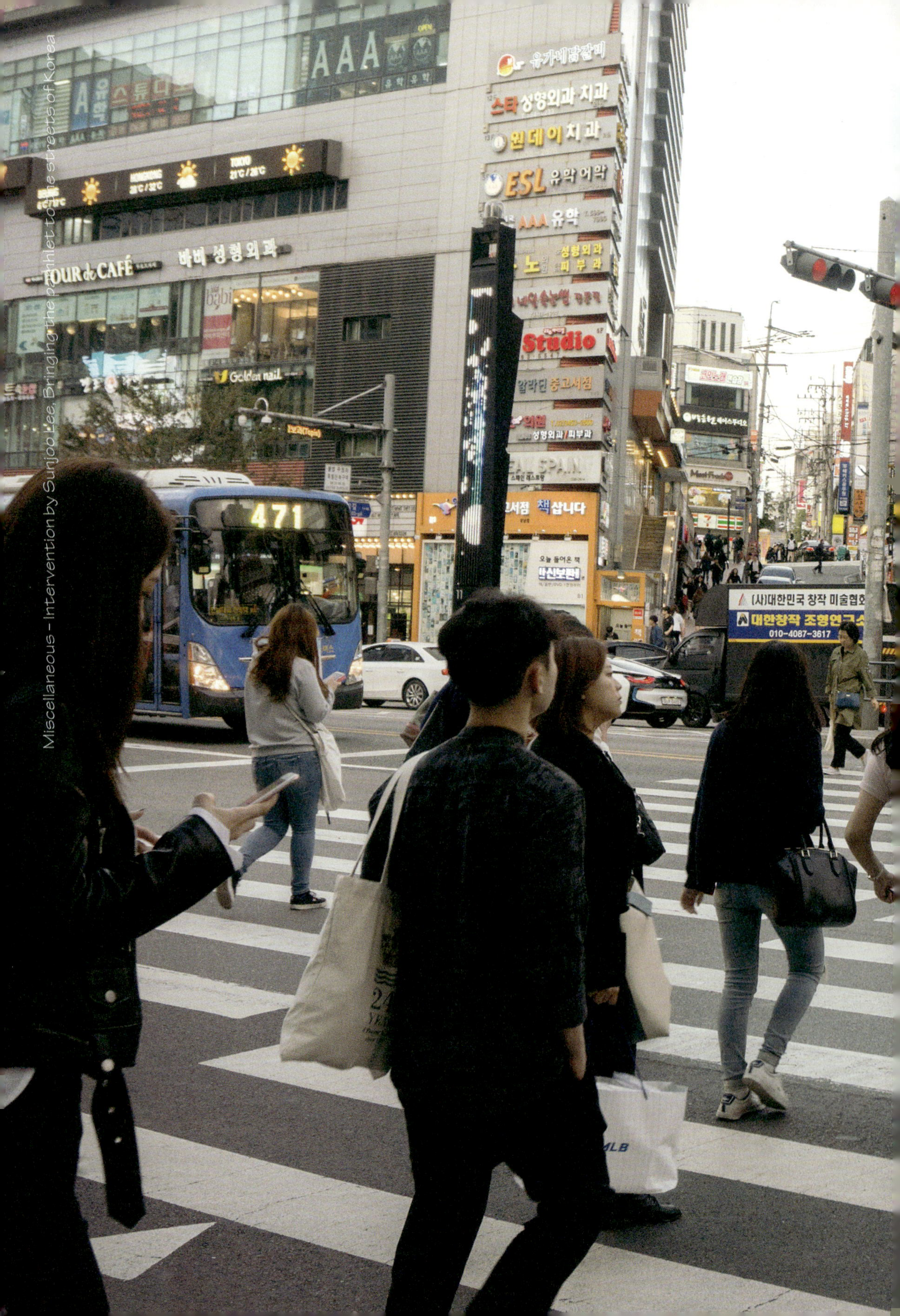

Miscellaneous – Intervention by Sunjoo Lee. Bringing the pamphlet to the streets of Korea

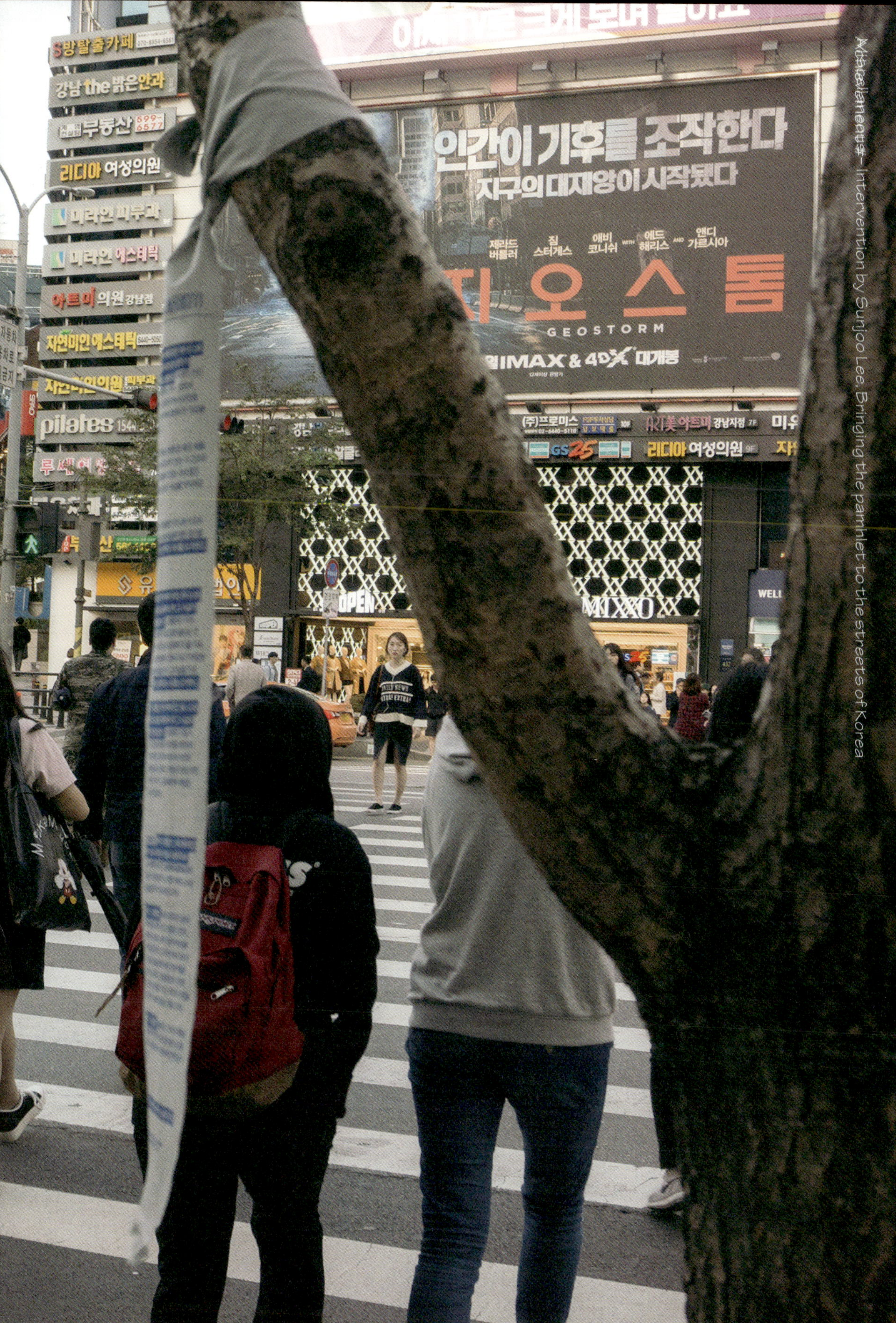

Miscellaneous – Intervention by Sunjoo Lee. Bringing the pamhlet to the streets of Korea

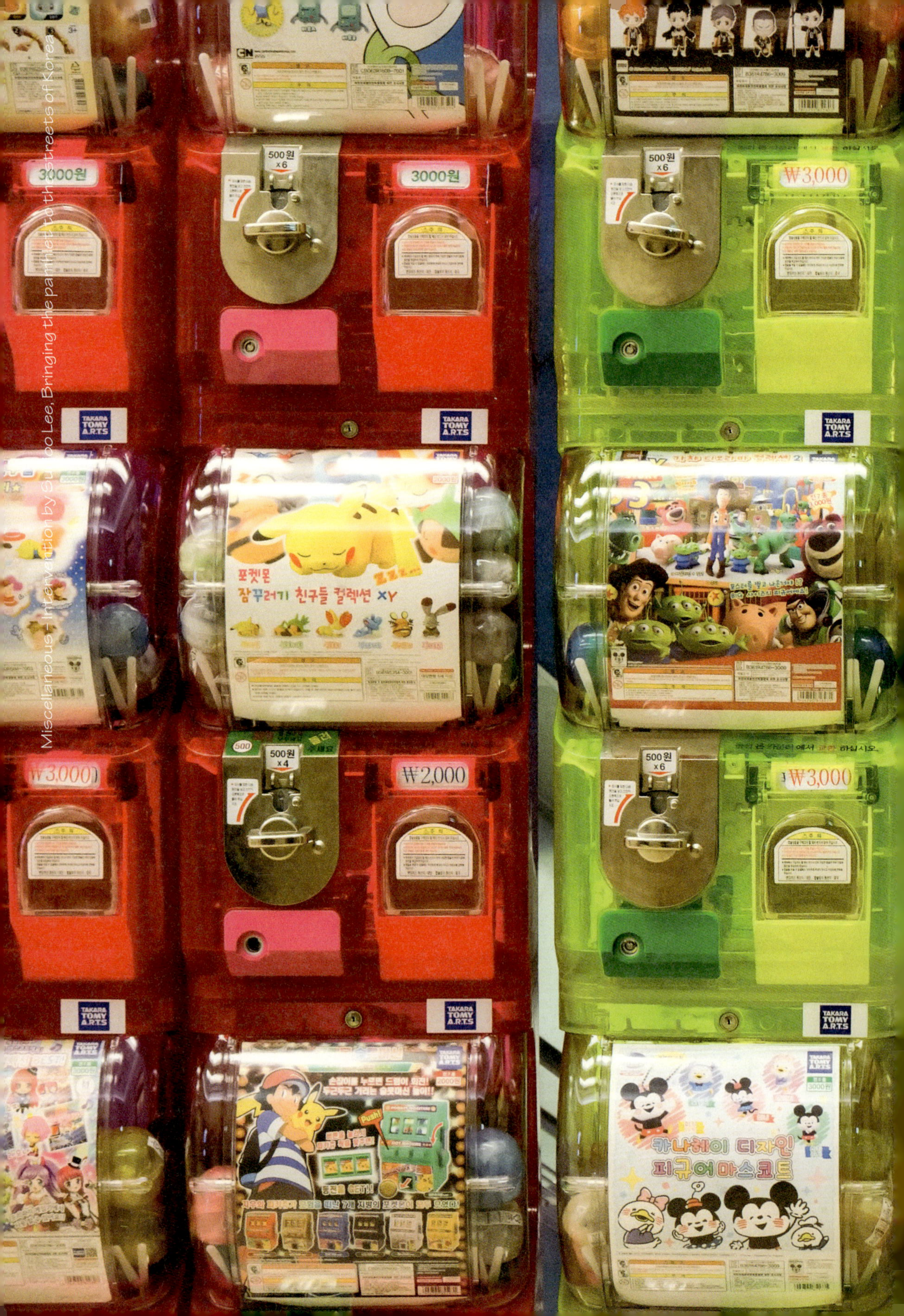

Miscellaneous - Intervention by Su[illegible]oo Lee, Bringing the pamphlet to the streets of Korea

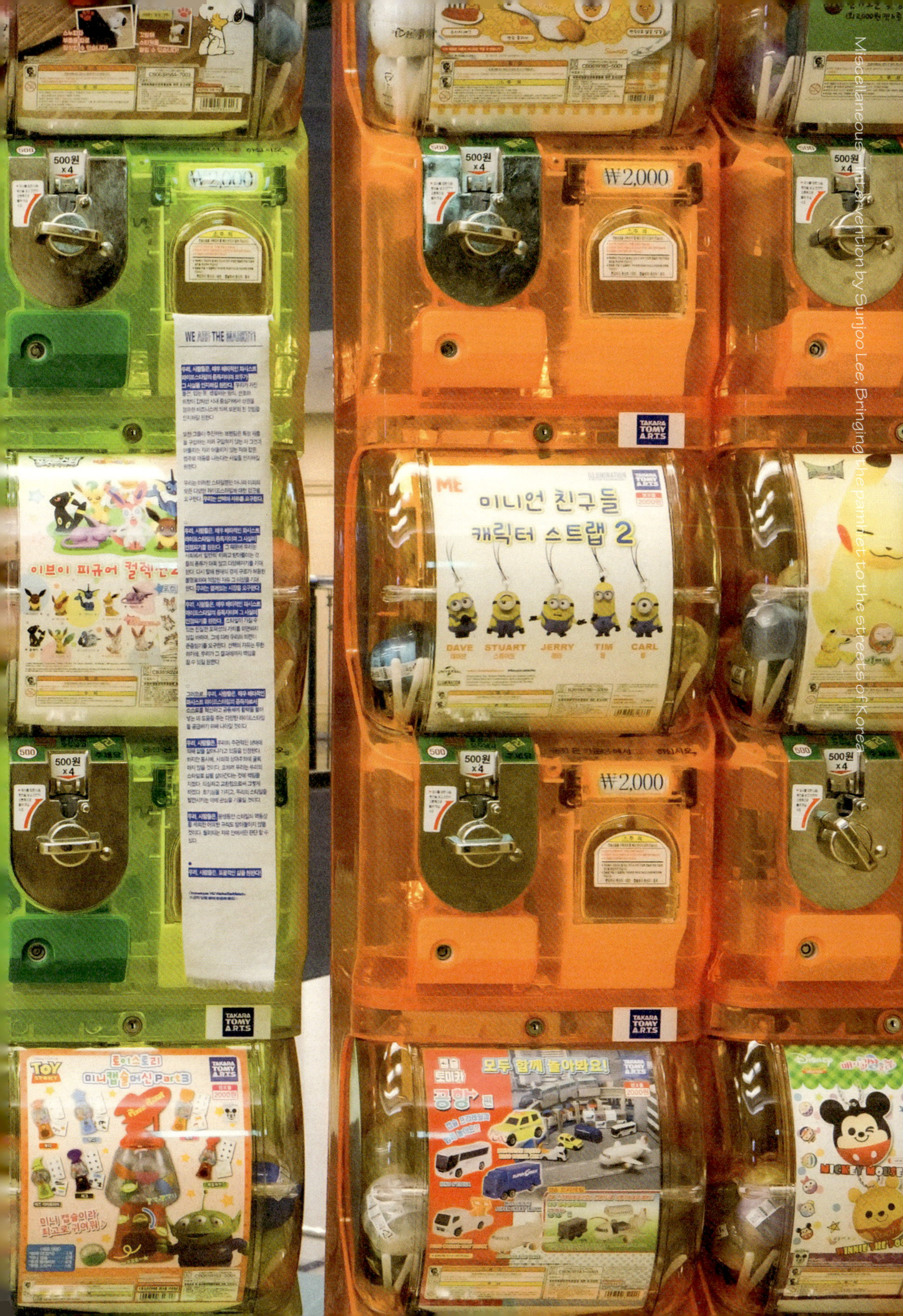

Miscellaneous Intervention by Sunjoo Lee. Bringing the pamphlet to the streets of Korea

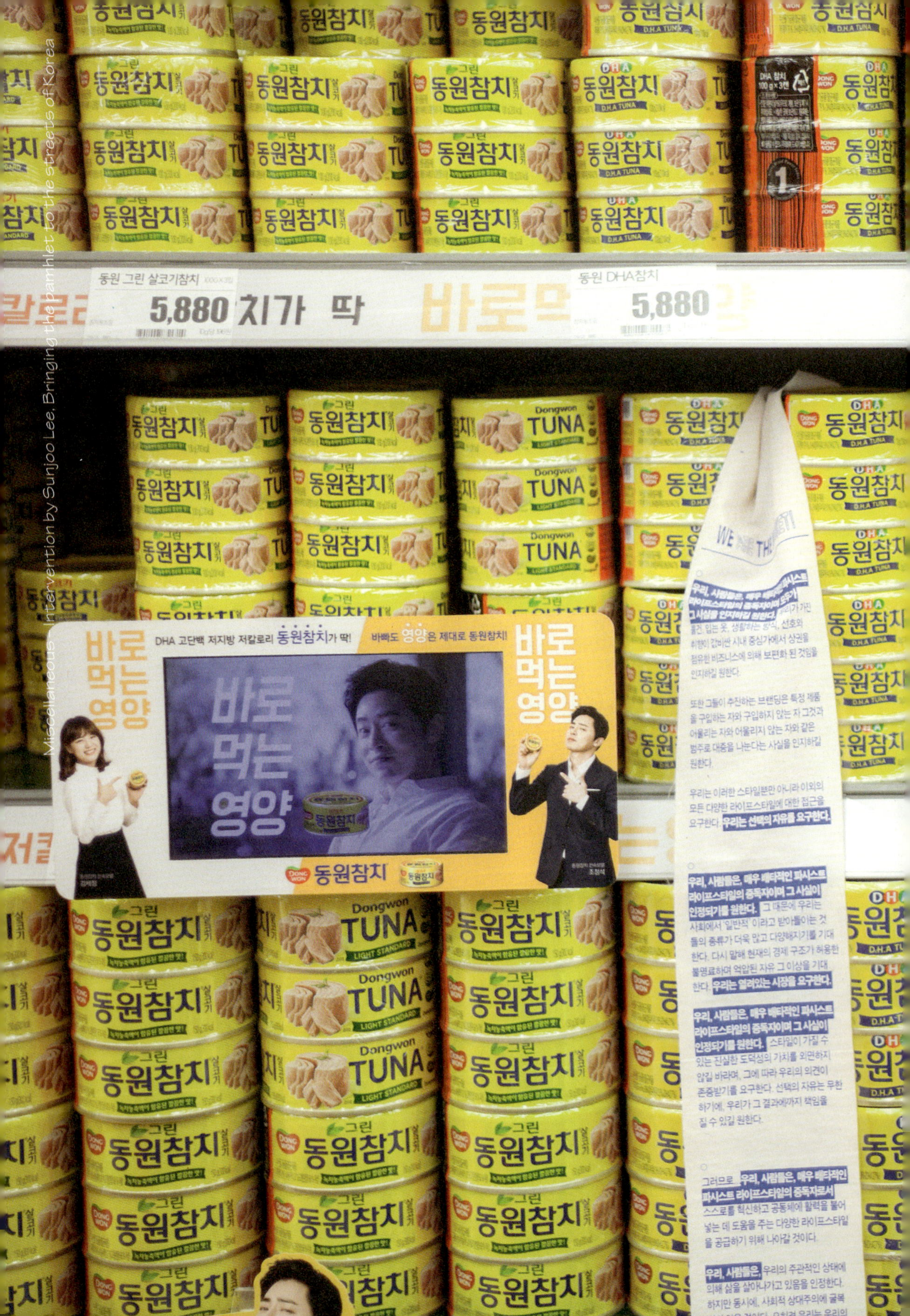

Miscellaneous – Intervention by Sunjoo Lee. Bringing the pamphlet to the streets of Korea

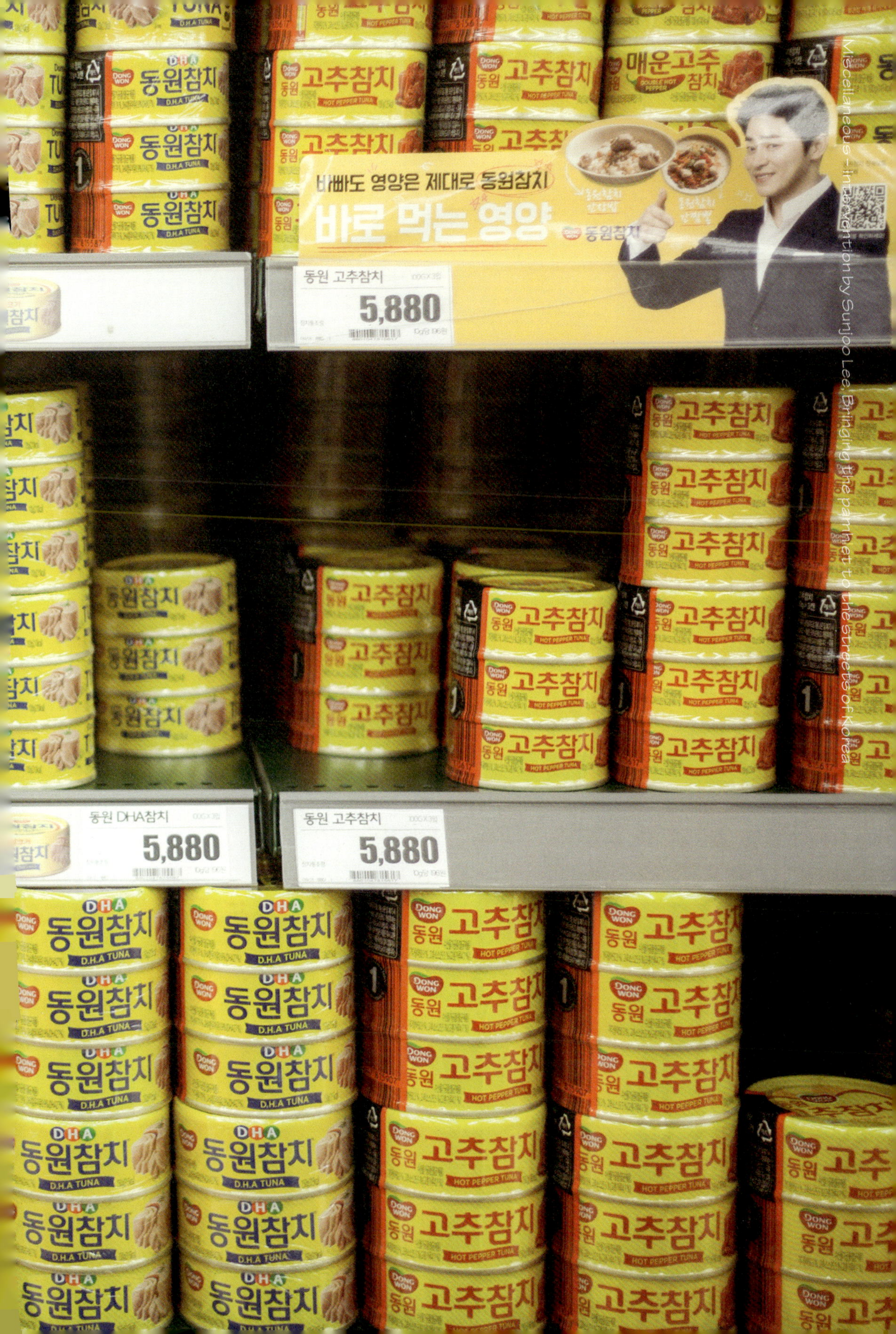

Miscellaneous - intervention by Sunjoo Lee. Bringing the pamphlet to the streets of Korea

Colophon

Onomatopee 142
WE ARE THE MARKET!

The commercial city centre
as the final commonplace

ISBN: 978-94-91677-87-8

Curator/editor:
Freek Lomme

Assistant curator/editor:
Josh Plough

Project assistants:
Lucy Rose Nixon, Mook Attanath and Delany Boutkan

Technical support exhibition:
Guus van der Velden

Graphic design:
Bart de Baets and Nina Schouten

Printer: ArtLibro | Coers & Roest

Paper:
Neobond
UPM Sol Matt

Typefaces
Tekton

Made possible thanks to the generous support of the Province of Brabant, the Mondriaan Fund and the Creative Industries Fund NL.

www.onomatopee.net

Provincie Noord-Brabant

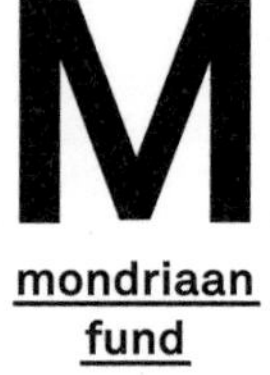

creative industries fund NL